Goodbye to All That

Goodbye to All That

BRYAN GOULD

MACMILLAN

First published 1995 by Macmillan
an imprint of Macmillan General Books
25 Eccleston Place London SW1W 9NF
and Basingstoke

Associated companies throughout the world

ISBN 0 333 63800 X

9 8 7 6 5 4 3 2 1

A CIP catalogue record for this book is available from
the British Library

Typeset by CentraCet Limited, Cambridge
Printed by Mackays of Chatham plc, Chatham, Kent

CONTENTS

PREFACE

WHEN I TOOK THE DECISION, at the beginning of 1994, to return to my native New Zealand after 32 years in Britain and 20 years in British public life, I surprised myself as much as anyone else. Yet, in retrospect, I now see that there was a growing inevitability about the decision.

This was partly because, as I grew older, I found that my New Zealand roots called to me more and more strongly. I had returned to the country increasingly often over recent years. My links with my family had grown closer. We had acquired some property there. When the offer came of an attractive job in New Zealand, I suddenly realised that my native country offered much of what my wife and I wanted from life.

Throughout my political career, I had never concealed the fact that I came from abroad. I was intensely proud of the fact that I am a New Zealander. I felt that it gave me a particular advantage: the ability to see Britain more clearly as outsiders see it, yet from the viewpoint of one whose origins are exclusively British.

I had often been asked, during my political career in Britain, whether I felt that my New Zealand origins were a handicap. I had always replied that I had virtually never encountered any overt prejudice (though it was no doubt sometimes whispered behind my back that I was somehow disqualified from a proper understanding of British life). The only disadvantage I suffered was that I lacked the natural power base which assisted a Labour MP from, say, the North or from Scotland or Wales. It meant that I had to rely very much on my own resources, but I never made any complaint about that.

My decision to go back to New Zealand was, naturally enough, interpreted in Britain as less a statement of enthusiasm for New Zealand and more a comment on my view of Britain and of the Labour Party. But if disenchantment played a part in my decision, as was suggested, it did not take the form of a loss of affection for Britain. Indeed, it was my continuing affection for my adopted country which in some senses led to my departure.

I had arrived 32 years earlier as a young man with perhaps an idealised view of Britain. The reality naturally fell short of the ideal, but I remained convinced that Britain could be the country I wanted it to be. I saw in Britain a country of incomparable qualities and riches – advantages which, if properly exploited, could transform British society and British national fortunes. The opportunity for Britain was for an old industrial society to rejuvenate itself and become a modern, efficient, socially cohesive and just democratic state.

What prevented the country from achieving this transition, so it seemed to me, was the dead weight of history, the inertia and apathy produced by a stultifying class system and a continuing attachment to attitudes and institutions which reflected an imperial past but which had long since outworn their relevance to modern conditions. I naturally looked to what claimed to be the principal political force for reform – the Labour Party – as the instrument for casting off these burdens and bringing about the real political change which Britain needed.

I wanted to make my own contribution to this process. I developed, as I joined the Labour Party and became active politically, my own analysis and my own prescriptions as to what was needed. But over the next 20 years, the hopes and ambitions I had nurtured of helping towards real change were frustrated. The path I wanted to follow increasingly diverged from the one that was actually taken. Both Britain and the Labour Party abandoned the goals I felt were both necessary and attainable.

Britain opted not for change but for resignation, not for seizing

control of and shaping its future but for sub-contracting the management of that future out to others. The Labour Party, which briefly
promised to kick-start a process of change, gradually yielded up its
ambitions to build a different and fairer society. Today's Labour Party
no longer promises a different Britain, merely a Britain which will
uncomplainingly accept its declining fortunes.

Britain and the Labour Party seem content with a future which I
am unwilling to accept and to which I can make little contribution.
My sentiment is regret, not disillusion. I had higher hopes than I
could persuade others to share.

ONE

A New Zealand Upbringing
1939–62

EVERYONE SHOULD HAVE a New Zealand childhood. The New Zealand into which I was born on 11 February 1939 had – in common with the rest of the advanced world – recently emerged from a debilitating recession in which many people had suffered real hardship. Later that year, it was to enter the most destructive war in world history. Many writers have attested to the tribulations they endured during these times of stress and strife. But, for myself, New Zealand during the war years offered a haven of peace and stability, untouched by the dangers and difficulties which afflicted the rest of the world.

I was fortunate in being born into a loving and stable family, and an economic and social milieu which meant that, while we lived simply – even frugally, by today's standards – we were nevertheless free from the financial and other worries which troubled so many other people. Life was simple and slow-paced. We had the space and time in which to grow up. The psychologists tell us that a secure and happy childhood is the best possible start in life. That is exactly what my parents, and New Zealand, gave me.

Outside events did, of course, intrude. My father, a bank official, volunteered to serve in the armed forces when war broke out. He was mortified to discover that he could not serve overseas on health grounds, but he nevertheless joined the Royal New Zealand Air Force and spent most of the war at air force bases around the country. He would occasionally get leave to come home (and sometimes came home anyway – I remember one illicit weekend when my parents agonised as to whether the railcar would make an unauthorised stop to enable my father to get back to camp undiscovered) but essentially my mother raised me and my sister, Ngaire, on her own during the war.

The war did more than take our father away from us. I remember my mother taking Ngaire and me into the hallway of our small 'state house' (the equivalent of a British council house), pointing to the trapdoor in the ceiling and saying, 'When the Japanese come, I'll put you up in the roof and you're to be very quiet.' My father, in common with all the neighbours, had dug an air-raid shelter in the back garden. Fortunately, we never had to use it.

The war also meant that we lived very simply. My mother was proud of being a 'good manager', and there was no money to spare anyway. Even if there had been, there would have been little to spend it on. My parents had sold their little Morris 10 at the outbreak of fighting. We made very occasional journeys by train: to see my grandparents just outside Wellington, and on one memorable occasion to spend a weekend in a boarding house in New Plymouth where my mother got dreadfully sunburned on the baking iron sands. Otherwise we walked everywhere.

We ate well and we were convinced that my mother was the best cook in the world. But eggs were in short supply, since most egg production was earmarked for Britain and the war effort, and the occasional gift of half a dozen fresh eggs from friends was an event to celebrate. I well remember the excitement of being able to buy sweets (or 'lollies' as we called them) from the local Woolworths on VE Day.

I took it for granted throughout my childhood that New Zealand was the centre of the universe. We were dimly aware that there was a wider world out there somewhere, but the only bits of it that concerned us as we grew up were Britain (which loomed large as mother country and major trading partner), the United States (to which many – like my father – looked as our saviour and protector when Britain failed to defend us against the Japanese) and Australia (which we regarded as a larger but inferior version of New Zealand).

I was born in the Taranaki province on the North Island, in a small dairying town called Hawera. It was, and still is, a somewhat undistinguished, flat and featureless place, with a single main street boasting some fifty or sixty shops. However, it nestled on the plain under the slopes of Mount Taranaki (or Mount Egmont, as we then called it), an almost perfectly conical, snow-covered mountain of great beauty. We grew up with the instinctive expectation common to most New Zealanders that there would always be mountains on the skyline.

It is hard to credit now, but when I was born, Hawera had been settled for less than a hundred years. Yet it was a substantial town: my father's bank was an impressive building, approached by a magnificent set of steps; the main roads were sealed; we were served by efficient postal and telephone services; we had a railway and a water tower which was the tallest building in town. We grew up in a new house subsidised by the state, we enjoyed state-provided health and dental care, we attended a comprehensive state-funded school and we boasted a local daily newspaper whose coverage of world news would put to shame most of today's leading quality broadsheets.

In other words, Hawera, in common with the rest of New Zealand, was truly a miracle – a monument to the extraordinary energy of the early European settlers. Their story was a remarkable one. Unlike their Australian contemporaries, they were neither convicts nor conscripts, nor were they refugees from persecution or economic hardship. They chose to come.

Nearly all of them began their journeys in rural Britain. Most of my own forebears came from the West Country, but they also included Scots and Welsh. In mid-nineteenth century Britain, for most people, a journey to the nearest large town would have been a once-in-a-lifetime experience. Most likely never having seen the sea, these early pioneers embarked on tiny sailing ships to travel 12,000 miles to the farthest corner of the earth, facing hardship, disease and death on the voyage, to a land clad in impenetrable jungle and inhabited by warlike tribes. What made them do it?

Within a few decades, the settlers had cleared the bush, planted pasture land, developed herds of cattle and flocks of sheep, and were exporting meat, dairy produce and wool back to Britain. The air of prosperity and stability which I remember from my childhood reflected the riches produced by this immense effort.

My parents must have made a lively young couple – attractive, sociable and sporting. They had met in Wellington, where they were both good badminton and tennis players. They had married in 1938 and moved to Hawera when the bank posted my father there. I was the first-born, followed 18 months later by Ngaire. We grew up very close. My brother Wayne, nearly seven years younger than me, was born as the war drew to its close.

Although my parents had met as a consequence of moving in the same social circle in pre-war Wellington, there was always a sense of a slight social divide between their respective families. The Goulds justifiably liked to think of themselves as a family of some standing. My great-great-great-grandfather, George Gould, had come to New Zealand in 1850. His father and grandfather before him had been lock-keepers on the River Thames at Hambleden. His grandfather, Caleb Gould, who had been a famous figure on the river, lived to the age of 92. His gravestone, in Remenham churchyard, just above the river, bears the verse from John Gay: 'Life is a jest; and all things show it./ I thought so once; but now I know it.'

George turned his back on the older world of water transport and obtained employment with a railway company. He embarked for New Zealand as a young family man and settled in what is now Christchurch, where he became a prosperous merchant. The firm he founded, Pyne Gould and Guinness, is still the premier stock and station company in the South Island.

My great-grandfather married Kate Ballantyne, from another established Christchurch family. My father had been the apple of his wealthy grandmother's eye, and had been sent to two of New Zealand's leading schools, Christ's College and then King's College. His father had been a none too successful farmer, but I well remember his mother, whom we called 'Gran'. She was a somewhat distant old lady who attached great importance to the schools people had been to and was clearly disappointed that my siblings and I only went to local schools.

This assumption of social superiority on the part of the Goulds was felt keenly by my mother, yet it is hard to see why she should have allowed herself to be put at a disadvantage in this way. She came from an equally long-established New Zealand family. Indeed, her great-grandfather on her mother's side, Thomas Duck, had been born in Wellington in 1841. Her forebears had been farmers and merchants in Britain, largely in the West Country. Her own father, Frank Driller, was a prosperous Wellington businessman who drove the most impressive cars in New Zealand. I always remember Grandad at the wheel of an enormous caramel-coloured American Hudson, which caused a sensation wherever it went, and I recall listening entranced to his stories of driving at more than 100 miles an hour.

Grandad Driller was an altogether more interesting figure than the genial but rather dull Grandfather Gould. I say he was interesting, but he was in fact rather terrifying. He was a domestic tyrant and my mother lived in fear of him. This communicated itself to us children. We loved to visit my mother's parents, because they were so kind to us, but we were always a little nervous in case we angered Grandad for any reason.

My mother's mother, 'Nana', was, by contrast, someone we could love unreservedly. She was kind and wise, more a friend to my mother than a parent, and every child's ideal grandmother. My Driller grandparents lived in a 100-acre paradise in the Akatarawa mountains outside Wellington. A Christmas school holiday spent with them was an idyll of swimming, catching frogs, climbing mountains, running through pine forests, gorging ourselves in their soft fruit gardens, and eating Nana's freshly baked scones for tea.

Once a week, we would drive into Wellington so that Grandad could meet his business friends and Nana and my mother could go shopping. At the beginning of the holiday we would take an evil-smelling sack into the Ministry of Agriculture. The sack contained the ears and nine-inch strips of pelt from a hundred possums which Grandad had killed after trapping them in his fruit trees. The Ministry paid 2s. 6d. for each skin. We children were allowed to keep the proceeds, with which we then financed our modest spending for the rest of the four- or five-week holiday.

On the face of it, then, my mother had every reason to feel the social equal of my father and his family, but for two things. One, she had not been to secondary school, and two, she did not have her own teeth. She felt both deficiencies keenly. Both were directly attributed to her tyrannical father. He it was who had decreed that she leave school at the first opportunity, and who insisted – against the pleadings of a reluctant dentist – that the correct response to a little tooth decay at the age of thirteen was that she should have all her teeth out. When my father told his parents that he had become engaged to my mother, he dutifully reported that his bride-to-be was uneducated and had false teeth. My mother's reputation never recovered in my Gran's eyes from this betrayal. Or at least, so my mother thought.

Nevertheless, my mother was a forceful and intelligent woman, and a considerable beauty in her younger days. She had left school to work as an office girl in my Grandad's business. Over the years, she demonstrated an aptitude for office administration and ended up virtually running the business. She was active in the Red Cross and was a leading tennis and badminton player. She had been pursued by a large number of suitors, and eventually got married, I believe, because she felt that, at 27, time was passing. She was in any case intrigued by my father's rather laid-back courtship and by his air of refinement and social superiority.

My mother was in many respects the dominant partner in the marriage. She was made for motherhood and established herself as the sun around which the family solar system revolved. She was aided in this by my father's absence throughout the war years. By the time he returned, he was an outsider. He seemed content to remain so. He was totally absorbed by the family – my mother saw to that – but he was also curiously peripheral to it.

We children worshipped our mother. She loved to talk, and we would sit for hours as she busied herself in the kitchen, listening to her reminiscences and observations on life. These were not, in retrospect, very profound. She had, in truth, a rather narrow range of interests, but she had a good eye for the human condition and her main interest was people. We learnt a great deal about human foibles, as viewed through her sharp eye.

My father was a much more mysterious figure. On the surface, he was the archetypal bank official – conventional, loyal to the bank, a pillar of society. He spent all his working life at the bank and eventually rose to become the manager of one of its larger branches, in New Plymouth.

But it was always known that my father was 'artistic'. He rarely talked about it, but we discovered much later that, as a boy, he had wanted to become an architect, that he had at some point enrolled in art school, that his grandmother (who financed his education) had lost patience with his artistic leanings and had simply arranged a job for him in the bank. When we were young, he produced in his spare time intricate Maori-type carvings, and after the war, he made wonderful jewellery – rings, bangles, tie pins, cufflinks, napkin rings – which he would fashion out of a large lump of titanium (somehow acquired, we were told, from an aeroplane propeller) and inlay it with polished paua shell.

As he grew older, this evidence of my father's artistic bent diminished. My mother, in any case, had little patience with it. This partly explained, perhaps, the air of detachment and self-containment my father had. It was not that he actually lived a separate life – he was in his own way a loving and dutiful father and husband – but he seemed to be sustained by some sort of inner resource which he did not need to share with anyone else.

A conscientious servant of the bank, my father was occasionally required to socialise with his colleagues and customers. He would sometimes go to the pub with them after work, incurring my mother's bitter hostility if he did, but he never gave the impression that it came naturally to him. He enjoyed a glass of beer but my abiding memory is of him relaxing in an armchair with the crossword, sitting quietly while family life went on around him.

In English society, everyone is assigned and accepts a place in the social hierarchy. Social standing is a matter of nice judgements and the careful weighing-up of a myriad of social indicators. In these terms, we would have been impossible to identify. The social and class indicators were too contradictory.

On the one hand, I was born into a 'state house' and went to the local state schools. On the other, my father had been to some of the country's best-known fee-paying schools, he was the product of one of the country's oldest families, he was a professional man. My parents soon bought their own – modest – house and my mother never worked in paid employment once she married, and spent her later years playing bridge and golf and visiting her lady friends for tea.

These confused social signals were not peculiar to my family but were true of quite a large part of New Zealand society. The most important aspect of our place in society was that we were brought up to believe, or rather to take for granted, that we were at least as good as, and very probably better than, most other people.

We were a family of decided preferences. We ate pork sausages not beef, Cadbury's chocolate rather than Nestlé's, Aulsebrooks biscuits not Griffins, Ovaltine not Milo, Tip Top ice cream not Peter Pan. We preferred Roma, the Dust-Freed Tea, until the day when, for some mysterious reason, we switched to Choysa. These choices we regarded not so much as consumer preferences but rather as expressions of moral virtue and superiority. Families like ours, we felt, just knew which were the best brands.

In fact, we knew very little, even of the limited society in which we lived. We went to the local school with all the local children, but we played with our own friends. We knew little of the poorer children, those who came to school bare-footed and shoddily dressed, and we took virtually no interest in the Maori children who shared our classroom. We led a sheltered, not to say privileged, existence.

My parents established a modus operandi which suited us all well. My mother ran the household and my father was accorded full respect as the breadwinner. They rarely quarrelled, and then only about some aspect of disciplining the children (my mother was very strict and quick to punish, my father much less so) or about my father's occasional forays to the pub with his pals.

It was also an extremely secure family life. My parents' marriage, their love for us, the absolute stability of the family relationship, were simply taken for granted. My mother was the source of all knowledge and wisdom. She inculcated in us a strong sense of moral values. We were brought up to believe absolutely in the usual virtues – honesty, thrift, and so on – but, perhaps more unusually, in the importance of thinking of others.

This came, it must be said, less out of genuine thoughtfulness and compassion than a concern for what others might think of us. We were always brought up to try to earn the golden opinions of everyone with whom we came into contact. This certainly made us behave well in company and pay great attention to the opinions of others, but in some ways we were too eager to please. It was only in later life that I felt fully mature, in the sense that I was able to identify what I wanted to do rather than what I thought others would expect.

Although our home life was rich in love and security, it was actually rather poor in cultural or intellectual activity. My mother was, although very intelligent, no intellectual. She respected intellectual achievement but had little understanding of intellectual life. There were books in the house, but I can't recall my parents ever actually buying one. There was no music, or painting. My father had a broad knowledge of current affairs – he was good at general knowledge quizzes in the newspapers – but we rarely discussed anything serious.

My mother was, however, very keen that I should do well academically. I somehow managed to learn to read before I went to school. I have no recollection of actually being taught to read, but I remember a visitor to the house being startled to hear a four-year old Bryan read out loud – indeed, at the top of his voice – from a book called *The Story of the Life of Jesus*. At that point, if asked, I would have said that my ambition was to become a bishop. Heaven knows why. We had been christened, but apart from that I had only occasional contact with the church.

My mother's ambitions for me extended beyond schoolwork. She sent me to elocution lessons where I learnt to recite poetry. The high point of the year for my elocution teacher, and for my mother, was the 'Competitions'. These took place over two or three days in the Hawera town hall. Devoted mothers brought their largely untalented offspring to sing, dance and recite poetry and to be judged in deadly earnest by the somewhat elderly judges. The results were faithfully reported in perfect detail by the local paper.

In my first year, at the age of four, I acquitted myself tolerably well but had to make do with a 'Highly Commended'. My mother vowed that I would do better next year so I was transferred to a different, supposedly better teacher. It speaks volumes for the seriousness of purpose of all those involved that a small town like Hawera could boast more than one elocution teacher.

This time, I was schooled to recite a poem called 'My Dog' which I can recite to this day. The great day came. I made the final. I had to repeat the performance in the evening. It was a triumph. My mother's cup of happiness brimmed over. My glorious victory was duly recorded in the paper the following day.

This taste of success convinced my mother that she had a genius on her hands. A woman of powerful personality who had never been able to achieve a great deal in her own right, she threw all her considerable energies into becoming the perfect mother, and she made a pretty fair job of it. No child ever received more encouragement and support than I did. It was a daily ritual that I should be asked, when I came home from school, what had happened during the day. What my mother was hungry to hear was how I had been the only one able to answer a particularly difficult question or how the teacher had commended me for an especially good piece of work. I duly obliged, usually truthfully, and my mother basked in the vicarious pleasure of my teacher's praise.

I was reminded of those days by an experience I had shortly after I returned to New Zealand in 1994. I received through the mail a small parcel with an accompanying letter. The writer introduced herself as a Mrs Walker who, as Miss York, had been my first teacher at primary school in Hawera. She still lived in Hawera. She enclosed a school exercise book, in remarkably good condition. It bore a picture of Mount Egmont on its cover and the legend, in pencil: 'Composition, Bryan Gould, 1945'. Inside were the childish essays I had written in my second year at school. It almost beggars belief that my teacher should have been able to produce that book nearly 50 years later. When I replied to her letter, however, and expressed surprise as well as pleasure, she simply said that she had found it one day when clearing out a cupboard.

Success at schoolwork came easily to me, and because it seemed quite natural, I took little notice of it. Because I was brought up in a family with few pretensions to cultural or intellectual sophistication, I was able to regard my scholasticability as a sort of happy accident, and I spent most of my time pursuing the same interests as my schoolmates.

I was small for my age and young for my class, a problem which was exacerbated in later years when I skipped a year or two because I was academically advanced for my age. I avoided being labelled the class swot (something that occasionally worried me) because I could run fast, fight well and was tolerably good at and even more enthusiastic about sport.

My father's job at the bank meant that he was transferred from one branch to another at regular intervals. This meant in turn that we children had to go to a new school every three or four years. We always viewed such a prospect with a mixture of excitement and apprehension. There was something rather daunting about joining a new class, usually halfway through the term. I had a particularly testing time when we moved from Hawera to Palmerston North and, at the age of seven, I arrived at my new school with all my hair shaved off – the treatment prescribed for a bad case of ringworm contracted from a stray cat I had brought home. I was the object of fascinated curiosity for some time – until my hair grew again.

The experience of starting a new school from time to time was, however, on balance beneficial. It made us adaptable, and stimulated us to new achievement. New people, new situations, new challenges held few fears for us. It created a pattern in our lives which, in my own case, has persisted. After I have lived in one house for about five years, I begin to get restless, even to this day.

My school career continued to prosper. I was *dux* of Central School, Palmerston North, in 1949. This gave my mother great satisfaction since my main rival for this distinction was the son of a childhood acquaintance of hers. From Standard Four at the primary school, I went to an intermediate school which served the whole city of Palmerston North. The school was strictly streamed. I found myself in the top stream and challenged daily to produce my best work.

My teacher there, Darcy Dale, was really the first person to open my eyes to the pleasure of academic pursuits for their own sake. About now, I began to realise scholarship might result in more than mere parental approval.

Although I was the smallest boy in the class, I was elected class counsellor – a sort of class prefect. This was, I suppose, my first experience of elected office. I had to act as a sort of liaison officer between class and teacher and I took the task very seriously. I was generally pretty well-behaved and didn't get into many scrapes. On one occasion, however, I was caught for some minor offence (I have a vague recollection that it was something to do with chewing gum) and was taken outside the class to be caned. I felt the humiliation keenly. On returning to the classroom, the object of scores of curious eyes, I made a public statement, at the age of eleven, to the effect that I was sorry that I had let the class down as their class counsellor!

I had only two terms at that school before my father was transferred to Tauranga. Here, I was again bumped up a year and my parents were delighted at this further evidence of my academic prowess. Within a couple of months, just before my twelfth birthday, I was on my way to secondary school, in a town still new to me, with classmates who were in many cases two years older than me and in every respect bigger and more physically and emotionally mature. I survived the experience reasonably well, but it is not, I think, to be recommended. In general, children should be allowed to mature at their own pace, however tempting it might be to exploit a particular talent.

Out of school, we had very little with which to entertain ourselves.

There was of course no television or any other gadgets or devices which occupy so much of the time of modern children. We had no money to spend on going out. Our principal means of passing the time was 'going out to play'. Most days, there would be a tap on the back door, a neighbouring child enquiring politely whether Bryan or Ngaire or both could 'come out to play'. And off we would go, to do nothing in particular.

Tauranga, however, was a town with an excellent climate and a lovely beach. We spent hours swimming and fishing. I was allowed to join the local tennis club, of which my mother became captain, and I became passionately addicted to the game, spending virtually the whole of my summer weekends on the courts.

I also began to work for a living. I did numerous after-school and holiday jobs – mowing lawns, delivering telegrams, working as a shop assistant in MacKenzies, the local department store. I delivered newspapers for the *Bay of Plenty Times* after school, for 12s. 6d. a week with a 2s. 6d. bonus if there were no complaints. At one point, I had two other rounds as well, one in the morning for the *New Zealand Herald* and the other at about eight o'clock in the evening for the *Auckland Star*.

In order to do the paper rounds, I had to have a new bike. This cost me £19. 19s. 6d., which I paid off at the rate of ten shillings a week. In the course of my round, I became friendly with a beautiful rough-coated collie called Dandy. When he became too much for his elderly owners, it was agreed that I could have him, provided that I exercised him every day and paid for his food. The exercise was no problem – he simply accompanied me on my round; however, to be fair to my parents, I can't recall ever having to contribute to his food.

I was also something of a budding thespian. An English professional pantomine producer called Eddie Martin arrived in Palmerston North with his beautiful young New Zealand wife. He contracted with a local charity to put on a pantomine called *Mother Goose*. He played the dame, his wife, who was a professional dancer, the principal boy. He provided the set, the costumes and so on and produced the show. The rest of the cast was recruited locally. My mother noticed the advertisement and I was duly taken along to be auditioned. I landed the 'juvenile lead' part of Onyx, the goose who laid the golden egg, and spent a wonderful couple of months rehearsing most evenings followed by a fortnight of playing to packed houses in the town's largest theatre.

I was entranced by the whole thing – the chance to keep company with adults who rather fancied themselves as louche or bohemian, the fascinating contrast between the beautiful young dancer and the world-weary cynicism and raffishness of her much older pantomine dame of a husband, the tattiness of the costumes and sets in the cold light of day transformed by the glamour of the lights, music and greasepaint.

Shortly after we arrived in Tauranga, a year or two later, Eddie Martin turned up there as well, and repeated the performance. As an old hand, I waltzed into the slightly more demanding role of Simple Simon (I was clearly already marked out as a future vice-chancellor!). This involved a good deal more speaking (Onyx the goose had necessarily been a bird of few words) and also required me to sing a solo. By this time, I had fallen in love with a girl in my class called Maxine Tilby, a very promising young ballet dancer who had been chosen as a leading dancer in the corps de ballet. The glamour of the whole experience persuaded her to find some romantic interest in me as well. The only trouble was that she was a full head taller than me. The romance did not long survive the end of the pantomine season.

At the end of our third year at secondary school, we all took our School Certificate examination. I had pursued an academic course and was studying five subjects, English, History, Geography, French and Latin. I never regretted my three years of Latin, but I have often regretted the peculiarity which allowed me to avoid the study of mathematics altogether. As the examination approached, my father was again transferred, this time to Dannevirke. It was plainly unfortunate that I would have to change schools just a couple of months before the exams, so I boarded with neighbours for a couple of months and took the exams in Tauranga.

When school started in Dannevirke at the beginning of the next academic year, I faced the familiar challenge of starting a new school.

Dannevirke High School, like all the schools I had attended, was the local co-educational comprehensive. It had an excellent reputation, considering that it was a relatively small school in a rather obscure part of the country. The headmaster was a great enthusiast called T. Duncan Scott (or 'Dunc', as we referred to him) who had an uncanny ability to attract to the school some of the best young teachers in the country. He was a large, red-faced, irascible man who must nevertheless have had some appeal, since he was married to a much younger and rather attractive woman. As a couple, they were often referred to as Beauty and the Beast.

Dunc took one look at the academic record of his newly arrived pupil and decided that I was 'scholarship material'. He suggested to my mother that I should skip the lower sixth year and move straight on to upper sixth work. This would enable me to sit the national university scholarship at the end of the year, as a sort of 'dry run', and stand me in good stead to actually win a scholarship when I repeated the whole performance the following year.

By this time, still very small and young for my age, I was at least two and sometimes three years younger than the others in my class. It speaks volumes for their tolerance and, I suppose, my adaptability, that I enjoyed my new school. The work was quite hard. I had to drop Latin, which wasn't taught there, and replace it with biology, which I hadn't studied before. I was not a particularly gifted linguist and lacked enthusiasm for French, which was in any case taught by a charming but ineffectual teacher who could easily be distracted (and usually was) by invitations to tell us stories about his wartime experiences. I duly sat the examination at the end of the year. It turned out that I did poorly in French, moderately well in biology and geography, but came fifth in the whole of New Zealand in English and second in history. I was awarded a scholarship, one of thirty pupils thoughout the country to get the award.

The news was completely unexpected. We learnt of it only when a neighbour across the road phoned to say that she had just read about it in the paper. I can still remember my excitement as, scarcely believing what I had been told, I ran across the road to get the paper so that we could confirm that it was really true. Typically enough, my mother was delighted, but not so delighted that she did not want to apply to have my French paper re-marked. Wiser counsels prevailed.

At the age of fifteen, I was – in an academic sense – ready for university. My achievement made me something of a hero. Dunc was so delighted that he gave the whole school a day's holiday, which naturally rather raised my popularity with my schoolmates.

Dunc, however, was not satisfied with my success. He laid plans for me to sit the scholarship exam again the following year, this time in the hope that I would come top of the whole of New Zealand. I may have been only fifteen, with an ambitious mother and headmaster urging me on, but I quickly worked out there was little advantage in undertaking another year's hard study. I could not improve on winning a scholarship – and as for coming top of New Zealand, it might have brought prestige to me and more especially the school, but it was just as likely that I would do worse rather than better. I therefore declined to sit the scholarship exam again, but opted instead for a year of marking time.

I am afraid that I have always had a tendency to laziness. I am not sure that that extra year at school waiting until I was old enough to go to university did me very much good, since it encouraged me to believe that life was rather easier than it is. I nevertheless enjoyed myself immensely, playing rugby and tennis, falling in love with the beautiful leading lady in the school production of *Iolanthe*, and becoming a prefect and moreover the rather unlikely regimental sergant major for the school cadet battalion.

As the time came for me to go off to university, I began to make preparations. For a couple of months during the summer holidays I worked for a local painter who was contracted to paint all the farm buildings on a huge sheep station out on the coast. This meant going off for two or three weeks at a time and staying in a shearers' whare. We lived mainly on potatoes and cabbage, occasionally supplemented by lamb supplied by the farmer. I loved the outdoor life, and cheerfully put up with the hardships. The point of the exercise was to earn enough money to set me up for my first year at university. My earnings, plus the scholarship, went a long way towards covering my living costs.

My parents also made their contribution. As luck would have it, the local gentlemen's outfitters, Art Carr, suffered a disastrous fire over the Christmas holiday period. Most of his stock was damaged by smoke or the firemen's hoses. He accordingly had a fire sale, and readily agreed to open his shop specially after hours one evening so that my parents could kit me out for university. They spent £100 on my wardrobe, buying everything from underwear to cravats, waistcoats to trilby hats. I looked ridiculously young in many of the clothes I was bought, some of which, particularly the heavy winter-weight underwear, lasted twenty years. My mother laboured long and hard to sew my name tags into every item. There was just one drawback to this splendid wardrobe. Most of the clothes smelt strongly and persistently of smoke.

As I got ready to go off to university, I was nevertheless curiously unprepared. I had not really been away from home very much. I was still very young, and in some ways immature for my age. No one in my family had ever been to university. As far as my parents were concerned, I may as well have been going to the moon. I was well equipped academically, but even then it took me a full year at university to realize that my fellow students were not actually geniuses. My major handicap was that there was so little in my family background to prepare me for serious discussion of matters of real importance. Not only were my parents not interested in cultural matters, it was a rule in our family that good manners precluded any conversation about religion or politics, or indeed anything that might provoke disagreement.

I had briefly, at about the age of thirteen, shown some enthusiasm for Bible classes. That lasted about three months and could be said to have come to a natural end when, during a sermon in which the local vicar asserted that the name of Jesus was unique and was never encountered as the name of anyone else, I contradicted him by pointing out that I had recently read a report in the local paper to the effect that a South American by the name of Jesus had been convicted of theft. The vicar was neither impressed by nor grateful for the information.

As to politics, it was simply taken for granted that our family voted National (or Tory). Despite the fact that we never discussed politics, I was passionately interested in the subject. My hero was Winston Churchill, and I was delighted when I won the oratory contest at school with what I fondly imagined was a speech in the Churchillian mould. I remember being reduced to tears once when my terrifying Grandad accused me, on account of something I had said, of being a 'Labourite'. In our family, there could be no more damning indictment.

I had been friendly with a teacher at Tauranga College for whom I had occasionally babysat. Mr Mitchell was a forceful character who was widely believed to be a socialist and therefore a bit odd. I was fascinated to discover books on his shelves which bore the word 'socialism' in their titles, but I didn't get so far as to ask to borrow them.

Despite their unthinking allegiance to the conservative cause, my parents were not conventional right-wingers. Like many New Zealanders, they had a strong streak of egalitarianism. Although their decision not to send any of us children away to school was almost certainly taken on financial grounds, it was cloaked – in my mother's case, at any rate – in a healthy scorn for those parents who preferred to pay strangers to bring up their children, rather than face up to the job themselves. We children heartily agreed with this scepticism. We could think of nothing worse than being banished at a tender age from hearth and home.

My father, although a scion of a family which saw itself as a pillar of local society, was republican in his views. He had little patience with the Royal Family, or indeed with anything British. His wartime experiences had brought him to the view that the future belonged to America and that New Zealand would do much better to throw in its lot with them. For some reason, I differed from him sharply in this respect. I always saw myself as an anglophile.

In most other respects, however, my parents (and indeed all our relatives) were extremely conventional in their views. This was particularly true in their attitudes towards Maori. They were in no sense overtly racist, and strongly supported – if challenged – the notion of equality before the law, but they could never conceal a feeling of patronising superiority. They evinced no interest whatsoever in Maori language or culture, which might as well have been non-existent. As a consequence, we children, like most of our contemporaries, were completely at home with Maori as a familiar feature of the landscape but profoundly ignorant of anything to do with them, even to the extent of hopelessly mispronouncing Maori place names.

It was with this narrow base of experience that I set off on my seventeenth birthday to Victoria University in the capital of Wellington to read history and law. It would be wrong to suggest that I was a trembling naif. I was by temperament pretty self-reliant and could always conceal any doubt or nervousness. I had decided to do a law degree partly because my parents had always thought that the local lawyers did pretty well, partly because of the encouragement of a Dannevirke solicitor, Mark Poole, who had employed me during the school holidays, and partly because I thought it would be a good outlet for my talents at speaking and arguing.

I was to board at Weir House, a hostel near the University perched on the side of a steep hill (as are most buildings in Wellington) with a magnificent view over the harbour. In my first year, I shared a set of two rooms with John Gibson, a blond, ruddy-faced boy a year or so older than me.

John had been a boarder at Wanganui College and was well-used to living away from home. He was a good cricketer, swore with great delicacy, and his interest in girls had clearly gone a good deal further than my own rather ineffectual romanticising. He must have wondered what on earth he had been landed with, but he was very kind to me and we became good friends.

I quickly fell in with a group of lively lads who included Brian Brooks, a charismatic and amusing extrovert who later became prominent in New Zealand public affairs and is currently dean of the law school at Victoria. Brian, too, was a man of the world, and I was secretly flattered when he consulted me, in all my naiveté, on affairs of the heart or even such esoteric subjects as sex. I was eventually to be his best man.

Our group was quickly recognised, I believe, to be exceptionally talented. Brian Brooks, another pal, Roy Peach, and I made up a formidable debating team. I only regret that, in those days, there was no wider arena in which we could have displayed our talents. In due course, we were also elected as the student representatives whose principal task it was to represent the student interest to the Warden. I regret to say that we made life for Ted Harvey, the Warden of the time, pretty difficult.

I passed my first year exams with very good results, and it was, I suppose, the respect accorded to this by my contemporaries that encouraged me to realise that I could go on to do well at university, which I duly did. I was doing a conjoint BA/LlB degree which required me, in effect, to do a history degree as a preliminary to going on to the law units of the LlB. I completed the BA in my first three years. However, there was a slight hiccup in my third year. I had undertaken five units, including the third year of history and four of the main law subjects – Contract, Torts and so on. This was a substantial burden for anyone, and especially for someone who was by now as self-confident and as easily distracted by other interests as I was. I did very little work and left much essential preparation until the few days before the exams. I then found that, because of constant interruptions, I could not do all that I needed to do during the day – one of the disadvantages of living in a hostel.

I conceived the idea of sleeping during the day and working at night. This worked all right for a couple of days, but the real test was to be Company Law, for which I had done no work, and which required a full night's work if I was even to have a nodding acquaintance with it.

I took a short rest before beginning my night's work. The next thing I knew, it was breakfast time. I was panic-stricken and, feeling genuinely ill, spoke urgently to the Warden to say that I was too ill to take the exam (to say nothing of the fact that I knew no Company Law whatsoever). He advised me to sit the paper and apply for an aegrotat afterwards. I sat the exam, which didn't seem to go too badly, so I forgot about the aegrotat. I was astonished to get a mark of 94 per cent – one of life's great mysteries.

I had an enjoyable although low-key social life. Every Wednesday, my grandparents came to town. I would meet my Nana and her older sister, Auntie Marjorie, for morning coffee at James Smith's, the department store. I then went on to meet Grandad and some of his business cronies for lunch at a restaurant called Garland's. Grandad had apparently helped finance the proprietor and we were always made a great fuss of. Apart from that, and a Saturday foray to Athletic Park to watch the rugby, however, I didn't venture far from Weir House. I had no money and, of course, no car. I played quite a lot of tennis, represented the university at badminton and in the law moots competition at the annual university tournament and occasionally went to the pictures, but my main social interest was debating and generally messing around with my friends.

For the first time in my life, I found myself engaged in real debate about current issues. We had little knowledge of or interest in domestic politics. Our arena was the world. I generally took a rather imperialistic and pro-British view of international affairs, to the extent that I was a passionate (though secretly rather troubled) defender of the Suez adventure. I remember being somewhat shaken a little later when a Czech refugee I met while working at the dairy factory during the summer holidays told me what a blow to the British reputation Suez had been among those in Eastern Europe who prized liberty.

We drank beer occasionally, within the limits of our resources, and for some strange reason I acquired the nickname of 'Alky', short for 'alcoholic'. I found this quite amusing, especially when I thought how aghast my parents would be if they knew. I was very interested in girls, but had little idea of how to do much about it. This was the late Fifties, just before the permissive era, and to ask a girl out, let alone establish any sort of physical relationship (which was what we all dreamt about), was regarded as an almost impossibly difficult exercise.

One of my great interests was pop music. I followed the hit parade closely. I had bought myself a piano accordion just before I left school and painstakingly taught myself to play – not very well. It was not an instrument which endeared itself to my friends, however, so I decided, in recognition of the modern era, to buy a guitar. I was not much good at that either. I could strum a few chords and sing at parties, which, in the days of three-chord tunes, was good enough to be going on with. My great talent was mimicking the pop singers of the day. My specialities were 'Heartbreak Hotel', 'Be Bop A Lula' and 'Great Balls of Fire', which I would sing as a floor show at the termly Weir House dance.

I had very little money, and would often try to eke out my meagre resources by taking on casual work. Sometimes I went down to the Wellington wharves for what was called 'seagulling', where I joined a crowd of other men just before 8 a.m., hoping to be given the nod for a day's work. Since I was small and young-looking, I guess they needed to be pretty desperate before they chose me. I found the work hard but I have always enjoyed physical labour and I was quite strong for my size. I had no sense that I might be doing work which should have constituted a proper permanent job for someone. My political horizons were very limited.

In the long summer holidays, I worked at the local dairy factory, first in Dannevirke and later in Te Awamutu, when my parents moved there. I enjoyed this work enormously, although the first few days of the season were quite hard, until I toughened up. I worked at various times on making butter, milk powder and casein (a sort of industrial plastic made from milk solids) and, at Te Awamutu, I worked on a shift system which sometimes meant working through the night.

I learnt a great deal from mixing with working men. It was possible to earn their respect by working hard. For the first time in my life, I found myself in the company of people who took for granted a set of values, and a political outlook, very different from my own. When politics were discussed, I prudently kept my own – or rather my parents' – opinions to myself.

This conflict between my parents and my workmates came to a head one summer. It was the custom at the end of the season, as workers left or were laid off, to 'shout' your workmates to a keg of beer and some fish and chips at the end of your last shift. As my last shift approached, there was a good deal of anticipation on the part of my workmates. It so happened that the date coincided with a Junior National Party dance in town which my mother was particularly keen for me to attend, in the hope, no doubt, that I would meet some wealthy farmer's daughter. I insisted on the beer and fish and chips with my mates. This was achieved only at the cost of a bitter row with my mother who was not accustomed to being denied.

By this time, I had moved from Victoria University to Auckland, partly because my parents had moved to Te Awamutu, which was much closer to Auckland, and partly because I had reached the point when law students obtained part-time jobs in law firms, and I had somehow obtained through a connection of my father's a job in an Auckland law firm.

Changing university halfway through a degree may appear an odd thing to do, but it didn't seem strange to me, what with my history of moving from one school to another every few years. I rapidly fell in with a new group of friends, mostly, but not all, law students and law clerks like myself. I boarded for a year in a boarding house near the University in Princes Street, then moved to a bedsit in Grafton Road where for the first time I did my own cooking and learnt to look after myself.

I enjoyed my work as a law clerk, even though it meant attending lectures at eight in the morning and for a couple of hours in the evening. I rapidly established a reputation as a good student. I still had no money (law clerks were very poorly paid), but managed a fairly active social life.

I also fell in love with a girl who worked as a secretary in the law firm where I worked. Diane was small, pretty and bright. We had a wonderful time. She lived with her parents about a mile and a half from where I lived. I spent a good deal of time walking backwards and forwards to and from her house.

I took a job in my spare time as secretary of the Auckland region of the Legal Employees Union. This was mainly a matter of getting in subscriptions from the members, but once a year I was required to negotiate a wage settlement with the employers. I had taken the job more in order to supplement my income than for reasons of trade union solidarity, but the experience was another step in my political education.

On Friday evenings, my friends and I would meet in the Occidental, a pub in Vulcan Lane. We gathered as soon as we could after five o'clock when our offices closed, and drink as much beer as possible before closing time at six o'clock. We were part of a milling throng, crammed into a large square room which was tiled like a men's urinal. Along the far wall ran a straight bar, behind which sweating shirt-sleeved barmen ran up and down with hoses, filling jugs and glasses with beer. We would then spill out on to the street at six o'clock, half-drunk, and go for a 'curry' at the Chinese restaurant.

This was the infamous 'six o'clock swill'. Every three years, a referendum was held on whether the licensing laws should be changed. The result was always the same. The women of New Zealand calculated that if their husbands came home drunk when the pubs stayed open till six o'clock, they would come home even drunker if the opening hours were extended.

I celebrated my twenty-first birthday after I had been in Auckland a year. My parents put on a family dinner party for me, at which I tasted wine for the first time. My father had, rather improbably, obtained a bottle of sparkling red burgundy, a wine which I have never since come across. It was opened with a satisfying pop and sparkled very prettily in our glasses. The only thing I had seen before which looked anything like it was raspberryade, and I was bitterly disappointed when it tasted somewhat different.

My sister married in 1961 and I was best man at her wedding. Her husband was a young dairy farmer from the district named Doug Short, a tall, handsome man and, at six feet three, an excellent rugby player. Doug became one of my best friends.

About this time, I conceived the idea that I might try for a Rhodes Scholarship. I knew very little about the scholarship but my mother had somehow got to know something about it and had occasionally mentioned it as the pinnacle of any student's achievement. My interest was further stimulated by the fact that at Dannevirke High School a boy named Colin Beer had won a Rhodes Scholarship a year or two before I had arrived, and his name was still being mentioned in tones of reverence.

I knew that the scholarship was awarded to all-rounders who had a good academic record but could also demonstrate some sporting prowess and wider interests. I was concerned that, as a recent arrival at Auckland University, I might take some time to make my mark. I took the precaution of going to see the Dean of the Law School, a powerful university politician called Jack Northey, to tell him that I intended to do a Master's degree. I hoped this would induce him to look out for my results. Whether helped by this or not, I duly got A passes in three of my four final-year subjects. I was tremendously excited, since I knew this was good enough to win me the Senior Law Scholarship, conclusive evidence that I could meet the academic requirements for a Rhodes Scholarship.

I was less confident of my other qualifications. I had a good but not outstanding sporting record. I had not played competitive tennis for some time but I decided that I should try for the university team. I enquired about qualifying, only to discover that I was too late and that the team had already been selected. Further enquiries revealed, however, that the tennis club was almost defunct and that the team had been made up of the club captain and his cronies. I challenged the club captain to a match, and persuaded him to agree that if I beat him, I could be in the team. He had a tennis court at his home and I duly arrived to play him. We played a tense match, with no spectators and umpiring ourselves. I won. I not only made the team but supplanted the club captain as number one in the team.

At about this time, I attracted the attention of S.W. Tong, president of the Auckland Law Society. He was a kind and gentle man, who had an extremely prosperous one-man practice in Queen Street. The question of whether or not they were to be offered jobs which would lead to partnerships was one which very much exercised my friends as they qualified. I was therefore regarded as extremely fortunate when Mr Tong offered me a partnership.

My parents were, as usual, very excited at my success. They had always seen my law degree as the passport to a comfortable life as a successful professional man. They had envisaged me as a respected country solicitor. A Queen Street lawyer exceeded their wildest dreams.

For me, however, the offer created a dilemma. To turn it down would be madness, yet to accept it would mean giving up the dream of a Rhodes Scholarship, of going up to Oxford, of seeing a wider world. I resolved to keep that dream alive and take the gamble of turning down what might have been a once-in-a-lifetime chance. And the difficulty was that I could not even explain, except to my immediate family, why I was taking what seemed such an irrational step.

By this time, I was doing my Master's degree. On Jack Northey's advice, I was writing a thesis on the subject of declaratory judgments, a little-known remedy whose major significance was in administrative law. As always, I was troubled by laziness. It was always so tempting, in setting one's own schedule, to take just one more half-day off. Yet I enjoyed the work, and for the first time developed a genuine scholarly interest in researching and thinking.

The time came to apply for a Rhodes Scholarship. I prepared my application carefully, and was shortlisted. I was invited to Wellington for the interview. About eight of us gathered to go through the ordeal. I was in a state of high excitement. It was my first important interview, but I somehow knew that I would do well. I remember taking a few risks. When asked about books I had read recently, I confidently talked about a book by the American author Michael Harrington which I had in fact only glanced at. When asked what foreign languages I spoke, I said that I could speak French and could count up to twenty in German.

The day seemed to pass very quickly. I have a hazy recollection of being called back into the interview room late in the afternoon and being told that the two Rhodes Scholarships for the year had been awarded to myself and to a younger student called Colin Jeffcot. I suddenly felt very tired and keen to escape. I stayed just as long as politeness demanded, accepting the congratulations of the interviewers (mainly past Rhodes Scholars) and of the unsuccessful candidates. I then made my excuses and left, going out to meet my mother who had been waiting patiently for me in her car outside.

I told her the joyous news. She was thrilled but not surprised. She had come to expect that I would achieve whatever I set my mind to.

In New Zealand, in those days at least, the annual award of the Rhodes Scholarships was national news. I received telegrams of congratulation from everyone from the Prime Minister downwards.

I also wanted to celebrate my success with my girlfriend Diane. I asked my mother whether I could invite her home for the weekend. She reluctantly agreed. The two had never met, but my mother was instinctively hostile to the notion that another woman might have some claim on me.

Diane duly arrived. I was delighted to see her and we had a lovely time. She was a very presentable girl and keen to please. There was no conceivable reason why anyone should dislike her, yet my mother immediately took against her. Diane, however, was rather nervous, and when nervous, found difficulty in eating very much. My mother took offence: either her cooking had been slighted or Diane was on a silly diet which she was unwilling to abandon. From that viewpoint, the weekend was not a great success.

I began my preparations for going to Oxford. I had only the haziest notion of what Oxford might be like, so I eagerly accepted advice from anyone. It was agreed that I should apply to go to Balliol, where the law tutor was a New Zealander called Don Harris.

My thesis was going well. Diane typed it for me, a herculean task, since every page had footnotes of varying length, as well as copious case references, in each of which the underlinings, commas and brackets had to be got exactly right. It was, I suppose, a real labour of love. She and I were rewarded by my being awarded an LlM with first-class honours.

The date for my departure approached. I was to sail on the maiden voyage of the new Shaw Savill liner, the *Northern Star*, at the end of August 1962. I was travelling with a number of New Zealand scholars bound for Oxford, including Ian Ramsay, another Auckland lawyer who had won a Shell Scholarship to Wadham College. We were to share a cabin.

On the night before my departure, I found myself caught in an emotional dilemma. I was keen to spend the evening with Diane, and that was naturally what she expected as well. My mother, on the other hand, was adamant that I should spend my last night in New Zealand in the bosom of the family. I unwisely tried a compromise, in which I took Diane out for a meal but cut the evening short in order to return to the family. Neither party was satisfied.

The problem got worse the following day. My family came on to the ship to look it over and see me installed in my cabin. Diane and her family did likewise. I spent a tense couple of hours sharing my time between the two parties whilst doing my best to keep them apart. At last, to my intense relief, the time came for them all to debark. The passengers crowded on to the decks to wave to the crowds of well-wishers gathered on the quayside. The bands played, and the crowd sang 'Now Is the Hour' as the great ship began to move, almost imperceptibly at first, away from the quay.

It should have been an emotional moment, as I embarked on the great adventure which would take me 12,000 miles away to the other side of the globe, to an older and more worldly civilisation. Instead, my emotional travails continued to the end. I could see the two little knots of people, my family and Diane's, on the quay below. As was the custom, I threw coins to them from the passenger rail as the boat pulled away. I was scrupulously fair to the last, throwing a coin first to one, then to the other. As the distance between us increased, I saw that they edged ever closer together, trying to shorten the distance between themselves and the passenger they had come to bid farewell.

I learnt subsequently, in tear-stained letters from both my mother and Diane, that the evening had ended in disaster. The two groups had eventually collided, words had been exchanged, my young brother and Diane's father had jostled each other and my mother had – accidentally – been pushed to the ground. I was glad to leave it all behind, and to look forward to a new life.

TWO

A Student at Oxford
1962–64

THE NORTHERN STAR took five weeks to reach Britain. We called at Fiji, Tahiti, Panama, Georgetown and Port of Spain, before arriving at Southampton. I had never before ventured out of New Zealand. To me, this range of new sights and experiences was like looking through a kaleidoscope.

Shipboard life was itself a revelation. There were many young people on board and a great deal of social and sporting activity. My travelling companion, Ian Ramsay, was someone I had known slightly in Auckland but now grew to know very well. He was a large, slightly clumsy young man, with a slightly off-beat personality which some people found offputting but which I very much liked. He was someone of independent, not to say unpredictable, views, and unexpected talents. He was, for example, a very good amateur wrestler. We became firm friends. Later, when he married in England, I was his best man.

We were assigned permanent seats in the dining room with two Australian girls who were travelling together. I was, incredibly by today's standards, determined to remain faithful to Diane, and therefore avoided any romantic entanglements. Ramsay (everyone called him by his surname) was in a similar situation, with the slight added complication that he was being faithful to two girls, one an English girl he had left behind in New Zealand and the other a New Zealand girl holidaying in England.

We and the two Australian girls nevertheless struck up a friendship.

On one occasion, Ramsay's size and physical presence came in handy. We had disembarked in Tahiti and were visiting a pretty disreputable bar in town. A tough-looking man, slightly drunk, took a fancy to one of the girls and in a gesture designed to attract her attention tipped the sunhat she was wearing over her eyes. I remonstrated on her behalf. To my dismay, the man turned on me and invited me outside to continue the argument. I was much relieved when Ramsay rose to his considerable height and offered to take over our side of the argument. The man slunk away.

Five weeks of leisure were an unaccustomed luxury. I was, however, keen to make some constructive use of my time. I had always been a voracious reader. As a boy, holidaying with my grandparents, I would start at one end of the bookshelf and work my way along it. I set out on a similarly eclectic exercise on my voyage to England. I read books about Oxford, including *Zuleika Dobson*. With its highly coloured account of life among the gilded youth, it prepared me in my imagination for an Oxford of which (thankfully) I found only faint echoes when I arrived. I read the Bible from cover to cover – not very rewarding. I read works of philosophy, including, for some unfathomable reason, *Thus Spake Zarathustra*. I can only imagine that it happened to be available. I read novels endlessly, including *The Alexandria Quartet*.

The reading, and the amount of time I had to ponder on what I was reading, where I was going, and what I really believed in, made for a somewhat unsettling experience. By virtue of the absolute security of my childhood and the certainties of my upbringing, I had rarely, if ever, doubted. Now, however, I began to ponder the great questions, not so much political (although there, too, my ideas were in a ferment of change) as philosophical, moral and religious.

I spent a great part of the voyage agonising (not too obviously – I still managed to have a pretty good time) about the possible basis of a personal morality whose validity could be asserted to others in the absence of any external, God-given commands. I reached the bleak conclusion that it was very difficult, without God, to postulate a morality which would bind others – and I had the greatest difficulty in believing that the concept of God was anything other than a way of rephrasing a question to which we humans had not yet found a satisfactory answer.

I was quite depressed, in my quieter moments, by this conclusion. I have often returned to it, with only slightly more encouraging results. Most of the time, though, I choose to ignore the question and remain cheerful.

The voyage across the Atlantic was slightly prolonged by the fact that the *Northern Star* developed engine trouble. We limped into Southampton a few days late. I was astonished to find that the sky was blue and the sun was shining as we sailed up the Solent. I had developed an image of Britain in which the sky was always dark and full of belching chimneys.

I was by now 23 years old, but still in some ways remarkably naive. Most young New Zealanders travelling abroad seem to have a sort of childlike innocence about them which, to others, is both engaging and irritating – and I was no exception. I gazed at the world with wide eyes, mentally (and sometimes verbally) comparing everything I did and saw with the range of limited experience I had gained back home.

I was immensely proud of New Zealand, and determined that people should know about the delights of my home country – and with good reason. New Zealand at that point had arguably the highest living standard in the world. Our social reforms led the world. New Zealand's health and education services were of a very high standard and were basically free. We seemed free of social or racial conflict. New Zealand appeared to be a country which had solved all its problems.

This impression I had of my home country was further reinforced when I encountered such obvious poverty in the ports we stopped off at on the way over.

My first impressions of Britain were pretty confused. We took a train to London and I spent a night or two on the floor of a flat occupied by some New Zealand acquaintances of Ramsay's. I found London crowded, dirty and tiring, but undeniably exciting. I was, however, disappointed by Piccadilly Circus, which I had somehow persuaded myself was the hub of the world. I was not prepared for the rather drab and undistinguished intersection I found. I was also appalled at the price I had to pay to go to the pictures in the Dominion Theatre on Tottenham Court Road.

After a couple of days in London, Ramsay and I went for a day trip to Oxford just a few days before term started. It was a lovely golden October day. The sunshine was rather pale and lacked warmth, but the trees glowed with autumnal colours and there was a slightly acrid smell in the air, as though peat fires had been burning. Ever since, the early autumn has been my favourite time of year in England. There is something about the pale and faded beauty, the air of faint melancholy, which suits the English character.

I visited what was to be my room at Balliol. By a curious coincidence, the room – which was empty – was being visited at the same time by a distinguished-looking man, whose name I promptly forgot, who had occupied it as a New Zealand Rhodes Scholar before the war and who had stayed on in England to pursue a career with Shell. He was very encouraging about the prospect of enjoying myself at Oxford.

My room was on the ground floor of staircase 17, and looked out over the main quad. It was to become home for me for the next two years, apart from the time I spent in the long vacation at the Balliol hostel at Holywell Manor. It was a large square room, plainly furnished and heated only by a two-bar electric radiator. In my first term, I kept the radiator going most of the time. It cost me £2 a week – a huge sum on my limited resources.

I quickly settled in to college life. I was considerably older than most of the English undergraduates, the majority of whom I found rather juvenile. They were also unlike anything I had yet encountered. The public school boys, in particular, seemed to have quite a different set of social values from mine. I was astonished at their lack of sensitivity, their assertiveness and their self-obsession. I could hardly believe the braying tones in which they addressed each other.

I remember on one occasion shortly after I arrived hearing two young men talking in the quad outside my bedroom window. They were speaking in the exaggerated upper-class accents which I had only ever heard on radio comedy shows. I was convinced they were playing some sort of joke on the newly arrived colonial boy, and surreptitiously went outside to check. They weren't.

I did, however, make a number of friends amongst the English undergraduates, although I naturally found it easier to mix with the other overseas graduates who were more my own age and shared more of my background. I became particularly friendly with an American named Reid Chambers who shared many of my interests, particularly in politics and foreign affairs. Reid was in every sense a liberal. He was committed to the civil rights cause and, after Oxford, obtained a top degree at Harvard Law School which he put to use in advancing the rights and interests of American Indians.

Shortly after we arrived in Oxford, the Cuban missile crisis came to its dangerous culmination. I was shaken to discover that even someone as civilised and tolerant as Reid had a blind spot so far as Castro was concerned. He clearly believed the US government's propaganda to the effect that Castro was the devil incarnate. It was a powerful lesson in the way that prejudice can make prisoners of us all.

I saw quite a bit of my fellow Rhodes Scholars. Indeed, I was somehow selected to serve on the dance committee which organised the termly dances at Rhodes House. These dances were the only purpose for which Rhodes Scholars came together as a body. Organising them required very little work, since they followed a pretty well established pattern, but the committee meetings, and the dances themselves, were great fun, and there was some competition among the women at Oxford to get themselves invited.

I discovered that I had been earmarked for special attention by two young women who had had access to the files of students from overseas who were about to come up. Caroline Hudson worked as a secretary at Rhodes House and Jane Ross was a secretary at Balliol. They and two others shared a flat together in North Oxford, well brought-up girls whose families had clearly decided that Oxford was the place to find good husbands.

I was invited round to tea. I was intrigued by their Englishness, and only partially concealed flirtatiousness. I invited Jane to the Rhodes dance in Michaelmas term, and from that point on spent most of my spare time with her.

In those days, the rules about having women on college premises were still pretty restrictive. Since Jane worked at Balliol, however, I was the only student in college who could legitimately have his girlfriend on site. Not only was it difficult to entertain girlfriends in college, it was equally difficult to stay out late. The lodge was locked at midnight. The ground-floor windows looking out on to the street were barred, and the drainpipes leading up to the first-floor windows were fitted with fearsome spikes. There were blood-curdling stories of drunken undergraduates trying to scale the drainpipes and being gored as they fell. I discovered, however, that these heroics were quite unnecessary. A tap on the lodge window, a half crown pressed into the palm of a hand, and access to the college was possible at any time of night.

I very much enjoyed the Oxford social life. I again had very little money, but, as always, this did not bother me. I took particular pleasure in going out to eat, something I had done very little in New Zealand, where restaurants, particularly licensed restaurants, had only just begun to make an appearance. I remember one evening cycling down the Banbury Road in a foursome on our way to the Moti Mahal for a 4s. 6d. curry and registering that I was completely happy. It was one of those moments of no particular significance which powerfully evoke a mood and stay in the memory.

My social life took me into areas I had not previously explored. I rapidly discovered that, while class seemed to matter enormously to most people, I myself was difficult to categorise in such terms. I found myself invited, on occasion, to places where my lack of social sophistication became apparent. I remember passing the port the wrong way at a dining club called the White Tie Club and, on another occasion, having bought a bottle of wine for an outing with a college friend – a Wykehamist called Tommy Cookson – being told rather sharply that in future he would buy the wine.

Yet in most respects I felt no sense of inferiority to the people I mixed with. Quite the contrary. For the first time in my life, I was actually older, more mature and in some senses more experienced than most of them. By the time I got to Oxford, I had, for example, sat nearly forty final examination papers. The academic work held few terrors for me and I was able to enjoy the Oxford tutorial system to the full.

My tutors were principally Don Harris, whom I found a stimulating guide to the higher reaches of the law, and occasionally Theo Tyler, a legendary Balliol figure who was nearing the end of his teaching career. Theo was blind and very set in his ways. A tutorial with him was like a tour around an ancient monument.

He once revealed an unexpected emotionalism. I recall an evening when he and his sister (with whom he lived in north Oxford) invited a few students back for tea. It was a stilted and uncomfortable occasion which was suddenly transformed when, on Theo's insistence, we all sat and listened to a radio commentary on a championship boxing match in which a British boxer named Dave Charnley came from behind to win a dramatic victory. Theo was enthralled and, as the fight reached its climax and patriotic intensity filled the air, he began to sob, great tears falling from his sightless eyes.

I was reading for a Bachelor of Civil Law, a post-graduate degree which was regarded so highly that few post-graduate students felt able to avoid it in favour of a research degree. I found it full of unexpected pleasures.

Non-Oxford graduates were obliged to take two years over the degree, spending the initial year on subjects they might not have covered in their first degrees. I found myself, for example, studying Roman law, and using my schoolboy Latin in order to analyse Justinian's texts. As an intellectual exercise, it appealed to me enormously.

I worked just hard enough to keep things under control while I enjoyed the rest of my life. I played regularly in the college tennis team, whose composition reflected Balliol's cosmopolitan flavour – an Englishman, a Scot, two Australians, my Indian doubles partner Bheeshma Rajagopalan, and myself. I played badminton and ran cross-country for the college; I also took up squash for the first time, making such rapid progress that I made the college team in that sport as well. Again, I found it easy to reach a certain state of competence but the very top levels of the sport were beyond me.

An organisation called, I think, the Victoria League used to offer hospitality in members' homes to Rhodes Scholars. It was arranged that I would spend my first Christmas with a family called Barnett. The son, David, was an old Etonian, an undergraduate at Magdalen. The father, a stockbroker in the City, was the cousin of the Earl of Verulam. They had a large house just outside St Albans.

They were extraordinarily kind to me. I took it all – the rolling acres, the profusion of rooms, the silver cutlery, the candlelit dinner parties – in my stride. I was by this time not easily discountenanced, even when, on one occasion, I went to pour the port into my claret glass and had to be stopped.

We went pheasant shooting one day on the Earl of Verulam's estate. I was of course not allowed anywhere near the guns and mercifully saw nothing of the carnage, but it was an interesting day out and gave me the chance of further social observation. I stayed in touch with the family throughout most of my time at Oxford.

My wanderings through the English class system taught me a number of things, one of which was that I should not condemn anyone for the way they spoke or behaved. The public school boy could no more help the disadvantages of his upbringing than anyone else. I did feel able, however, to condemn the system which produced such wide social divisions, and so many social casualties as well. I felt particularly sorry for the minor public school boys, always aping the Etonians and Harrovians, but never really being accepted by them, while at the same time feeling that the money their parents had spent on social exclusivity (rather than education, which in most cases their parents would have been incompetent to judge) would have been wasted if they had mixed with the grammar school boys. In addition to these difficulties, they were socially handicapped in wider terms: they were immature when it came to dealing with women, and ignorant about how their own society worked.

The early 1960s were, on the other hand, a time of liberation for working-class boys made good. Britain was in a state of social ferment. Suddenly, with the rise of the Beatles, regional accents became acceptable, even fashionable. Pop music, Carnaby Street clothes, the mini-skirt and the Mini car were the icons of the age. It was an exciting moment for a colonial boy to come to Britain. The country had suddenly become – for young people, at any rate – the cultural capital of the world.

I felt very much in tune with the spirit of the age. When we crowded into the Junior Common Room on a Saturday night to watch *That Was The Week That Was*, I was fascinated by the programme's iconoclasm, the almost palpable sense of a society on the move. There were many aspects of Britain that I felt impatient about. Some issues were relatively trivial. I recall my incredulity at the fact that shops in Oxford closed during the lunch hour, just when most people might be expected to want to go shopping. Other issues, however, were more fundamental, or so I thought. I had a New World impatience with the English attitude to problems. To me, they existed to be solved, or at least addressed. I had little understanding of the old world cynicism and world-weariness which accepted that problems were to be tolerated and accommodated.

I was, in particular, shocked by the pervasiveness of the class structure. I found it embarrassing to be looked after by a grown man (a 'scout'), whose job it was to make my bed, until I dispensed with his services. I condemned not only the obvious waste of human talent which class made inevitable, by refusing opportunity to those who could have developed their true potential, but also the cost to society of pushing inadequate people into positions of responsibility and influence.

I was also depressed by what I saw of urban life in Britain, the slum housing, the struggle people faced to get to work, the dirty streets. Oxford, or at least my part of it, was something of a haven, and most of my friends came from well-to-do families. They seemed impervious to what was going on around them, but I could never return from an occasional visit to London without feeling that life was unfairly stacked against the majority of people.

I was also aware that the class or political struggle was much more serious and deeply felt in Britain than it ever was in New Zealand. My parents' unthinking conservatism was just a pale image of the aggressive class warfare I met on the lips and in the actions, not so much of the working class, who were for the most part surprisingly quiescent, but of the privileged, who made it plain that they were determined to defend their position and hated and feared those who might challenge it.

I became very sensitive to the social freemasonry that enables one Englishman to recognise another in class terms. I recall going to stay with Jane at her parents' home in Portsmouth. Her father was an anaesthetist at Portsmouth Hospital. Her mother was extremely charming. We went one morning to a fête of some sort (I suspect it may have been in aid of the Conservative Party). Jane's mother remarked to a fellow helper as they cleared up afterwards that it had been a successful and enjoyable occasion because there had been so may of 'us' there. Class is never far from the English mind.

My political views were only gradually taking shape now, but they were definitely moving leftwards. I was friendly with a bright English law student called David Keane who was doing the BCL with me in my first year. He was politically ambitious and became president of the Oxford University Conservative Association. He was due to speak in an Oxford Union debate on one occasion. The motion for debate was to the effect that the Conservative Party lacked a social conscience. He asked for my advice on how to tackle the topic. I did my best to help him but I was interested to find that I had little enthusiasm for the task, still less any real idea of what arguments to advance. He must have shared my doubts. He subsequently became a Labour candidate, narrowly failing to win Taunton in the 1980s.

My first year at Oxford was a period of great political ferment. The newspapers were dominated by the Profumo affair. We were clearly entering the fag end of what subsequently became known as the thirteen wasted years of Tory rule. There was the stench of decay in the air, an almost palpable sense of a new Britain, a new social order, thrusting its way through the rubble of the old order, and demanding its place in the sun.

Undergraduate politics held little appeal for me, however. I found the aping of parliamentary debates in the Oxford Union rather puerile. I did, however, listen to one debate, shortly after Macmillan had axed half his Cabinet in a desperate attempt to regain the political initiative. I heard a brilliant speech from Stuart Holland, who affected an air of dismissive superiority towards his opponents. It served him well on that occasion but did not transfer so well to the House of Commons when he became a Labour MP twenty years later.

One of my English undergraduate friends at Balliol was Robin Wilson, Harold Wilson's son. We were both members of the Balliol choir. Robin was much more musically educated than I was (though my lack of musical experience did not prevent me from deriving great pleasure from my first exposure to choral music). He was a rather shy young man, and I cannot claim to have known him well. I do recall, however, sitting in a friend's rooms with him one day, listening to the radio news. The radio bulletin announced that Harold Wilson had defeated George Brown for the Labour Party leadership. I had hardly even registered Hugh Gaitskell's death, but my interest in British politics was rising sharply and I became greatly interested in Harold Wilson and his prospects in the forthcoming general election. I remember Robin telling me, a few days after the leadership result was announced, that his father had been holding George Brown's hand aloft (as shown in a well-used photograph, recording Harold's moment of triumph) so that George Brown could not stab him in the back.

As a law student, I was a member of the Balliol law society, which was called the Younger Society. The society occasionally invited speakers, usually old members, to address us on a legal topic. The meetings were very informal, usually took place in the small college law library, and were preceded by a meal. Our guest one evening was Dick Taverne, a Balliol lawyer and rising star on the Labour back benches. He was an attractive character, tall, good-looking, bright and articulate. He made a considerable impression on me, not so much for what he had to say on the law (of which I have no recollection) but for the fact that he was a Labour MP. I remember a group of us walking him back to his car in the late evening and hanging on his every word.

In my second year, I became president of the Younger Society and spoke at the annual dinner, which was a rather grand black-tie affair, held in hall, and with a number of senior judges as guests. It was my first major speaking occasion. I acquitted myself well enough, but criticised myself, feeling that I had tried too hard, my jokes were too laboured, and so on. I envied the relaxed ease and polished wit of more experienced speakers.

My political views, in response to these various influences, however, were now shifting quite fast. I realised that I was not, and could not be, a Tory. I flirted for a short time with the idea that I might be a Liberal, but since I had little idea of what a Liberal might be, that did not last long. It gradually became apparent that my sympathies lay with Labour. Once I realised this, I began to devour the political news with zest, analysing every development from the vantage point of my new allegiance.

My life was pretty much based in the college, and, apart from the occasional foray to London, or stay with friends for the weekend, I did not get around a great deal. The main problem was lack of money – not that it occurred to me to think of this as a problem, since I had never had any. In any case, my Rhodes Scholar's stipend made me better off than most English undergraduates.

I did, however, manage to travel abroad on two occasions. Reid Chambers and I planned a trip to Florence for the New Year of 1963. He made his own way to Europe and I met him in Munich. We looked around Munich for a day or so and then hitchhiked across the Alps to Florence, which came as a complete revelation. I had little idea of what to expect and no interest in things artistic or cultural. Reid, however, had studied the Renaissance as part of his first degree at Amherst. I don't suppose he knew a great deal, but he was a walking encyclopaedia by comparison with his ignoramus of a travelling companion. I learnt a healthy respect for the easily derided American college education system.

We spent hours in the Uffizi. I hardly knew what I was looking at, but, without my realising it, it was the starting point of an inexpert interest in painting which I have enjoyed ever since. I suppose it was rather like the hours I spent in English lessons as a schoolboy, learning poetry. They have repaid me many times over as my enjoyment of poetry has grown.

Reid and I lived very frugally, but we decided that on New Year's Eve we would hit the town. We began to wander the streets at about 9 p.m., looking to celebrate the New Year in the company of others. We wanted somewhere convivial and cheap, where we could get a meal and a drink.

Our wanderings produced no result. Everywhere seemed full. Restaurant after restaurant turned us away. (Perhaps we were not helped by the fact that Reid had decided to grow a beard for the holiday which by now had become an untidy stubble.) We became desperate. Finally, to our great relief, we passed a restaurant which, though crowded, undeniably had an empty table for two in the window overlooking the street. A rather reluctant waiter showed us to the table, but before we could order, the manager approached us and, with smiles and gestures, led us into the kitchen. We sat on a couple of stools and ate well, but out of the gaze of the restaurant's other customers and passers-by. The kitchen staff celebrated with us when midnight came.

I made a further trip abroad during the summer. I had heard from friends about a scheme which offered a return fare to Denmark in return for a couple of weeks' work on a farm. My friends had had a wonderful time. The farm work had been a doddle, they said. One had found himself on a farm on the coast and had spent most of his time at the beach, surrounded by beautiful Danish girls.

I signed up enthusiastically. I spent a day or two in Copenhagen, visited the Tubörg brewery and heard a concert by Sarah Vaughan at the Tivoli Gardens. The farm, however, was nowhere near the coast. The couple of hours of light work I had been promised turned out to be a dawn-to-dusk marathon. My farmer was a tough young man with an eye to cheap labour. I don't think I have ever felt as physically exhausted as I did at the end of the first, long, day. On my one day off during the fortnight I cycled the 40 kilometres to Esbjerg in a vain attempt to find the beach and the beautiful girls.

By now, my personal life had become slightly complicated. I had continued a correspondence with Diane, my girlfriend in New Zealand, and she had decided that she would come to England for an extended holiday. By this time, however, I had also become very involved with Jane. I had never made any promises to Diane, and had told her about Jane. Jane, in turn, knew about Diane, of whom I was still very fond.

The All Blacks were touring Britain in the autumn of 1963 and their opening match was against Oxford University. I and a party of friends went to the match, where we unexpectedly ran into Diane and some of the New Zealand girlfriends with whom she was travelling. After the match, I invited them back to college for tea. A large party assembled in my room. My friends were very interested in Diane, of whom they had heard a great deal. As luck would have it, Jane turned up in the middle of the proceedings. The room fell silent as realisation dawned that a confrontation was inevitable. Fortunately, the two girls handled the situation very well, greeting each other politely and then ensuring that they kept out of each other's way.

My academic work progressed well. At the end of my first year, I sat a preliminary exam, which I am afraid I did not take very seriously but passed satisfactorily. I settled down to more resolute work in my second year. By now, I felt I was at the height of my intellectual powers, and attacked the work with enthusiasm. I enjoyed the stimulus of wrestling with knotty problems and feeling that I was on the frontier of knowledge in my subject. Even subjects like the law of trusts I found intellectually fascinating.

As I approached the end of my second year, I began to think about my future. I remained passionately patriotic about New Zealand, but I was enjoying myself enormously in Britain and didn't feel quite ready to go home. I had made contact with the New Zealand External Affairs Department, through New Zealand House in London, and they had made it clear that I could have a job with them. I could also, of course, go back to legal practice in New Zealand, or go to the Bar in England.

However, I was particularly interested in foreign affairs, and conceived the idea of joining the British Diplomatic Service. I reasoned that in that way I could keep my options open, since I could always move with relative ease from the Foreign Office to the New Zealand service.

The notion seems odd today, especially now that New Zealand has a much better-defined sense of national identity, but in the early 1960s, many New Zealanders still referred to Britain as 'home'. As a child, I had often watched the London newsreels and the images of Big Ben, and had thought that one day I would go there. I was intensely proud of my British heritage. I felt, when I came to London and Oxford, that I was visiting the heart of my civilisation, rather as a Roman citizen might have felt when returning to Rome from some far-flung corner of the Empire. *Civis britannicus sum* – and that is exactly what my passport said. I was a New Zealand citizen but a British subject.

I made a tentative enquiry to the Foreign Office, asking what their attitude might be to an application from a New Zealander. They seemed to think that my nationality was a non-issue. I was advised to contact the Civil Service Commission and apply for entry in the ordinary way. This I did, and accordingly found myself in the spring of 1964 spending three days in London going through the then equivalent of the old 'country house weekend'. The candidates (most of them Oxbridge) were divided into groups of six. Each group had attached to it a chairman, an observer and a psychologist, all from the Civil Service Commission. We went through a large range of exercises, always under the watchful eyes of our three supervisors. I remember, for example, having to chair a meeting of my group with a view to deciding some complicated issue which arose from a detailed set of briefing documents we had been provided with.

I enjoyed the exercise. I was, I suppose, a little older than most other candidates, and again my wider experience stood me in good stead. I tried to raise the question of my nationality, but again the issue was dismissed as of no consequence. It was simply assumed that it was the most natural thing in the world for anyone to want to join the British Diplomatic Service.

In the event, I passed this entrance examination as the top entrant of my year. I calculated that I would be foolish to ignore this clear signal that a successful career beckoned me. I thought to myself that if I encountered any prejudice on account of my New Zealand origins, I would simply leave.

A month or two after I had been notified of my success, I was vetted for security purposes. I was interviewed by someone who seemed to be about 150 years old. He asked me a number of questions whose purpose appeared rather obscure. He wanted to know what newspapers I read and what weekly journals I took. When I replied that I did not read any weekly journals since I could not afford them, he nodded approvingly. He enquired about girlfriends and seemed pleased to discover that I had one. He positively beamed at the information that she had been to a good girls' public school.

In my last term at Oxford, I began to work quite hard. However, this didn't prevent me from enjoying myself. I took Jane to the Magdalen Commem Ball, and continued to play tennis for the college. Although I was working hard, I paced myself carefully and gave the impression, I think, of being fairly relaxed.

Nothing, however, could have prepared me for the sheer physical burden of taking six final exams in three days, followed – after a day's break on the Sunday – by two more. I had always had some trouble sleeping before exams. It was not so much fear of exams but rather the fear of not sleeping which prevented me from doing so. I was exhausted by the time Sunday arrived. I found myself in a curious state of mind. I felt that all my senses were heightened yet they were at the same time unreliable. I decided that I needed some relaxation, and Reid kindly agreed to give me a game of tennis. I felt as though I was floating on the court and played – for me – almost perfect tennis. I won a set against Reid without losing a point.

I had left my revision of international law until that Sunday. I had a good set of notes but I had not looked at them since Easter. On that Sunday, I was just too tired to do more than simply read through them once. I did so, however, in the knowledge that I would not see them again and that whatever I retained from that single reading would be all that I took with me into the exam. I concentrated hard. To my astonishment, I found in the exam the following day that I could see in my mind's eye every word on every page of my notes. I had always had an excellent memory, but this was totally unexpected. Since then, I have never been surprised at anything that human beings are capable of.

The results of the exams were posted on a notice board in the Schools building in the High Street. A number of my fellow candidates and I crowded around. I had got a first. My one disappointment was that I had failed to win the Vinerian prize, awarded to the best BCL of the year. That honour went to a good friend of mine, Jeff Hackney, who almost immediately became a law don at St Edmund Hall and subsequently at Wadham. I was told that the examiners had found his work a little more scholarly than mine. I had no quarrel with that. I was also told some years later (with what justification, I am not sure) that my degree was rated at that time as the second best BCL since the war. If that was true, it was my bad luck that the best degree was awarded to a candidate in the same year as mine.

I had loved my two years at Oxford. It was not only a wonderfully pleasurable experience which, even now, arouses in me powerful feelings of nostalgia. It also endowed me with a privilege which I was able to take with me through life. In English society, getting a good Oxford degree is almost like a magic talisman. It wards off evil spirits and is as effective as abracadabra at opening doors.

Oxford left me ambivalent, however, about its impact on British society. The university makes a tremendous contribution to scholarship, research and civilised values. It confers great privileges on those fortunate enough to go there. But it does so at a price.

Oxford and Cambridge are still so dominant, educationally and socially, in British society that they distort the rest of the education system. They sit at the apex of the educational pyramid. Other universities, the rest of higher education, the leading secondary schools, all judge themselves by Oxbridge standards. They find themselves aping, perhaps sub-consciously, the way Oxbridge does things. Because Oxbridge dons like to teach school leavers who have already done quite advanced work, the whole education system specialises early. Those who satisfy Oxbridge's exacting standards are regarded as successes. Almost by definition, those who none the less meet some other standard of excellence are marked down.

In the light of my exam success, discreet enquiries were made as to whether I might be interested in becoming a don. I had, however, decided to go into the Foreign Office. I was keen to see the wider world. The Foreign Office offered travel, politics, London, power. Oxford was beautiful but cloistered. I was ready to spread my wings.

First, though, I had to spread my wings in a more geographical fashion. I had written to my parents to tell them of my decision to stay in Britain for the time being and to take up a job with the Diplomatic Service. They were disappointed, but bore their disappointment bravely. I felt I could not simply just stay indefinitely on the other side of the world without making some effort to see them.

I still had very little money, but I had managed to save enough to buy a one-way air fare back to New Zealand. I would have to work in New Zealand to earn enough to pay for the return journey. I was to fly on the new Comet. The days of the passenger liner were over.

The flight took 38 hours and was excruciatingly uncomfortable. I was cramped and miserable, largely because whenever we took off again after the innumerable touch-downs for refuelling, I made the mistake of eating the indifferent food we were offered.

I was met at Auckland airport by the whole family. No one had ever heard of jet lag. It never occurred to them that I would not be as fresh as a daisy. I was driven from Auckland to Te Awamutu, where we had a celebratory meal at my sister's home. Then on for another lengthy drive to my parents' house in New Plymouth. We arrived late in the evening. My parents had acquired while I was away their first television set. It was their pride and joy. I was sat down in a darkened room and the television set was switched on. After more than 48 hours of sleepless travel, the inevitable happened: I nodded off. My parents were mortally offended. Somehow, they felt, I had insulted their television set.

My visit home was, however, a happy one. I was delighted to see my family. My sister had had her first baby and I enjoyed helping to teach young David to walk. New Zealand seemed familiar yet different. The images I had cherished in my memory proved to be ever so slightly inaccurate. I looked at the country through the eyes of one who had seen other beauties, other landscapes. I was struck by how unformed it all was. The English landscape is a monument to a thousand years of human endeavour, its gentle contours showing in every swell and curve the imprint of a civilisation which has grown with the land. New Zealand, by contrast, is rough and raw. The pastures are still littered with tree stumps, evidence of how recently the bush has been cleared. The rugged hills give the impression that, at any moment, they may shrug their shoulders and all mankind's puny works will slither off into the sea.

In order to earn enough money for my return fare to Britain, I did a number of jobs, principally as a school teacher at a secondary school called Spottiswood College during the day, and as an announcer on station 2XP, New Plymouth, by night. Those were the days of full employment, when it was relatively easy to get temporary jobs.

I enjoyed my teaching. I was reasonably well equipped to teach English and history, but unfitted to teach mathematics. I was nevertheless required to try. I took the text book home each night and learnt just enough to get me through the next day's lesson.

As a radio announcer, I did everything – played the records, read the commercials, linked to the national station from time to time. I made one gaffe. I was very keen on pop music, and kept on my desk a rack with all the latest hit singles. If I needed a 'filler', I would pluck out my current favourite and play it. One evening, I had linked in to the national programme at 9 p.m. for a classical concert. The concert finished a few minutes before 11 p.m. when we were due to close down. I took the chance to play 'The House of the Rising Sun' by The Animals. The station manager had been snoozing in his armchair, listening to the programme at home, when he was suddenly aroused by the strident tones of rock music. He was not best pleased.

I stayed in New Zealand for nearly three months. I was impatient to get back to Britain and start my new job at the Foreign Office. I was also missing Jane, who had left Oxford and moved into a flat in London. One night, I had a sort of nightmare in which I dreamed that I was unable to leave New Zealand. It was not that I did not love my homeland – quite the contrary. But I had seen a wider world. It is one of the paradoxes of New Zealand's situation that the greater the ease of foreign travel, the more isolated New Zealand can feel. I said my farewells and flew back to Britain.

THREE

The Foreign Office
1964–66

IN OCTOBER 1964, while I was still in New Zealand, Harold Wilson had won a dramatic and tensely narrow election victory. The British people, hardly daring to trust themselves, had rejected what Wilson called the 'thirteen wasted years' of Tory rule and responded instead to his inspirational promise to use the 'white heat of technology' to bring Britain into the modern age.

I had watched the election campaign from afar, but with a growing conviction that Britain's future depended on there being a Labour government. I did not vote but I would certainly have voted Labour had I been in Britain. When I divulged this to my parents, they were intrigued. I think they felt that I was indulging a youthful aberration.

I was convinced that the moment was ripe for major change. The fag end of the Macmillan government and the bizarre passing of the premiership to Lord Home had given the unmistakable impression of an *ancien régime* in its last days. One could almost smell the odour of decay.

Harold Wilson promised a new start – not just the end of thirteen years of Tory rule but a real revolution. The country was already in the throes of exciting change. Society was in upheaval, popular culture was bursting out before our very eyes. New people – young people, people with strange hair and clothes and accents, people who dared to do and say new things – were rising like corks to the surface.

Harold Wilson himself, with his flat Yorkshire accent and Gannex mac, was a new phenomenon, a sort of classless technocrat who seemed to embody in his own person the way the new Britain would go. The country was crying out for change, not just in fashion and pop music, but in the more fundamental matters of how it governed itself and how political power was exercised. The 1960s were Britain's decade, and Britain was ready to show the way to the post-war world.

I still understood little of politics and even less of economics. I had done a year's economics at university but, with its emphasis on concepts like perfect competition, very little of it seemed to have any relevance to the problems which real governments faced in the real world. And the Wilson government ran into some of those problems as soon as it was elected.

It appeared that the balance of payments was in much worse shape than anyone had realised. A Tory press which had conveniently affected ignorance of this difficulty before the election piled on the pressure afterwards. The City took fright. A Labour government was bad enough, but a Labour government with a balance of payments deficit was a nightmare. There was a run on sterling. The balance of payments deficit bequeathed by the Tory government became a sterling crisis for its Labour successor.

I was outraged, not just by the unfairness of saddling the new government with the magnified problems of its predecessor but by what seemed to me to be the deliberate attempt by the press, and more particularly the City of London, to overturn the results of a democratic election. The Labour majority was wafer-thin. The onslaught on an inexperienced government was a serious matter. There was a real sense of the possibility of a counter-revolution in the air, something that dogged the first Wilson government throughout its term.

What seemed to me to be an attack by the City on the very viability of the new Labour government made my support for it even more passionate. I went and joined up. At least, that's the way I like to tell the story. Joining the Labour Party proved a more difficult and protracted process than I had expected. The 'penny-farthing' Labour Party excoriated by Harold Wilson was simply incapable of handling anything as complicated as an application for membership. My visit to Transport House produced no results for several months and I had to make several repeat calls before I was finally signed up.

Meanwhile, it had been decided by the Foreign Office that the first thing I should do on my return from New Zealand was to improve my French. I was accordingly sent off to the *Institut de Touraine* in Tours to do a three-month course for foreigners learning French. Accommodation was arranged for me in the home of a Monsieur and Madame Janelle, who lived a couple of kilometres from Tours, on the other side of the Loire. They were an elderly couple who were almost caricature French. Monsieur Janelle was small and gnome-like, with a wide and expressive mouth. Madame looked as though she had just stepped from a Simenon novel. She had grey hair, pinned up, and glasses. She always seemed to have a neat apron tied tightly around her dark dress. She looked rather severe but she had kind eyes.

They looked after me very well. The house, though large, was rather dingy, and the plumbing left a lot to be desired. The food, however, was excellent, although it took a little getting used to. I had never before tasted, for example, the natural yogurt which Madame Janelle made every day, and I was not sure that I liked it.

Monsieur Janelle was a French nationalist with a particular scorn for the Americans and – by extension, though to a lesser degree – the British. I was never quite sure whether his extreme views were known to the Foreign Office who had perhaps calculated that exposure to them was good experience for a budding diplomat, or whether they were simply unaware that their French boarding house was run by a virtual fascist.

In any event, Monsieur Janelle was a stimulating companion. It was good for my French to engage him in argument, something he was always willing to be drawn into. His contention was that France had lost the war to the Germans, the Americans and British. He was full of stories of Mers el Khebir and the British scuttling of the French fleet. He quickly linked this episode with earlier instances of English perfidy. His version of Anglo-French rivalry seemed full of instances and place names, like Fashoda, which are virtually unknown in the British version of history.

As for the Americans, he could hardly contain himself. He would describe with great scorn the American bombers unloading their bombs over France from high altitude, as though – and here he would rub the tips of his finger and thumb together in a gesture of exquisite contempt – they were sprinkling sugar. The British, he grudgingly admitted, were at least brave and skilful enough to fly low and bomb with greater accuracy.

Paradoxically, Monsieur Janelle had little time for de Gaulle. I could never work out whether this was merely because of de Gaulle's record on Algeria or whether Monsieur Janelle had been in some sense a Vichy sympathiser.

I was staying *chez* Janelle when Churchill died on 24 January 1965. The televised account of his funeral was broadcast on French television. The slow beat of the drum seemed to echo throughout the day. I was profoundly moved. Monsieur Janelle commented acidly that Churchill had been a war criminal, like Hitler. He nevertheless remained glued to the television screen all day.

Before then I had been back to Britain for Christmas, which I spent with Jane and her family. The gossip was all of Harold Wilson and Marcia Williams. I was assured that the *Daily Express* was about to publish the full exposé. The belief in those quarters was that Wilson could not long survive. It was hard, I think, for people like that to accept that a man of Wilson's lowly origins could be taken seriously as leader of a great country.

I often caught the flavour of this sentiment. One of Jane's friends had married someone I could only think of as a public school twit. On hearing that I had joined the Foreign Office, he remarked that he had always believed that people like me would not be allowed into the Foreign Office. I rejoined that 'people like me' were now governing the country.

I went back to France to complete my language course. I achieved a fair degree of proficiency, but I would never claim to be a linguist. I can only marvel at the ease with which some people can pick up a new language. It must be something to do with a lack of self-consciousness. I think I try too hard and am unwilling to run the risk of appearing foolish through making mistakes.

I travelled a little in France, spent a weekend in Paris with Jane and saw most of the *châteaux* along the Loire. Once again, though, lack of money prevented me from making the most of my opportunities. I also had a brief romantic entanglement with a French girl which, I am ashamed to say, I did not reveal to Jane but which was no doubt good for my French. It was something of a shock when she and her mother pursued me to London!

On returning to London, I began work at the Foreign Office. I was given a job in the Western Organisations and Co-ordination Department, on a desk called European Political Co-operation. The only problem with this was that there was none, and if there had been any, it would have taken place at a level far above that of a new entrant like me.

This was the era of the Gaullist veto. The British interest in the Common Market had flickered briefly under Macmillan, but had rapidly been extinguished. Most of Whitehall regarded the issue as a dead letter. Only the Foreign Office kept our interest in joining Europe alive and, even then, only against sustained French opposition.

My appointment to a desk in WOCD – the department which dealt with Nato and our principal allies – was meant to signify my status as a 'high flier'. The department was headed by a brilliant and irascible man called John Barnes, who surrounded himself with similarly intelligent people.

I confess that I was a little overawed to start with, which wasn't helped by the fact that there was, in truth, very little for me to do. The battle against the French for a seat at the European table was conducted at a very high level, mainly through an obscure organisation called the Western European Union which had originally had some defence objective linking the six Common Market members and Britain. Although its purpose had long ago passed into history, we saw it as an opportunity to breathe life into a relationship with the Six. The French were equally determined that the WEU should moulder quietly away.

I spent most of my day reading the telegrams which came in from posts abroad. I had the occasional glimpse of high-level activity, usually in the person of Viscount Hood, a tall and languid nobleman who was the under-secretary responsible for WOCD. The nearest I came to the real action was when I joined the British delegation attending a WEU conference in Luxembourg. The Labour government had had difficulty in appointing a foreign secretary. Patrick Gordon Walker had had to give up when he could not secure a seat in Parliament. The job had eventually gone to Michael Stewart, a rather dull but competent man whose reputation rested on being a 'safe pair of hands'.

It was Michael Stewart who led the delegation to Luxembourg. I tagged along as a sort of bag carrier. However, I did manage to participate in the briefings which preceded the conference, and even had some slight input into the speech the Foreign Secretary was to make. I enjoyed the conference enormously, but found it hard to understand why every tiny detail of the communiqué was regarded as being of such importance.

There was a great deal of goodwill in the Foreign Office towards the Labour government. The Tories were generally regarded as having run their course. Labour was looked upon as a breath of fresh air, and Labour ministers were reckoned to be, on the whole, rather cleverer than their Tory counterparts.

It was an interesting moment of transition at which to observe British foreign policy. The older generation still had an attachment to the American alliance. They held a view of the world based on their wartime experience, in which the British and Americans would impose their view on events and jointly resolve most issues. The British might be junior partners in this arrangement but they made up with experience what they lacked in material muscle.

The younger generation, however, just reaching the senior levels of the Foreign Office, were looking for a new role. They found riding shotgun for the Americans less than wholly fulfilling. Some of them flirted briefly with the idea that leading the Commonwealth might provide Britain with a world role commensurate with our experience and status. But most were moving decisively towards the view that leadership of Europe was our true destiny.

What was never really questioned was the view that Britain should exercise a world role. Inevitably, because they were professional diplomats committed to the furtherance of British interests and influence in the world, they sought the widest possible stage. It simply never occurred to them that Britain might do better to forsake such illusions of grandeur and concentrate on the difficult domestic business of turning the country into an efficient and socially cohesive modern state.

The attachment to the European connection was also based, to a large extent, on institutional and professional self-interest. The Foreign Office saw the danger that, in a world in which Britain's role was shrinking, its own influence in Whitehall would also diminish. If, on the other hand, Europe were to become the main arena for the pursuit of British interests, and if the whole of British domestic policy were to be conducted through European mechanisms, there would be a much more powerful role for the Foreign Office, as intermediary on all such matters between the national government and the European institutions. There was a sense in which the European commitment induced the Foreign Office to become an agent for Europe in Britain, rather than the other way round.

This, however, in 1964, was largely for the future. The immediate task in hand was to keep the European idea alive in Whitehall and to find the means of overcoming or circumventing the Gaullist veto in Europe. I was myself wholly committed to this task. I shared the enthusiasm of those who felt that the European project was an expression of idealism and internationalism. In any case, this was the way in which history was inevitably taking us.

I became impatient with the lack of anything to do. I remember writing a memorandum in which I recommended that we should seize the initiative, and bypass the French veto, by proposing a plan for European political unity. I had not, of course, thought through what European political unity might actually involve. My concern was solely for the immediate tactical advantage which such a proposal might bring us. My paper was no doubt naive in the extreme. Mercifully, I had enough judgement to realise this and, although I had it typed up, I wisely sent it no further. I sometimes recall this episode somewhat wryly whenever I am accused of being irredeemably anti-European.

Fortunately for me, my inactivity and boredom came to an end pretty shortly afterwards. A new department called the Defence Supply Department was created. Its task was to promote collaborative ventures with our allies in the production of defence equipment and, I am sorry to say, to lend diplomatic support to our efforts in selling arms abroad.

I was moved to the junior desk in the new department. Its head was a charming man called Leonard Figg. He and I were its only two members and my experience there taught me a number of lessons.

First, I learnt that it is always a good thing to be an expert. In WOCD, I had known less than everyone else. In my new job, I knew more about my subject than anyone else, largely because no one else knew anything at all. Whenever someone needed to know about our policy in the area of defence supply, I was called in. My confidence soared. I became genuinely knowledgeable. I found myself working to very senior people since, whenever there was a conference which might need to know about defence supply at however high a level, I was required to attend.

One of those I worked with occasionally was Sir Con O'Neill, a very senior diplomat of almost legendary reputation. He was regarded as something of a visionary and was looked up to by the younger generation of diplomats who believed that he offered them and the country a path to a new future. He was perhaps the principal European enthusiast in the Foreign Office. I admired his personal qualities and did not question his policies.

Another advantage of my new job was that I saw something of the way Whitehall worked. The policy area I was responsible for often involved the interests of other departments – the Ministry of Defence, the Ministry of Aviation, the Government Chief Scientist and, inevitably, the Treasury.

I remember one meeting called to discuss a project called Nadge which was meant to provide Nato with a new radar capability. The British interest was in something called passive detection. Our interest was especially keen since it was an area in which we had a technical lead. If we could ensure that passive detection was an element in the scheme, there would be rich pickings for British industry.

Before we could press hard for this outcome in the negotiations with our allies, however, we had to be sure that passive detection really worked. Accordingly, we sought technical advice from the scientists who were working on the project. It was a most unsatisfactory dialogue. The scientists, figuratively blinking in the light, were unable to answer our simple-minded questions, since they were halfway through a complex process of research whose outcome was still uncertain. Yet on the basis of this confused evidence, we had to make a decision. It has always remained with me as an example of the difficult interface between the complex real world and the exigencies of politics and government.

I learnt other lessons in the Foreign Office. I discovered that it always pays to know how things work. One of the tasks most commonly undertaken was the drafting and eventual despatch of telegrams to posts abroad. Very often, there was a deadline to meet. The usual practice, once the draft had completed its process through its various stages in the department, was to summon a messenger. A black-coated figure who moved slowly down the long corridors, the messenger was the same person who arrived with the coal to feed the little stove in our office. I discovered that the deadline for the despatch of telegrams could be extended by an hour and a half by taking the telegram to the mail room myself. The mail room was in the bowels of the earth on the other side of the building and virtually no diplomat of the administrative class knew of its whereabouts. I saved myself many an anxious moment by acquiring and acting on this piece of information.

I also learnt to draft. A draft paper would begin its life with a particular officer and would then proceed upwards, across a number of desks, until it reached the head of department or even an under-secretary. Each person wrote a comment on the covering page; each comment was subject to a silent process of judgement as the paper crossed the various desks. It was an elegant form of instruction.

I spent nearly two years in the Foreign Office in Whitehall before being posted abroad. Throughout this time, I lived in Earl's Court. I had settled in this area largely because it was one of the few parts of London I had heard of, and it was handy for the Foreign Office – just five stops along on the District Line.

I had started out in a bedsit in Redcliffe Gardens, but rapidly discovered that living by oneself in London can be very lonely, especially since I had broken up with Jane. I answered an advertisement for someone to share a flat in Philbeach Gardens and moved in immediately. I resolved that I would accept every invitation I received, however unpromising it might seem, and quickly developed a circle of friends, beginning with my flatmates, and then the girls in the flat upstairs, then all the people they knew, and so on.

My flatmates (who tended to come and go) worked at various jobs in London and I found myself with introductions to the worlds of advertising and the theatre. The main constraint on my social life was the usual one: lack of money. For the first time, however, this was a real worry. Hitherto, I had simply adjusted my lifestyle to what I could spend. In London, however, certain expenditure was inescapable, and sharing a flat meant also sharing costs, of food and other things.

I was desperately hard up. My mother had come for a holiday in the summer of 1965 and had persuaded me to take out a bank loan in order to buy a car. She had earlier given me £150 with which I had bought an elderly Ford Prefect, but this was not, she felt, reliable enough to take us on extended trips around Britain. I accordingly sold the Ford Prefect, borrowed the money and bought a brand-new Austin 1100. I was delighted with the car, but the cost of the monthly repayments meant that I had virtually nothing left from my meagre Foreign Office salary to live on.

In an attempt to increase my income, I took on some part-time teaching. Every Friday night, I taught commercial law (not something I knew much about) to a group of law students. I can't actually remember under whose auspices the course was arranged and I can't pretend to have done a very good job. It did, however, produce some useful extra income.

Still pretty broke, I remember on one occasion being invited to the theatre by one of the girls in the flat upstairs. She had apparently been given a couple of tickets and wanted someone to take her so that she could join a party of friends. She was not someone I particularly fancied but, partly for reasons of politeness and partly because it promised a free night out, I agreed to go. I remember nothing of the play, but I do remember that, to my horror, the party decided to go to a Soho restaurant after the show. I could hardly eat my meal for worry as to how I was going to pay for it or, for that matter, my partner's. It cost, I recall, £5, which represented all the money I had in the world.

When it came to my turn every three days or so to buy food for the flat, I found myself having to pawn or sell my books, a few at a time, in order to find the 4s. 6d. needed to buy the mincemeat which was our staple diet. Gradually, all my possessions – including my camera and tape recorder – went in this way.

On one visit to the butcher's shop in Earl's Court Road, I stood behind a striking-looking girl in the queue who had a brief altercation with the butcher over her change. I intervened on her behalf. She suggested as we left the shop that we have a cup of coffee. I agreed but had to reveal rather shamefacedly that she would have to pay since I had no money. Over coffee, she invited me to a party that Saturday night at her flat in the Cromwell Road. So began a relationship with Paulina Inverno, an Australian-Italian school teacher on a working holiday in London. She was the sort of girl who attracted attention wherever she went. She was rather more accustomed to appearing on the arm of a professional tennis player or racing driver than slumming it with an impecunious Foreign Office Third Secretary. Rather to my surprise, we eventually became engaged.

My social life was by now flourishing and picked up still further when I eventually paid off the debt on the car. My other activities developed more slowly. My involvement with the Labour Party was still rather tenuous. I had eventually managed to make contact with the local party in Fulham. I went to a few meetings, which were generally ill-attended and irregularly held. I was also careful about my involvement, since there were quite strict rules about the participation of civil servants in party politics.

I recall one meeting at which the guest speaker was Norman Hart, a sort of public relations activist for the European cause. I had recently returned from the WEU conference in Luxembourg and could not resist revealing, when he discussed the speech made by Michael Stewart at that conference, that I had written part of that speech. It was gratifying to see that he was impressed!

I was a strong supporter of the Wilson government and followed its fortunes closely. I was particularly interested in the Rhodesian issue. In some ways, I sympathised with Ian Smith. I could understand his impatience with the British, and his insistence that he should be allowed to resolve his own problems in his own way. But I was deeply opposed to racism and wanted to see the Wilson government take strong and decisive action to bring down the illegal regime. I was disappointed that Wilson seemed unwilling to act.

I understood little, however, of the other policy issues the government confronted. I was blithely unaware of the seminal decision that had been made, in its first few days, that sterling should be defended and that Labour must on no account be saddled with a reputation as the party of devaluation. Nor did I understand that the long struggle against the economic odds in which the Wilson government was engaged, and the long process in which that government's supporters became disillusioned by the deflated expectations and deflationary emphasis of policy, were the direct consequence of the decision to put the City's opinions and monetary targets ahead of the interests of those who had elected the government.

There was little evidence to the world outside, even to those like me who reckoned themselves to be students of politics, of the struggle going on within the government over these central issues. Treasury ministers like Joel Barnett and Robert Sheldon conducted a long and unsuccessful campaign to get the government off the sterling parity hook. Within the Cabinet, there was probably a majority in favour of devaluation, but they lacked the political weight, unity or firmness of purpose to make sure that their view prevailed.

I was, however, much more aware of the tactical situation in which the government was operating. I took pleasure in Wilson's mastery of the House and his general image as a modern and clever political leader. It was clear that he would choose his moment to call another general election and that his high approval rating and control over the timing were very likely to give him a greatly increased majority.

I have never forgotten this period in my political education. I suspect that most political activists are much as I was then: keen, fascinated by the day-to-day developments of party battles, but almost wholly ignorant of the fundamental issues which divide politicians at the highest level and determine the fates of governments and countries. Political commentary in the media provides little help, since the commentators are equally preoccupied with the minutiae, and even less able to escape the limits of debate laid down by establishment opinion.

There was a great interest at the time in the concept of a British 'establishment' which, it was felt, dominated much of British life through the cohesion achieved by a large number of well-placed and powerful people who shared a common social, financial and educational background and outlook. There was an equally popular feeling that the election of the Wilson government presaged an end to, or at least curtailment of, the influence of this 'establishment'.

I now believe in restrospect that by opting for financial orthodoxy ahead of the interests of his own supporters Wilson had decisively thrown in his lot with the establishment, which had once again demonstrated its power to determine the course of events and to disarm those who threatened it. The moment had passed, the opportunity for real change had gone. Never since then has there been any real challenge to establishment power in Britain. If anything, the snuffing out of the challenge in the mid-1960s consolidated orthodoxy and discouraged the political left (in its most general sense) from trying again.

To make these points is always to run the risk of being accused of paranoia or of adhering to some sort of conspiracy theory. But such charges entirely miss the point. It is precisely because there is no plan, no conspiracy and – much more importantly – no need for one, that the British establishment is so powerful. It achieves its aims because it truly reflects the views and interests of a stable but, at the margins, permeable grouping who genuinely believe that their interests are identical to those of the country as a whole. Its very flexibility and lack of dogma are its greatest strengths. It makes recruits and disarms opponents through a long process of social conditioning. To be defeated by the establishment is not painful. Most victims find pleasure in the process of absorption.

None of these considerations, however, weighed with me very much in 1966. It was a thrilling time to be in London. I enjoyed the freedom of flat life. My car gave me a mobility I had never before experienced. I had an interesting range of friends, my job was going well, and I knew that I was shortly to be posted abroad.

My main circle of friends built up around my flatmates and Paulina's flatmates, a mixture of Brits and colonials. Some of the people I met then remain among my closest friends today. Occasionally, I found myself breathing rather rarefied air. Once I attended a rather grand dinner at the Guildhall. I cannot remember what it was for, but I do remember somehow being provided with a very large chauffeur-driven car in which I called to collect the somewhat startled young woman whom I was to partner for the evening.

On another occasion, I was invited to a party in an elegant Westminster flat given by an American friend of mine from Balliol called Scott Thomson. Scott was one of those go-getting Americans to whom self-doubt seemed totally unknown. He was clearly destined, in his own and others' estimation, to become President (a not uncommon condition among Americans at Oxford) and he conducted himself accordingly. He had invited half the glitterati of London to his party and, what is more, most of them seemed to have accepted. I found myself chatting to a group which included, I recall, Selwyn Lloyd and Prince William of Gloucester.

I thought little about my long-term plans, but I suppose I was already relegating any eventual return to New Zealand to the distant future. I was absorbed by British life, by British politics, by my job in the British Diplomatic Service. I was still proudly and noticeably a New Zealander (my accent was even now quite pronounced) but my achievements at Oxford and my growing sense of comfort at the Foreign Office led me to feel increasingly integrated into British society.

I continued to write home once a week and looked forward eagerly to receiving letters from my mother. She was a wonderful correspondent. She could cover reams of paper with nothing very much, all in her small, perfect handwriting. But New Zealand seemed a very long way away. I was preparing to see the world.

When my posting came, in July 1966, it was, I suppose, just a tiny bit disappointing. I was to become Second Secretary (Commercial) at our embassy in Brussels. I had hoped for something a little more exotic. However, I have always had the capacity to look positively at every situation, and so I consoled myself with the thought that my superiors had clearly decided to launch me on the Western European circuit, which was reputedly the career path trodden by those destined for the top.

By this time, I was sharing a top-floor flat in Ulster Place, near Regent's Park. It was here that I held my farewell party – a highly enjoyable and somewhat alcoholic affair. I remember that certain of the departing guests found it impossible to negotiate the stairs and some of the girls had to be carried down.

For the first time in my life, I was not actually penniless. My tastes were still very simple, but I could at least afford to go out to restaurants occasionally, which became one of my greatest pleasures. I began to develop an interest in food and wine. Brussels, of course, promised a further step in my education in that respect.

My greatest thrill was the purchase of a new MGB sports car. As a diplomat going abroad, I was entitled to a number of allowances, amongst which was the duty-free purchase of a British car. To the surprise of my friends, who seemed to think it was completely out of character, I decided that I would put all my newly acquired cash, plus the proceeds from selling my Austin 1100, towards the purchase of a dark blue MGB with both a soft top and a removable hard top. I had great fun driving it round London in the few weeks before my departure.

On my last weekend in London, England won the World Cup. I watched the match with a large group of friends at Paulina's flat. I remember literally falling out of my chair when the Germans scored the equalising goal. I have always been an avid sports fan, and, although I had never played the game, I was now a keen football supporter. England's victory was a thrilling moment. On the day I arrived in Brussels, *Le Soir*'s headline was '*L'Angleterre est Championne du Monde*'.

FOUR

The Brussels Embassy
1966–68

BRUSSELS MAY NOT have been the most exotic foreign posting for a young diplomat thirsting to see the world, but it was good enough to be going on with. I was in a state of high excitement as I drove my MGB down the motorway from Ostend. I suppose I was looking forward most of all to the experience of simply living in a non-English-speaking foreign country.

Brussels itself I knew little about. In 1966, it still felt like a somewhat limited provincial city, rather than the international capital it is today. The Nato headquarters had only just been transferred there, and the Common Market had not yet reached its present level of importance.

Yet, for me, arriving from England, it had all the charm of a European city. Europe – indeed, the world – had not yet been homogenised. Brussels still had the appeal of something new and different. The city looked different, the shops stocked different goods, and the restaurants were superb. It was true then, and probably still is now, that one could eat better in Brussels than anywhere else in Europe – even Paris. One could step off the street into a completely unknown restaurant and be absolutely assured of a meal of top quality and value.

I approached each meal with a mixture of trepidation and exhilaration. I occasionally tripped up, as when my order for steak diane produced a mound of chopped raw beef, but I learnt a lot. I was impressed with how the Belgians had taken what had to be done anyway – the preparation and consumption of food – and converted it into an art of civilisation. The British certainly possessed the civic virtues, but they had little understanding of the pleasures of good food and wine.

I had arranged with the young diplomat whom I was replacing that I would take over his two-bedroomed flat in the avenue du Prince Héritier. It offered a level of comfort and space which I had never before experienced, but it would not be ready until a couple of weeks after my arrival. I was accordingly put up in a small hotel named the Marie-José, in the rue du Commerce, just a block or two from the embassy.

The hotel was a delight. My room at the back of the hotel was large and airy. The bathroom down the corridor was exclusively for my use. It, too, was a big room, with an old-fashioned bath standing in the middle. There was a large window along one wall, looking out over the back of a row of buildings. I felt as though I was taking a bath on a stage set. It seemed both exotic and the height of luxury.

The embassy was an anonymous office block in the rue Joseph II. I had an office on the floor occupied by the commercial department. The First Secretary was a laconic but humorous man called Colin McGurk. John Wraight, the Commercial Counsellor, had an office on the next floor up. He was a small, dapper man, with a large moustache – one of the most genuinely charming and courteous people I have ever met. The Ambassador was Sir Roderick Barclay, a diplomat of the old school and a scion of the banking family. Despite his aristocratic bearing, he was a man of liberal outlook. His most treasured memories in a diplomatic career which was coming to an end while I was there were of the period he had spent as private secretary to Ernest Bevin in the post-war Labour government.

The most important people in the embassy were, however, the locally engaged staff. One of my responsibilities was to help British businessmen penetrate the Belgian market, but the real work was done by half a dozen French- and Flemish-speaking locals who knew the market intimately. I often felt that I, an Oxbridge law graduate, had been miscast for a job which the locals were so much better equipped to undertake.

The secretarial work was done by local Belgian women. I was assigned a secretary called Madeleine Aliphon, a charming and attractive Mauritian woman who became one of my closest colleagues. She was intelligent and well-informed and in truth did half my job for me.

The internal administration of the embassy was in the hands of a general factotum called Archimede. He was a man of genial good humour who had seen innumerable British diplomats come and go, and had difficulty sometimes in concealing the fact that he saw a strict correlation between their competence on the one hand and the transience of their presence on the other.

Although I felt that I was not particularly well fitted to meet the strictly commercial requirements of my job, I was much more comfortable in some other aspects of the post. One of my tasks was to report on the state of the Belgian economy. I was a careful reader of the financial pages and used my recollection of first-year economics at Victoria University to write a fairly credible series of reports. I also wrote the occasional speech for the Ambassador.

A few months after I had moved to Brussels, Paulina and I went on holiday to Spain. We returned an engaged couple. The news was greeted with less than enthusiasm, I think, by the British girls who worked at the embassy, for whom the loss of an eligible bachelor was something of a blow. The engagement did not last long, however. I spent the Christmas of 1966 in London with Paulina, and came back to Brussels in the New Year a free man.

I was by now, however, to some extent consciously looking for a wife. I had some degree of financial security, a good job and a home. Despite the years I had spent living away from home, I was very much home-oriented. It has always been my greatest pleasure to spend an evening in the bosom of my family, and, wherever I go, I usually manage to create some reasonable approximation of home life.

I made many friends in Brussels, perhaps less among the local Belgians than with other young diplomats. I was particularly friendly with a young Indian diplomat named Mani Shankar Aiyar. We have remained friends ever since. I also saw a lot of Denis Doble, who was slightly older than me and working in the embassy in Chancery as First Secretary. Denis was a bachelor who was even more evidently looking for a wife than I was. His trouble was that he had a penchant for young, glamorous girls who were a long way from settling down.

I played a good deal of tennis of a social sort, both at the local club and on privately owned courts. The Ambassador was a surprisingly good tennis player for his age and we played the occasional enjoyable doubles match against visiting opponents.

I remained fascinated by British politics and became a more and more partisan supporter of the Labour government. I followed its fortunes closely, though still without any great understanding of the reasons for its difficulties. I was concerned, however, at the growing evidence that the British economy was losing competitiveness. This was being said openly in the columns of the Belgian and other international financial papers.

One of my tasks was to attend trade fairs of various sorts. I remember once going to a motor show in Brussels, and overhearing a Belgian saying to another, as he looked at a British exhibit, '*Comme ils se retardent!*' I resented this sort of, I thought, unjustified comment.

The Wilson government was displaying a renewed interest in joining the Common Market. I remained an enthusiastic supporter of the idea and much of the reporting I was required to do pertained to this. I became aware, however, that things were moving on, and that de Gaulle seemed intent on concluding deals with the Germans before we British could have our say in how Europe might develop.

In June of 1967, for my annual leave I decided to go on a motoring holiday in Ireland. I was attracted by the accounts I had heard of the peaceful countryside, the excellent food and the uncrowded roads – all the requirements necessary for some enjoyable open-top touring in my MGB. It was a relaxing holiday, but I was lonely. I have always enjoyed my own company for a short time, but I am essentially a social animal and a fortnight was too large a dose of solitude. I was, in any case, quite keen to get back to Brussels. Just before I left, I had been told by a member of staff who had recently been in the Foreign Office in Whitehall that there was an exceptionally pretty girl on her way out to the embassy in Brussels. I was interested in meeting her when I got back.

I was due back in the office on the Monday, but actually arrived back in Brussels on the preceding Friday. I called in to see my friends and took the chance of going upstairs to meet the new girl. She was called Gillian Harrigan. She was indeed very pretty and, more than that, lively and intelligent. She wore, as was the fashion, a very short mini-dress. I stayed and chatted to her for some time.

Within a fortnight, we were madly in love. We must have been a bit hard to take, since we had eyes only for each other and seemed to spend the summer in a cocoon. Our friends and colleagues, however, treated us with commendable tolerance and we enjoyed a wonderful social whirl of parties, dances, restaurant meals and picnics. It was a golden summer, as I am sure the meteorological records will confirm.

I was preoccupied by this time with preparations at work for 'British Week'. British Week was actually much more like a fortnight. It was meant to be a great celebration of all things British, and its object was to promote British exports. There was to be a great trade fair, a football match, a large number of cultural events, a pop concert and a visit by Princess Margaret, who was to open the whole event.

My particular responsibility was to prepare the programme for Princess Margaret. This was a good deal more complicated than it seemed. It involved negotiations with Princess Margaret's private office (I made several trips back to London for the purpose) and with the equivalent figures at the Belgian Palace. Brussels at that time was divided administratively into a large number of communes, each of which, unbelievably, had its own police force. Each time the Princess was to cross from one commune into another, she had to be greeted by the appropriate mayor, and her security became the responsibility of the appropriate police force.

Added to this were the demands of local organisations and of the local British community, all of whom insisted on a piece of the action.

I also had to prepare a programme for Lord Snowdon, who was to accompany Princess Margaret but would, on occasion and particularly in matters cultural, do his own thing.

I brought the whole complex process to a reasonably satisfactory conclusion and a detailed final programme was printed. I still have a copy. Unfortunately, at the last moment, Princess Margaret fell ill and Lord Snowdon arrived on his own. A rearrangement of the programme had to be hastily organized. Lord Snowdon bore these vicissitudes with remarkable good humour. His main problem seemed to be that he had a weak bladder and was always anxious to know where the nearest loo might be. I remember running around the empty rear rooms of some vast building with him, desperately looking for a lavatory.

Princess Margaret eventually arrived a few days later, so that another rearrangement of the programme was required. It all went smoothly, however, and my stock within the embassy rose still further. Princess Margaret presented me with a pair of engraved gold cufflinks at the end of her visit. Gill was given a silver comb. All were stolen in a burglary some years later.

I felt very tired when British Week was over, partly because of the strain of seeing it through and partly because Gill and I were leading a pretty active social life which kept us up till the small hours most nights.

We decided to go on holiday. On a whim, we booked a fortnight in Tunisia, at the Hotel des Orangers in Hammamet. We had a wonderful time, marred only by the fact that, with my New Zealand passport, I discovered I needed a visa to enter Tunisia. I was eventually allowed in but only after numerous phone calls to the British Embassy. I had to leave my passport behind to have a visa added to it, then travel back to Tunis to pick it up. Gill nobly accompanied me on the long, hot train journey. We talked very seriously and at length. It was then, I think, that I realised we were going to get married.

When we got back to Brussels, we arranged our engagement. We drove up to Antwerp to buy a diamond ring from a diamond merchant recommended to us by Archimede. We climbed some rickety stairs to a scruffy little office. The merchant, dressed and coiffed in the orthodox Jewish manner, took two little screws of brown paper from his pocket and invited us to inspect the two stones which he then unwrapped. Gill and I were so excited that we could hardly focus on the diamonds. We selected one and then Gill chose a setting. I drove back to Antwerp a few days later to pick up the finished ring.

When I got back to the embassy, John Wraight had laid on a party in his office to celebrate our engagement. The Ambassador gave us a lunch at his residence, a beautiful house in the rue Ducale, and offered it to us for our wedding reception. We decided, however, to get married in London. The ceremony was at a registry office in north London and the reception at the Carlton Towers Hotel. No member of my family was able to be present but it was nevertheless a jolly occasion. I could hardly wait to get Gill away, to wave goodbye to friends and family and to drive off in the MGB to the West Country for our honeymoon.

As a married man, I was entitled to greatly increased allowances. Gill was not, as the wife of a diplomat, allowed to work (a sexist ruling which no longer applies). However, we were still better off than we had ever been. Gill moved into my flat, which was plenty big enough, and we therefore saved considerably on rent. We began to save very rapidly, although not at the cost of forgoing regular visits to our favourite restaurants.

Our social life extended into the upper reaches of Belgian society, since we were often invited to help entertain the Ambassador's guests at dinners in the residence. I remember once sitting at the end of the long polished dining table, glittering with silver and gold plate under the enormous chandeliers, and being offered by Archimede (who presided over the team of waiters at important occasions) a second helping of a particularly delicious main course. Since I felt I had somewhat stinted myself the first time round, I helped myself to a substantial plateful. As I looked up along the length of the table, I realised that every one of the other 30-odd guests had an empty plate and was looking expectantly at me. I hurriedly scoffed my food under the sardonic gaze of Archimede.

I felt a little better later in the meal when my neighbour, a rather snooty Belgian woman, attempted to remove a caramelised orange from a wonderful concoction of spun sugar. The orange slipped from the serving spoon, bounced across the table and splotted on to the floor. Archimede winked at me as he cleared up the mess.

From time to time, I would have to act as 'duty officer' for the weekend. This meant going in to the office on a Sunday morning and looking at any telegrams which came in. There would always be a cipher clerk on duty as well, and usually a 'friend' (a member of the secret service) would be around, too. The duty officer would then be on call for the rest of the weekend.

One Friday in November 1967, I was especially asked to be sure to come in to the office early the following morning. When I got in, I was handed a telegram. It announced the government's decision to devalue the pound by 14 per cent. I was to deliver a message to the Belgian minister of finance.

I duly telephoned the minister and arranged to go round immediately. I handed the letter over to a civil servant, presumably a duty officer like me. So ended the long and painful struggle of the Wilson government to defend sterling's parity. Wilson's credibility never fully recovered. Nor did his government's fortunes. The sacrifices required of ordinary people for the sake of a monetary measure and an ultimately unsuccessful campaign were rightly regarded by the British people as too high a price to pay.

I was aware that the government had somehow suffered a defeat, but I was still a staunch supporter and was inclined to blame largely unidentified outside forces. I had little idea of the true significance of what had happened, or of the irony implicit in this early link with an issue which was to become such an important factor in my subsequent political career.

Wilson had won a substantial majority in the 1966 general election. His new Foreign Secretary was George Brown, who was regarded with a mixture of exasperation and fascination by professional diplomats. He was recognised as a dynamic and original political operator, but his tendency to get drunk and his consequent outbursts of temper and irrationality made him a difficult boss to work for. When he came to Brussels, Brown stayed with the Ambassador at the residence. Although Sir Roderick was the soul of discretion, stories abounded of his grossness of behaviour – whether true or otherwise – which did George Brown's reputation no good.

Brown was passionately committed to the European ideal, and was anxious to make a further onslaught on the Gaullist citadel. He and Wilson planned a tour of Common Market capitals, in order to focus attention on British determination not to take no for an answer and to give courage to their European allies to stand up to de Gaulle. The tour was meticulously planned. I was myself involved in the arrangements for the visit to Belgium, which went off well. It produced, however, little by way of concrete results. It became clear that de Gaulle was determined to keep us out for as long as possible, if not for ever, and that the other Common Market leaders lacked the political will to do much about it. The break in the log jam would come only with the departure of de Gaulle, something which – unexpectedly, at least to me – the *évènements* of 1968 duly delivered.

In retrospect, I believe that de Gaulle recognised that he would not be able to keep us out indefinitely. He was determined, however, to establish the fundamentals of the Common Market in such a way as to ensure that they could not be challenged or overturned by British accession. He knew very well that France was essential to the project, in a way that Britain could never be. Provided that the central core of European co-operation was already solidly established, Britain would always be kept on the periphery.

That central core was of course the Franco-German axis. France would bind Germany to her, thereby removing the threat of further German attempts at invasion, and would offset German industrial power by the deployment of superior political and diplomatic skills (exploiting French centrality) and by setting the Common Agricultural Policy in concrete.

I remained an enthusiast for British membership of the Common Market, but it began to dawn on me that the Europe which was taking shape before my eyes was not necessarily one which would best serve

British interests. Indeed, it was not truly Europe at all, although the term was always used to describe what was being constructed. Instead, we were being presented with a trading arrangement, and a very particular one at that. It would provide industrial free trade but a very high degree of agricultural protection. Behind the grand sentiments, the 'Europe' which was being created was really the Common Agricultural Policy decked out with a few trimmings.

Furthermore, it was hard to conceive of any trading arrangement which would have been more inimical to British interests. For historical reasons, we had developed a very different economy from that of our Continental neighbours. We had had our industrial revolution first. We had moved our rural population into the towns. As democracy developed, the weight of the popular British vote reflected urban and industrial rather than agricultural interests. Our concern was for cheap food for factory workers, not high prices for farmers.

For Britain, therefore, the fall in the real price of food worldwide in the latter part of the nineteenth century was a godsend and a major benefit of empire. The great wheatlands of north America and the temperate grasslands of Australasia suddenly made possible the supply to the British market of cheap grain, and, with the advent of refrigeration, meat and dairy produce as well. We fixed the price of domestic British production in line with low world food prices and supported our own farmers through subsidy. Cheap food prices gave us a competitive cost advantage. The Empire, those same territories which provided us with cheap food, also provided us with preferential markets into which we could sell manufactured goods without worrying too much about competition from newly industrialising (and perhaps more efficient) manufacturing economies elsewhere.

On the continent of Europe, by contrast, the response to the fall in world food prices was very different. Their industrial revolution was only just beginning. They still had large rural populations whose continued livelihood was the most powerful single political consideration. They reacted to cheap food with protectionism. High food prices and the absence (at least to the same extent) of preferential markets for industrial goods forced them to become more competitive as manufacturing economies.

The Common Market was a trading arrangement expressly designed to serve the interests of the industrially efficient and agriculturally protectionist continental economies. The divergent paths pursued by the British and continental economies were not matters of right or wrong, but of simple historical fact. The adjustment of the British economy to the continental pattern may or may not have been inevitable or desirable, but it was always going to be painful.

The dismantling of trade barriers in manufactured goods through the 1960s provided a great stimulus to expansion and investment. By the end of that decade, however, some further stimulus was needed. The introduction of a major new market, Britain, whose domestic manufacturing industry was relatively uncompetitive, and which would pay two or three times the world price for otherwise unsaleable agricultural surpluses, could hardly have come at a better time for the founder members of the Common Market.

Very little of this, of course, was ever explained to anybody – not to the British people, and certainly not to our European colleagues. Our difficulties were always interpreted as British whingeing or as evidence of bad faith or malevolence. The Foreign Office saw itself as a proselytiser for the European ideal, and as a protagonist in the domestic debate. As a consequence, it lost sight of its proper role as the defender of British interests and as the interpreter of those interests to our allies abroad. I began to realise that to congratulate oneself on embracing what seemed to be idealistic or internationalist views was not a good enough substitute for proper analysis. A warm cosy glow of virtue was all very well, but not at the expense of the practical interests of the British people.

As Gill and I turned into 1968, I fell ill for the first time in my life. It had been a hectic few months – our courtship, British Week, marriage. Now, Gill was expecting a baby and there was the imminent prospect of a new posting. The talk was of Lima, or somewhere equally exotic and distant.

I developed a curious condition called glandular fever or mononucleosis. It began with swollen glands, and rapidly developed to the point where I could scarcely raise myself from my bed without feeling exhausted. I was confined to bed for nearly three months. I did not make a good patient. I found the sensation of being weak and helpless very unpleasant. It was a blow to my self-confidence from which I did not fully recover until long after the physical symptoms had disappeared. It was also an odd experience to be visited by a doctor who, despite a charming bedside manner, held out his hand for payment as he left.

As I recovered, the question of my posting later in the year moved more to the forefront of our minds. It was at about that time that I had a phone call from my former tutor at Balliol, Don Harris. It appeared that Worcester College were looking for a new law don. They had advertised and interviewed but had not been satisfied with the field they had attracted. They wondered, said Don, whether I might be interested.

It was agreed that Gill and I would fly over to England for the weekend to talk to Worcester. We calculated that, since there was no obligation, we could afford to enjoy a weekend in Oxford. As the moment approached, however, I began to think more seriously about the prospect. I had always imagined that I might eventually pursue a political career, but I had never really thought in practical terms as to how this might be achieved. And it was certainly true that I found it more and more irksome to be writing speeches and briefings within the political parameters laid down by others when I had increasingly strong views on these matters myself.

It began to dawn on me that to accept a new posting would be to delay for a further couple of years any prospect of becoming properly involved in political activity. Lima would hardly be the ideal launching pad for a political career in Britain. Oxford, on the other hand, would give me every opportunity to immerse myself in British politics.

First indications were not, however, very encouraging. We had a pleasant enough time in Oxford, but Gill was somewhat put off by the gloomy houses and rather precious conversation of those we met. I, too, was quite surprised by Oxford. I had forgotten how demanding the place could be. After the easy business of light conversation in Brussels, it was a shock to be pulled up and made to explain oneself on the basis of some inconsequential remark uttered as a social platitude.

Gill was rather less than enthusiastic but she was characteristically prepared to support any decision I made. At the end of the weekend, I had a long conversation with Lord Franks, Provost of Worcester College. He was a tall, patrician, rather forbidding figure. I was taken aback by his prescience when he said, 'I assume that you will go into politics. What the college needs is an assurance that you will give us a good five years before you do.'

We flew back to Brussels with the intention of returning to Oxford becoming ever firmer in our minds. I did not look forward to telling the Ambassador of my decision. Sir Roderick and Lady Barclay had been immensely kind to us, and I felt that I was letting them down.

Sir Roderick took the news well, but the Foreign Office were rather put out. There had apparently been a spate of resignations from people of about my age and at about my stage of career development. I was summoned to London, not so much to be talked out of it, as to explain what it was that had induced me to leave. In the event, the personnel department was very understanding. It was agreed that I would leave on the basis that, if I returned within five years, I could resume my career with no loss of seniority.

Our last few months in Brussels were a curious sort of twilight period. As a posting comes to an end, there is inevitably a slackening of interest in what one is doing. The excitement and novelty have long since gone. Many of the friends one made as a new arrival have themselves been posted elsewhere. It hardly seems worthwhile to get to know their replacements.

Gill and I were in any case increasingly preoccupied with the prospect of our baby's arrival. Gill had had an easy pregnancy and had handled the whole business very well. But we were in a foreign country and it was our first baby. We hardly knew what to expect, and we had no immediate family to turn to.

One night in July, at about two in the morning, Gill awoke with a sensation that labour had started. I made her a cup of tea while we decided what to do. When there was no longer any doubt, we dressed and packed her bag, and I drove her to the Edith Cavell Institute. We had some difficulty in finding our way into the building in the middle of the night. Once there, I was desperately keen that someone should examine Gill to see if she was all right. First, however, we had to fill in some forms and I had to write out a cheque for the equivalent of £400. Only then would anyone check to make sure that Gill was indeed about to give birth.

I had been with Gill to classes at which she had practised the techniques of natural childbirth. It became clear after a few hours, however, that her labour was not proceeding well. It seemed that the baby was in the breech position and was coming out bottom first. Her labour was long and painful. Today, I believe a decision to operate would have been taken very early. As it was, it was not until 10.20 on the following evening, that after twenty hours of labour Gill – exhausted and cradled in my arms – gave birth to a baby boy.

Gill's parents, whom I had been telephoning throughout the day, somehow miraculously (since they spoke no French) managed to get a telephone call right through to the theatre within a few minutes of the birth. They heard Charles's first cries over the phone. There were tears at both ends of the line.

We said our farewells to Brussels with many regrets. The city will always have the happiest of memories for us. It was as young parents that we made our preparations for life back in Britain.

FIVE

An Oxford Don
1968–74

WE HAD MANAGED to save enough money during 1968 to put down a deposit on a house in Wheatley, a large village about six miles from Oxford, and then to buy the basic furnishings. Gill had a building society savings account and that, coupled with the fact that I had a secure (though not very well-paid) job, meant that we qualified for a mortgage, even though there was something of a mortgage famine at the time.

The house was brand new, built of reconstructed stone by a local builder. We were thrilled with it. We worked hard on the garden, and every evening we would walk around it to marvel at a new shoot here or a new bud there. We spent every last penny we had on the house, its furnishings and garden. We waited anxiously for my first pay cheque at the end of the month. When it did not arrive, I made enquiries. I was told that Fellows of Worcester College were paid quarterly in arrears. It took us a long time to recover financially from this unexpected blow.

I found my first few months as a law tutor pretty tough. It was four years since I had opened a law book. We had left Brussels at the end of September and I had had no time to prepare before beginning my teaching in early October. I nevertheless enjoyed the teaching and found that I was reasonably good at it. The Oxford tutorial system suited me well. I would not have enjoyed going laboriously over all the detail of what could be pretty boring black letter law. The weekly tutorial, however, allowed me to assume that the student had mastered all of that in the weekly set reading. In the tutorial, I could then concentrate on the more interesting bits, engaging essentially pretty intelligent young men (Worcester was at that time entirely male) in discussion about disputed issues.

Although I was an effective teacher, I was not what I would call a born teacher. There were dons at the college for whom teaching was in itself totally satisfying. Each year, as a new crop of students came up, they were fired all over again by the challenge of shaping young minds. I found, by contrast, that I had difficulty in maintaining my enthusiasm after several years of delivering essentially the same tutorial eight or ten times a week. For, as one of the few law dons in the university who taught administrative law and international law, I did a great deal of teaching in these subjects for other colleges, in return for the teaching by them of subjects we did not teach.

The senior law don at Worcester was Francis Reynolds, a Wyke-hamist who was a fastidiously careful lawyer and an excellent colleague. We made for a pretty effective combination. Francis inculcated the necessary rigour, whereas I like to think that I helped to generate some real intellectual excitement. By the end of my time at Worcester, we had earned the college a reputation as one of the best of the Oxford colleges for law.

My particular pleasure as a teacher was to watch the development of a young mind as it grappled for the first time with real intellectual problems. I have a belief that, for many people of genuine academic ability, there is one period in their early lives of real academic flowering. It is exhilarating to teach someone at such a time. For many students, this flowering is artificially advanced. They are sent to schools which deliberately bring them to academic maturity early. They gain an advantage during their school days, but by the time they get to university, they have often become weary of academic study. I preferred to teach boys from schools which had not prepared them quite so thoroughly for Oxford. One such student was a young man called Paul Craig, who had been to a London comprehensive and thus represented a minority among Oxford undergraduates. He made rapid progress in the unaccustomedly rarefied atmosphere of academic excellence to which he was suddenly exposed. He eventually obtained a first class degree and succeeded me as a law don at Worcester.

The time of year I enjoyed most was the interviewing of candidates for places for the following academic year. It was fascinating trying to identify those school-leavers who would gain most from an Oxford education.

In addition to my teaching, I also took on some administrative responsibilities. I became the secretary to the Worcester College Governing Body. The college was a corporate body, comprising the Fellows of the college, which in effect governed itself. The Governing Body met every week during term time, under the chairmanship of the Provost, Lord Franks.

Oliver Franks, in addition to all his other great accomplishments, was a brilliant committee chairman, probably the best I have ever encountered. He had an uncanny ability to shape and guide a debate, and then – at the right psychological moment – to sum it up magisterially and produce a consensus. I watched and learnt.

Lady Franks was a considerable person in her own right. She had a strong interest in prison administration and reform, and persuaded me to become a member of the parole board for Oxford Prison. She became an important figure for our children, since she ran a sort of informal play school for dons' children every Tuesday on the top floor of the Provost's lodging. The children, who knew her as 'Bar' (short for Barbara), were very fond of her.

In the summer of 1969, my parents came to Britain for a lengthy holiday. We picked them up at Tilbury on a sweltering day and drove them through London to Wheatley. I was delighted to see them and had been looking forward enormously to introducing them to Gill. After they had been with us for a few days, however, relations became rather strained. My mother had brought over with her a collection of photographs, old letters and other memorabilia which, perhaps recognising the permanence of my stay in Britain, she wanted to leave with us. She was keen to go through these with me but for some odd reason appeared to resent Gill's quite natural interest. This inauspicious start to the relationship between mother-in-law and daughter-in-law was no doubt very typical, but caused a good deal of heartache at the time. In due course, however, both my parents grew to love Gill dearly.

By this time, Gill was pregnant again. Our daughter Helen was born at the Churchill Hospital at 6.30 one November morning. I was again with Gill but this time the birth was a much quicker and more straightforward affair. Her own parents had come to live in Oxfordshire, following her father's retirement, and her mother was able to give her invaluable support in bringing up two small children.

We again had little money but we loved to entertain and to go out to eat occasionally. I had acquired a Barclaycard, so that even if we had no cash, there was a constant temptation, to which we occasionally yielded, to go out for the evening. I remember once taking Gill to dinner at a restaurant called the Luna Caprese in Oxford and feeling guiltily extravagant as I paid the bill for £4.

Although I was carrying a very heavy teaching burden of at least 18 hours a week, I usually managed to get home at a reasonable time and accordingly saw a good deal of the children as they grew up. I was very willingly domesticated and Gill and I got enormous enjoyment from small domestic things. I even became something of a handyman and built a back porch – not very expertly, but it was effective enough.

I had always been interested in cooking and began to develop that interest further. Gill was also keen to learn more, so we learnt together. Our occasional dinner parties for friends became rather more ambitious as our experience and expectations grew. I still knew very little about wine but I was intrigued to discover that Worcester had an excellent wine cellar and allowed Fellows to buy individual bottles for their own personal use at the price which the college had itself paid.

So, we found ourselves one evening drinking a bottle of 1945 Château Latour which I had bought for 25 shillings. We were scarcely aware of what we were drinking but we knew enough to make an occasion of it. We had invited some close friends, Charles and Fran Russell, to share it with us and, as a slightly ironic comment on the reputation of the wine, had decided to greet them dressed in evening dress and carrying a lighted candelabra. They had had exactly the same idea and, to much laughter, solemnly arrived also attired in formal evening dress.

Apart from my teaching and other duties at college, we were entirely and enjoyably preoccupied by family matters. In the light of the way our lives developed subsequently, I have often looked back on this period as a wonderfully carefree time, full of laughter and pleasure.

Wheatley at that time still had very much the character of an old Oxfordshire village. We threw ourselves into village life, much of which centred on a community hall called The Merry Bells. We also joined the local Labour Party. Even though my earlier experience of Labour Party membership in London had been a somewhat desultory affair, I was confident that this time I would get to know the true Labour Party. I had envisaged that, by joining, I would somehow become privy to a wonderful corpus of political wisdom and ideals which would take my political education to undreamt of heights.

The reality was rather different. The local branch was a small gathering whose main preoccupation was to keep itself in being. Our finances were always in a precarious state and we kept afloat only by running a bingo session from time to time in The Merry Bells. Most branch meetings were taken up with lengthy discussions as to whose turn it was to perform various functions at the bingo.

Gill loyally joined as well, and sat through interminably boring meetings with as good grace as she could muster. She, too, took her turn at the bingo sessions. I at least had the consolation that it was all in the interests of pursuing a political career. If anything, the tediousness of the meetings and the small scale of our preoccupations somehow seemed to confirm the value of the effort we were making.

The local party was in fact in the hands of some excellent people with whom we became very friendly. Peter and Sylvia Freeborn were the leading lights. They were older than us, and had a lovely house and garden in Windmill Lane, on a ridge high above the village. We rarely had the chance to discuss politics at our branch meetings but we did so eagerly on our teatime visits to the Freeborns. We learnt not only about politics but also about gardening, which became an increasing passion for us.

The chairman of the branch was John Jackson, a retired trade union official. One of the few younger members was John Sheldon, an engaging young northerner and rugby league fan who subsequently became a leading figure in public service trade unions. The constituency party, at that time called Henley, was chaired by Mary Smith, a gentle and good person who demonstrated her socialism in the simple way she lived.

By the time we joined the Wheatley party at the end of 1968, a general election was again likely within the next year or so. The Henley constituency had just selected their candidate, a young, blonde 23-year-old called Maeve Denby.

Maeve became one of our good friends. She was a remarkably intense young woman with a fierce intelligence. I could sometimes find myself locked in hours of debate with her, often to the despair of our friends, who would find themselves spectators to what was virtually a fight to the death. Maeve was a moral philosopher by training, and an argument with her usually became a process of ever more detailed refinement of terms, so that, having begun with a disagreement on some broad and sweeping proposition, we would find ourselves eventually disputing the most arcane of semantic points.

The constituency was of course a Tory stronghold, with no prospect of Labour winning. Maeve nevertheless threw herself energetically into the campaigning. She had one or two friends in senior positions in the Labour Party, who sometimes came to speak for her. I remember on one occasion that Denis Healey turned up and delivered a characteristically rumbustious performance.

Wheatley, like most of the rest of the constituency, was dominated by the local Conservatives. They ran the county council, the district council and the parish council. The local Tory bigwig was Peter Audley-Miller, an Oxford antiques dealer. He was personally a very agreeable man, but he appeared to run the village with a rod of iron.

The local Tories were always very resistant to the idea that party politics should be a factor in local government. It was one of their main campaigning arguments against us that Labour was intent on introducing party conflict into local affairs. The fact that they were all known Tory activists and local party officials who just happened to have majorities on all the local bodies seemed to them to be of no consequence. 'Politics', a dirty word, was by definition something that others did. They were above such things.

Gill and I both felt ourselves to be political novices, and in truth we were. I was delighted to be selected by the local party to become a delegate to the general management committee of the constituency party. I eagerly attended the monthly meetings, but I felt myself ill-equipped for such heady heights so I decided to attend a residential course at Beatrice Webb House, and Gill agreed to accompany me.

We left the children for a week with Gill's parents and decided to treat the week as our annual holiday. Beatrice Webb House was near Dorking in Surrey. It was a lovely old house in extensive parklands which had been bequeathed to the Labour Pary. Although it was an attractive place, it lacked modern comforts and the catering left something to be desired. A week's course there on Labour Party organisation would not have been everyone's idea of a fun holiday.

We enjoyed it as best we could, however. There were sorties to the local pub in the evening, and a table tennis championship, which I won. It was also the opportunity to meet Labour activists from all over the country – something I have always found to be one of the true pleasures of belonging to the Labour Party. For the first time, I felt that I was part of a great nationwide movement – a movement with a beating heart and a living soul.

Our tutor was Walter Brown, a gregarious and worldly-wise party official who knew all there was to know about party organisation. Gill and I were avid students. By the time we got back to Wheatley, and a joyful reunion with our children whom we had missed greatly, we were keen to put our new-found knowledge into practice.

The county council elections were to be held in April 1969. I decided to offer myself as the Labour candidate. The local party were tolerant of this initiative, but not enthusiastic. They knew that there was a huge natural Tory majority. We knew, on the other hand, that with the typically low turnout in a local election, a candidate who knew where his support was and could get it to the polling station on the day stood a chance of winning.

Gill and I were left to canvass by ourselves. We did so methodically, using up most of the Easter vacation in this way. We covered every house in the small Oxfordshire villages of Horspath, Garsington, Cuddesdon, as well as Wheatley, which made up the electorate. It was soul-destroying work. The Wilson government had become very unpopular, and the revival in its fortunes had not yet taken place. We met with a great deal of bitter hostility, though no actual violence.

Gill hated the whole experience but loyally stuck with me. I remember at the end of a tiring day coming to the last house on the canvass sheet. The drive was a long and forbidding one, and we could glimpse an imposing house at the end of it. Gill said she was too tired and that there was no point. We would be rejected again by yet another hostile Tory voter.

I insisted, however, on walking up the drive and knocking at the door. I explained wearily to the woman who answered the door that I was standing for the Labour Party in the county council elections. To my astonishment, she fell upon me with cries of joy and invited me in. She and her husband, both doctors, joined the Labour Party on the spot and became two of our greatest supporters.

My opponent was Major Millar, the local squire, said to have been an equerry to the Queen. He was an elderly gentleman who lived in the large house called Shotover Hall and who owned a large number of tied cottages. He had never been challenged before for his county council seat, but he rapidly adapted to the new situation. His method of canvassing was to drive slowly down the main street of Wheatley and nod to his tenants as they doffed their caps and tugged their forelocks to him.

On election night, there was a freak snowstorm and most of our potential voters decided to stay at home. Even a distraught Gill could not persuade them to venture out. We lost by 1200 votes to 900. But the scale of the vote I received was a sensation. As Sylvia

Freeborn said to me at the count, if the local party had only realised I could get so close, they would have been out canvassing for me every night.

Buoyed up by our comparative success, Gill and I then decided to stand as Labour candidates for the parish council. We and three of our Labour colleagues romped in. By this time, we had become notorious as 'the Labour couple', and led the Labour Group on the council. We had a foretaste of the pressures, albeit on a small scale, of public exposure. It was at the same time exhilarating and oppressive.

The Wilson government had, by 1970, made a remarkable recovery in the polls. When Harold Wilson decided to go to the electorate in June, it was widely expected that he would win comfortably. I spent election day working in the local ward, but had to give up in the evening because I was expected at a college dinner for those who had just completed their exams.

The talk over dinner was entirely of the size of the expected Labour majority. I got home at about midnight, looking forward to watching the results with Gill. My first surprise was to find the house in darkness, Gill having gone to bed. I switched on the television. The first thing I saw was Keith Joseph being asked by the interviewer what job he expected in the new government. I watched in horror as the reality of the Labour defeat sank in.

My friend Francis Reynolds asked me the following day how I felt about the result. I think he was rather surprised at the vehemence of my reply. It was a tragedy, I said. The British people had briefly known what it meant to trust themselves and to govern against the wishes of their supposed betters, but they had been tricked and browbeaten into handing their future over to those who would again use the power of government to promote the interests of a powerful minority.

In 1970, I was selected by the constituency party as their delegate for the annual conference, held that year in Blackpool. Gill and I both went. We booked into a boarding house a couple of miles up the promenade. It was not very comfortable (we were kept awake most of the night by the wind rattling the windows) and the food was indifferent, but we had a wonderful time.

As luck would have it, we were allocated seats in the very front row, immediately below the platform. Gill and I were agog at the sight of so many famous faces, familiar to us from our black and white television screen, but now in living colour. We were the most assiduous delegates ever, sitting through every minute of every boring debate.

Conference was an uplifting experience. The sheer numbers of people there brought home to us that the Labour Party was indeed a great national party. Most of the delegates seemed to come from parts of the country where it was taken for granted that Labour was the party of government – a revelation to those like us who struggled on in the Tory heartlands. In the evenings, there was a veritable cornucopia of fringe meetings and receptions to choose from.

I had by this time become vice-chair of the Henley constituency party, and began to think that, after the next election, I might try my luck at becoming a parliamentary candidate. In early 1971, we moved house. With the aid of a £1,000 loan from Gill's parents and having sold our Wheatley house at a good profit, we bought a larger house in the village of Church Hanborough.

Shortly after we moved in, we received a caller, a charming gentleman who welcomed us to the village and introduced himself as being from the local Conservative party. He offered us some raffle tickets. The prize was a colour television set. I explained, as gently as I could, where my political allegiances lay. He was not at all discountenanced, and still urged me to buy a raffle ticket, explaining that it was 'not really political'.

The boundary changes which had long been delayed by Jim Callaghan were now implemented by the Health government, and we now found ourselves in the new constituency of Mid-Oxfordshire. I was made chair of the new constituency party and became friendly with Clive Lindley, chair of the neighbouring Banbury constituency, and Anthony Booth, who had fought and lost Banbury twice.

My friend Maeve Denby, having lost the Henley seat by a predictably wide margin, was now keen to find a better seat. She and I decided to join forces. We analysed all the winnable seats which did not have a sitting Labour MP. In practice, this meant seats which had been won in the *annus mirabilis* of 1966 but had been lost in 1970.

We duly applied for a clutch of seats – Dover, Gloucester and Northampton among others. We travelled all over the country, seeking the nominations of the ward parties which invited us to speak. I was gratified to secure a nomination from each ward I spoke to. I did particularly well at Dover, a mining seat which had been lost by David Ennals and where the party was anxious to replace him with a candidate who might achieve comparable prominence.

I was due to go to my first selection conference at Dover, where I was the hot favourite, when I received a call from Southampton Test. My application there had been very late, too late in fact to secure me any invitations from the wards, who had already made their nominations. The executive committee, however, was dissatisfied with the short list; there was some opposition to a local candidate who looked sure to have the beating of a weak group of rivals.

The executive decided, unusually, to exercise its power to add another name to the short list. I found myself invited to a selection conference without having a single nomination from a ward or trade union branch. A university lecturer named John Arnold, however, hurriedly got in touch and introduced me to one or two people in the local party. John and his wife Jenny remain friends to this day.

At the selection conference, I made my ten-minute speech and answered questions for a similar period. I then waited with the other candidates as they completed their turns. After what seemed to be an interminable time, we were summoned into the packed room. I was announced the winner and was asked to make a short speech. I did so as the prospective Labour candidate for Southampton Test.

The party in Southampton was extremely well organised. The city was divided into two constituencies, Test and Itchen, but for most purposes the two constituencies operated as one. The Itchen seat had been held by the former Speaker, Sir Horace King, and was a safe Labour seat. Test was really a Tory marginal, which we occasionally won in a good year. A local schooteacher named Bob Mitchell had won it in 1966 and, on losing it in 1970, had then had the good fortune to inherit Horace King's seat when he retired. Bob was a solid citizen and an excellent colleague, who sadly eventually defected to the SDP.

Itchen was the biggest local Labour party in the country in terms of membership and Test was the third biggest. This was because the two parties operated a very successful 'tote' scheme which required participants to join the party. The 'tote' generated enough money to pay a full-time agent and a couple of other staff, and to run good premises near the centre of town.

Shortly after I became candidate, the party appointed a new agent. He was Richard Bates, an experienced and competent organiser who eventually became leader of Southampton City Council.

I still had a lot to learn about politics and the Labour Party when I was selected. However, members of the local party were good teachers, Southampton was a good school, and I was a quick learner. Together, we campaigned hard and effectively, often supported by visiting speakers who found it reasonably easy to make the train journey from London. I learnt a great deal from the public meetings, the meetings with ward parties and the regular canvassing.

In Oxford, I had learnt of a free advice service being offered to social security claimants, and had gone along to help once a week. The service was run by Tony Lynes, the founder of the Child Poverty Action Group, and the author of an excellent handbook on the arcane world of supplementary benefit rules and discretionary powers. The work, which was absorbing and worthwhile, also enabled me to make good use of my legal skills.

When I became the parliamentary candidate in Southampton, I decided to start a similar service there. So began Southampton's first Social Security Advice Centre which, as far as I know, still functions. I would travel down by train every Friday lunchtime and spend the afternoon at the centre. The return journey was always a nightmare, involving difficult connections at Basingstoke and Reading. I shivered late at night on deserted railway stations on many occasions.

The centre was a great success, and was busy almost from the start. There was an almost insatiable demand for help of this sort. Although it was meant to be limited to advice on social security, people would in practice bring us problems of every conceivable sort. I was helped by a number of voluntary advisers, who ranged from Citizens Advice Bureau staff to lecturers from the law department at Southampton University. My most faithful supporter from the latter group was Malcolm Grant, a young New Zealander who went on to a distinguished academic career as a planning lawyer.

Gill and I had many good friends from the local party who helped me out with overnight accommodation and hospitality. Once, when I was required for a week's campaigning during the school holidays, we rented a caravan in the New Forest and the family treated the expedition as their annual holiday. On another occasion, our good friends Roy and Jeanne Butterfield lent us their house for a couple of weeks.

I was an enthusiastic and innovative campaigner. I remember on one occasion hearing on the local news that there was a glut of tomatoes and that a grower at Fareham was destroying great quantities. I got in touch with him and he agreed to let me have some, on condition that I would not sell them, for distribution to local pensioners. I drove over to collect them, packaged them in brown paper bags I had bought from Woolworths, inserted a little printed slip to the effect that they were a gift from their Labour candidate, Bryan Gould, and then left them outside each door in blocks of pensioners' flats. My Tory opponent was furious, but the local publicity was excellent.

Worcester College were pretty tolerant of my political activities. On one occasion, James Campbell, the history don, was approached by a Sunday newspaper which wanted to do a feature article on a day in the life of an Oxford don. He diverted them in my direction, on the grounds that I 'needed the publicity'. I duly featured in a full-page article, accompanied by colour photograph.

My friends Maeve Denby, who had been selected for Reading North, and Anthony Booth, re-selected for Banbury, and I formed a little organisation called the Labour Parliamentary Candidates Association. It never came to anything but during its brief life it did attract the attention of the BBC which decided to interview us for one of their programmes. A television crew duly turned up to spend the afternoon filming interviews with us in my garden in Church Hanborough. It was a wonderfully sunny afternoon and Gill spent most of it making and dispensing home-made lemonade. I was disappointed with the outcome, which I felt did us less than justice. It was my first lesson in the hard fact that the aims of the interviewee and of the programme maker are almost always different, and that the exaggerated expectations of the interviewee will almost always be disappointed.

On another occasion, we managed to persuade *Labour Weekly* that there was a story in the fact that in the tiny Oxfordshire village of Church Hanborough there lived within a couple of hundred yards of each other two Labour parliamentary candidates (myself and Anthony) and a Labour councillor (another good friend of ours called Peter George). Julia Langdon, then at the start of her journalistic career, with *Labour Weekly*, came to have lunch with us and wrote an excellent piece about this Labour stronghold in the heart of Tory rural England.

By this time, I had settled into my teaching, which had, I think, reached a pretty good standard. I was also fulfilling my obligations to deliver eight lectures twice a year to the University – something which took a great deal of work and which I found quite nerve-wracking. I was a reasonably accomplished public speaker, but lecturing for an hour at a time to a room of a hundred or more eager undergraduates is rather terrifying. My lectures were, however, a great success. It was one of the intimidating aspects of the whole business that the judgement made by undergraduates of the value of one's lectures was cruel and immediate. If they thought they were no good, they simply stayed away. I was glad to note that my numbers held up pretty well.

In my last year at Oxford, I became an examiner for the University, something which, although time-consuming, I enjoyed very much. It happened to be an *annus mirabilis* for law at Worcester College. We had a third-year group of truly exceptional ability. They achieved, because of the high standard across the group, a sort of critical mass which stimulated each individual to even greater levels of achievement. I had the pleasure of examining in a year in which no fewer than five Worcester men – half the college's lawyers taking Schools in that year – achieved Firsts.

Because of my other commitments, and because, I suppose, I knew I was unlikely to pursue an academic career for very long, I did less research and bothered less with publications than would a modern academic. I did, however, publish one article of which I was very proud. My special interest was in administrative law and, in particular, the question of judicial review – the power of the courts to review decisions or actions by public bodies which they believe are deficient in reasonableness or fairness or legality.

One of the great issues of the day was the concept of 'jurisdiction'. A public body was said to 'exercise jurisdiction' when it used the power given to it by statute to make a decision on some issue or other. The courts were entitled to ensure that the jurisdiction was correctly exercised, but not to substitute their own judgement for that of the public body. It was important therefore to define what 'jurisdiction' was. Did it include the power to be wrong as well as right?

The House of Lords decided a very important case called *Anisminic* v. *Foreign Compensation Commission* which bore directly on this point. I wrote an article for *Public Law* which used the case to show that 'jurisdiction' was that area of competence to act or decide which was defined by all the legal instructions given by statute or common law to the public body; that it was therefore impossible for the public body to make a legal error and yet remain within its jurisdiction.

This view was not widely held, but, if accepted, would greatly increase the efficacy of judicial review. It has given me enormous pleasure since to discover that the article is still found on reading lists for law students and that the view I then expressed is now widely accepted.

One of the major political issues over this period was Britain's imminent entry into the Common Market. The Gaullist veto had been lifted, and Heath had negotiated our entry. The Labour Party had decided that it was opposed to entry, and I had hardened my own view: I had heard Peter Shore speak at a meeting and he had articulated many of the concerns I felt about the appropriateness or otherwise for Britain of a trading arrangement which had been negotiated to meet French and German interests.

I met another senior politician at about this time when Roy Hattersley came to Southampton for a public meeting at which we both spoke. He stayed overnight for some canvassing the following day. We got on very well and he seemed to take a particular liking to me. Before he left, he said that if I got elected, as he expected I would, he would have 'something very important' to discuss with me. I interpreted this to mean that he intended to ask me to be his parliamentary private secretary. I was flattered and excited that a prominent MP who was so clearly on the way up should have noticed me in this way.

The Heath government was in dreadful trouble as we turned into 1974. The miners' strike threatened its credibility, and public opinion was sharply divided over Heath's handling of the issue. I began to realise that a general election might be called at any moment.

The last few days of January were an agony of uncertainty, but at last, as I listened to the lunchtime radio in my study in college, I heard the news I had been waiting for. There was to be an election on 28 February 1974.

Gill and I had arranged that we should spend the four weeks of the campaign staying at a boarding house in Southampton run by party members called Alan and Pat Cooper. Our children stayed with Gill's parents. The Coopers treated us very kindly, but it was nevertheless a great strain. Campaigning is stressful and hard work. It was an added burden living in a strange house with no chance of relaxing in one's own home.

Southampton Test, as befitted a marginal seat, expected a hard-fought campaign from the two leading candidates, and it duly got one.

My opponent, the sitting Tory MP, was a rather stolid former estate agent called James Hill. He had made no great mark in his four years in Westminster, but he had a certain political cunning which meant that he was no pushover. Even so, faced with someone who was fighting his first campaign, and with the advantage of four years' experience as an MP, he should have been able to dismiss me easily enough. In the event, on occasions such as that organised by the Council of Churches, where all the candidates appeared on the same platform, he made heavy weather of it and I comfortably outscored him.

My main concern was the Liberal candidate, Jack Wallis, a well-known local insurance broker. He always followed the well-worn Liberal tactic of letting James Hill and me tear each other's arguments to shreds, before coming in with the well-timed jibe that the two main parties always fought like cat and dog and only the Liberals could be trusted to apply sweet reason to the issue.

The campaign seemed to go well, notwithstanding our growing exhaustion. Gill, typically, worked extremely hard. As I now know is always the case, there is no time during the campaign to ponder on whether one is going to win or not. There is only one basis on which it makes sense to make the stupendous effort required, and that is the assumption (which one has no time, energy or disposition to question) that victory will be the end result. The candidate's main task in any case is to express unflagging confidence. No flicker of doubt must be allowed to dim the enthusiasm of the party workers on whose efforts so much depends.

As polling day approached, however, I began to detect worrying signs. Our own canvass results were still looking good and there was little evidence of a lift in Tory fortunes. But the Liberals seemed to be buoyant. I noticed one evening on a council estate in what should have been a safe Labour ward that the kids who swarmed around our car shouting various cries of approval or otherwise were all wearing Liberal stickers.

Polling day was a long one. Ordinary canvassing ceases on polling day but there is no rest for the exhausted candidate. Convention requires that the candidate should visit each polling station and committee room with the aim of exhorting the troops to try even harder. In the course of travelling from one location to another, I managed virtually to lose my voice as a result of the constant repetition over the loudspeaker of the injunction to 'Vote Gould, vote Labour'.

At last, mercifully, the polls closed. We were able to go back to the Coopers for a meal, a shower and a rest before arriving at the Civic Centre at about midnight for the count.

I have never been to a count which has been anything other than a nightmare. The exhaustion of the campaign, the burden of expectations from one's supporters, the hostility from one's opponents, the nervous tension as the votes are checked and then counted, all combine to create an atmosphere of dreadful emotional strain.

My first count was no exception. To the dispassionate observer, it was, I suppose, an occasion of excitement, action and colour, but I was too closely involved to feel anything other than a stomach-wrenching nervousness. The result, when it came at about 2.30 in the morning, was close, but not close enough. The Tory majority had been reduced, but it was still a decisive 1800 votes. The Liberals, whose vote had gone up substantially, had saved the Tories' bacon.

We all went back to Bob Mitchell's house for a party. There was genuinely much to celebrate. Bob had been returned in Itchen with an increased majority and there was at least a good chance that the Heath government had been defeated. I put a brave face on my own personal disappointment. Gill and I stayed for as long as we thought we must.

I followed the next few days with a mixture of fascination and exasperation. Heath tried hard to stay in office and attempted to persuade Jeremy Thorpe to negotiate the terms for a coalition deal with the Liberals. When the newly elected Parliamentary Labour Party met to consider the situation, I remember feeling a strong sense that I should have been there. I was impatient to make my contribution to the unfolding political situation.

My one consolation was that, when Harold Wilson was eventually asked to form a minority government, it was clear there would have to be a second general election before too long. Following on the precedent of 1966, it was also likely that that election would show a further swing to Labour.

As it happened, my seat in Southampton Test was now statistically the most important seat in the country. It was the seventeenth most winnable seat for Labour, and we needed to win just seventeen seats from the Tories in order to gain a Labour majority.

Although most of my thinking about the future was by now dominated by my political prospects, my day-to-day preoccupations were still with children and family. My mother had brought my eight-year-old nephew David over for a long holiday. It was a happy occasion and the beginning of the much better relationship which Gill and I established with her. Although she could never really approve of my political allegiance, she was proud of the fact that I had made such comparatively rapid progress in British politics.

My family gave me much pleasure. The mortgage repayments on our house in Church Hanborough kept us relatively poor, but we had a wide range of friends – from the university, from politics, from the village and from earlier times. The children were now both at the small village school at Long Hanborough and were a constant delight. By now, we had acquired the first of our West Highland White terriers, Dougal, who somehow completed the family picture. Dougal was in fact pressed into service as a political campaigner. He wore a red collar and lead, and sported a large red rosette whenever we went campaigning. When the October election was declared later in 1974, he threw himself into the campaign with enthusiasm.

There was a general expectation that this time we would win. The campaign, like most campaigns, followed much the same daily pattern. It became a confused jumble of endless meetings, canvassing, school-gate and factory-gate encounters, consultations in committee rooms, occasional interviews. We were always on the move. A moment's rest would be brought to an abrupt end by the sudden thought that a second more of inactivity might cost the very vote on which victory depended.

It is doubtful whether much of that frenetic activity makes any difference to the result. The only thing which a relatively unknown candidate can do to influence the result (apart from avoiding some catastrophic mistake) is actually to turn up in person and convince a doubting voter by making a favourable impression. The opportunities for doing that, for bringing about the particular combination of circumstances, are necessarily limited.

The count was again a terrible trial. As we prepared to go, we listened to the television commentators predicting that Labour would win by 100 seats. We arrived at the Civic Centre, nervous but excited at the prospect of victory. By the time we arrived, the votes had been tipped out of the ballot boxes and were being counted so that the total number of votes delivered could be checked against the numbers recorded at the polling stations. Only then would the count proper begin.

It is possible for an experienced campaigner to get some impression from this process as to how the result may go. If, for example, a ballot box from a safe Tory ward gives the impression of containing an unusual number of Labour votes, this is a hopeful sign.

As we entered the room, Richard Bates, my agent, was leaning over the tellers at one of the long trestle tables on which piles of voting slips were scattered. He was scanning the slips keenly. As we appro3ohed, he caught my eye, pulled a little face and silently, almost imperceptibly shook his head. I went cold; fear clutched at my heart. I could hardly bear the prospect of losing again, not, at least, with expectations running so high. I spent the rest of the night in a daze.

As the votes were counted, they were wrapped in bundles of 1,000 and stacked on the appropriate table. The Tory table grew steadily, and although mine did as well, we were always a thousand or two behind. I had warned Gill that we would lose and she felt the same sense of despair as I did.

The final moments approached. There were only a few bundles of votes left to bring to the table. I had noticed that, in the last few minutes, the Tory table seemed to have stopped growing. I had calculated roughly what they would need for a majority, and they had not yet quite got there. I quickly walked around the counting tables. With growing excitement, I saw that all the remaining bundles were Labour votes. Less than five minutes before the result was announced, I realised for the first time that we had won. I was the new Labour MP for Southampton Test.

SIX

Westminster
1974–79

THE BEST THING that can be said of winning is that it is better than losing. After the speeches from the steps of the Civic Centre and the cheers from my supporters. I was anxious to get away as quickly as possible. Gill and I set off back to Oxfordshire. We got home at about 5 a.m. and fell into bed.

I was woken at about 7 a.m. by a telephone call. It was a reporter from the Press Assocation who, after offering congratulations on my election, wondered if I would like to comment on an interview which my mother had given in New Zealand. 'Your mother,' said the reporter, 'says that you are a Communist.'

This was a little hard to take in after only a couple of hours' sleep and I laughed it off as best I could. It was my first experience of being transfixed by the unexpected glare of the media spotlight.

My poor mother had apparently been visited by a young journalist who had conducted a formal interview in which my mother had made all the right noises about how proud she was that her son had become a Westminster MP. She had then unwisely offered the journalist a cup of tea and, feeling more relaxed and assuming that the interview was over, had mused about the fact that I had been brought up in a conservative family but had turned out to be a Labour MP. It was, she thought, something to do with going away to university. Everyone knew, she said, that universities were hotbeds of communism. It was a gift to the journalist.

The next few weeks were truly exciting, and passed in a blur. I hardly recall leaving Worcester or saying goodbye to my friends there. My students gave me a farewell dinner, which I enjoyed, but my mind was set firmly on Westminster.

Bob Mitchell and I were photographed as we caught the train from Southampton to travel to London for the State Opening of Parliament. When we got there, Bob introduced me to a young Tory MP called Tom Arnold who had been elected in the February election. We agreed to be 'pairs' – an arrangement we maintained for the next twenty years.

Of all the wonderful and surprising things about arriving at Westminster as an MP, I suppose the one which stands out in my mind most clearly is the sense that one had suddenly become a great focus of attention. After a lifetime spent in decent obscurity, it is a heady experience to be courted by what one can easily think of as 'the world's media'. Wherever I went in Westminster, uniformed messengers would seek me out, carrying little notes to say that such-and-such a journalist had phoned and would like me to get in touch. Gill says that I didn't touch the ground for three months.

Immediately after the election, we began to think of moving. We had promised to live in Southampton and we were looking forward to the move, since we had already made many friends there. Some friends from the party, Margaret and David Teagle, had sent us a telegram the day after the election to say that the house next door was for sale. They lived at 8 Furzedown Road. 'Number Ten,' went the telegram, 'awaits a new occupant.'

It took us a little time to sell our house in Church Hanborough and to move in to 10 Furzedown road. It was a long, narrow, semi-detached house which had been divided into flats and needed a great deal of re-arrangement and upgrading. It was never an ideal house, but we were very happy there, largely because of its location. It was close to the university, and looked out on to the common. Our neighbours were mainly friends and party supporters, and constituted a wonderfully supportive and interesting community. Many of them – the Teagles, the Kings and the Butterfields, in particular – have remained friends to this day.

At Westminster, I quickly made my mark. My maiden speech was on housing, an issue of great concern to me since I had seen through my advice work how destructive poor housing could be to so many people. I have never been more nervous in my life than when I made that maiden speech. I think it was the sense that the Hansard writers were recording everything I said which added a special burden.

In addition, I had to wait a couple of days to make it, never quite knowing when I might be called. Gill had travelled to London to hear me speak, sitting patiently in the Strangers' Gallery throughout the afternoon. She was obliged to catch a particular train in order to pick up the children and had to leave the gallery just as I got to my feet. She left in tears.

The speech went well enough, and I received several congratulatory notes. A speech which made a greater impression, however, was one I made at the end of a debate on Europe a few weeks later. During my time teaching constitutional law at Oxford, I had become very interested in what I then described as the question of sovereignty. (I no longer use the term 'sovereignty' to describe this issue, since it has such a Diceyan and nineteenth-century ring that it is easily dismissed or ridiculed; it is better and more accurate to talk of democracy and self-government.)

Now I spoke quite powerfully on this issue. I said that the question of who made laws and imposed taxes in Britain was at the very heart of our constitutional concerns and was the very essence of democratic government. Jim Callaghan, the Foreign Secretary, and Roy Hattersley, minister of state, were both on the front bench, and rose to the despatch box to intervene. As Mike Thomas, another newly elected MP, observed to me, 'It takes quite a speech to provoke interventions from your own front bench.'

The fall-out from that speech was quite considerable. I was immediately marked out as an 'anti-Marketeer', and accordingly welcomed by one group and recognised as an enemy by another. These groups did not, of course, coincide with the boundaries between parties. As has remained true throughout my political life, the European issue has created strange cross-party alliances and even more significant intra-party divisions.

The speech also marked the end of my political friendship with Roy Hattersley. Roy felt passionately about the European issue. It has been, I think, the most important single issue in his political life. His friends and enemies, those whom he felt he could trust and those he could not, have all been identified according to their views on Europe. As far as he was concerned, my concerns about Common Market membership meant that he and I could never be on the same side.

As a result, I believe that Roy has at all times worked against me. This is something I regret since, in many ways, Roy and I were natural allies. I have always liked him personally and enjoyed his voracious appetite for politics. We share a common interest in the ideas of politics (something which is surprisingly rare amongst senior politicians) and have often agreed on issues of principle, such as the importance of both equality and individual freedom as socialist objectives, and the synthesis to be achieved between them.

It is probably true that I have in most senses been to the left of Roy. However, apart from Europe, the most significant difference between us has probably been on the in-fighting which is always an important part of political life, for which I had little appetite or talent and of which Roy is a great enthusiast.

There was one other important issue which involved me in my first couple of months. The IRA had carried out the infamous Guildford pub bombings and the new government decided that it needed special powers to help them catch the terrorists. The Prevention of Terrorism Bill was introduced. I spoke in the second reading debate, expressing considerable concern, not only about the obvious implications for civil rights, but also about the efficacy, from the strictly anti-terrorist viewpoint, of risking the criminalisation of large numbers of people of Irish descent.

Alex Lyon was at that point minister of state at the Home Office. He approached me after the debate and asked whether I was particularly interested in home affairs. He followed this up a little later with a more specific inquiry as to whether I would be prepared to act as his parliamentary private secretary. I replied that I would. I was very excited and flattered. The appointment would have meant a major step forward. I would have been, I think, the first of my intake to gain such recognition.

Nothing, however, happened. Alex mentioned to me from time to time that there were difficulties. It was only later that I learnt that Roy Jenkins, then Home Secretary and Alex's boss, had refused to give his approval to the appointment. I was given to understand that this was on account of my anti-Market views – another example of how the pro-Marketeers always looked to this criterion whenever decisions of this sort were to be made.

There was another consequence of the terrorism debate which was of more immediate and local significance. Over the Christmas of 1974, a cache of arms was discovered in Southampton and a number of local people with Irish connections were arrested and detained under the new Prevention of Terrorism Act. One of them was a man called Tommy McAllister, who lived in the eastern part of Southampton and was therefore Bob Mitchell's constituent.

As luck would have it, Bob was away on holiday. McAllister's family were distraught at his arrest and loudly proclaimed his innocence. They were also concerned about his health and how he would stand up to the shock of being incarcerated in Winchester prison and eventually being deported to Ireland. They sought political help and – in Bob's absence – that meant me.

I could easily have ducked the issue. I was a new MP in a highly marginal seat. McAllister was not my constituent and I could have advised him and his family to wait until their own MP returned from holiday. Bob and I had an informal arrangement, however, that we would, whenever necessary, deal with each other's constituency cases. I was also intrigued by the fact that McAllister not only claimed he was innocent of any offence (though it was clear that he was a republican sympathiser) but also maintained that he had been resident in Britain for twenty years and so was beyond the reach of the Prevention of Terrorism Act.

I yielded to no one in my abomination of terrorism but I felt that

McAllister was entitled, like everyone else, to the proper application of the law. If the Act specified that those who had been resident for twenty years could not be detained under its measures, then he was entitled to that protection. I went to see him in Winchester prison and on the basis of what I then learnt, I took up his case with Roy Jenkins.

The point at issue was whether McAllister was entitled to count as a period of residence a few months before he actually held an address in Southampton but during which he was working on a ship which sailed from Southampton. I argued that he was. I wrote letters to Roy Jenkins and had many phone conversations with John (Lord) Harris, the Minister of State, who, like so many Jenkins acolytes, sounded on the phone exactly like Roy himself.

The upshot was that McAllister was released. The case was headline news in the local paper and the comment on my role was by no means favourable. I lived in fear for years afterwards that McAllister would be subsequently arrested and this time convicted of some terrorist offence. On the rare occasions I came across him, however, he always appeared genuine in his expressions of gratitude and his assurance that he was involved in no terrorist activity.

I had made up my mind, in any case, that if I allowed concern for my 530-vote majority to dictate what I did, I would never do anything. In the long run, my action paid off, even in strictly electoral terms. Years later constituents would turn up in my surgery saying, 'We thought that if you were prepared to help that IRA bloke, you might be ready to help us as well.' I had learnt an important lesson – that one should not trim for the sake of short-term popularity.

We eventually moved to Southampton in April 1975. Gill and I were both suffering from severe flu and were scarcely able to get out of bed, let alone pack up all our wordly goods and move 70 miles. Somehow, we struggled through the couple of days which saw us leave our comfortable home in Church Hanborough for a cold and comfortless building site in Southampton.

The house in Furzedown Road needed a great deal of re-arrangement if it was to become a family home. Each ex-flat, for example, had a separate electricity meter. We could not afford to have the work done while we lived somewhere else. Accordingly, we lived in the house while the builders replaced floors, removed chimney breasts and rewired. We became used to picking our way through rubble and brushing down the sheets to remove brick dust before we got into bed.

My constituency work absorbed me immediately. I remember on the day we arrived saying goodbye to the packers and hearing the telephone ring as I closed the front door. I struggled to the phone over a pile of packing cases, to deal with the first of what turned out to be many thousands of calls from constituents.

We had hoped that the children would go to the highly regarded church school in the street behind our house. When we took them in to enrol on the first day of the new term, however, it turned out that there was room for only one of them. We decided to keep them together and took them instead to Portswood School, about a mile away.

It was a cold and miserable day, the old brick buildings looked depressing and our hearts sank as we approached the entrance. Inside, however, the corridors and classrooms seemed bright and cheerful. The headteacher was welcoming and our spirits rose. When the children came home from school that night, they seemed very happy. They never looked back. Portswood School treated them wonderfully well. Their schooldays in Southampton, which could have been difficult for them at times, as the children of the local MP in a marginal seat, were made very happy by good and caring teachers.

Southampton was a city which was used to fighting its politics at the margin. Control of the city council changed hands from one year to the next. My own parliamentary seat was of course highly marginal and it was generally assumed that it would return to the Tories next time. This meant that there was nothing one could do or say which was not perceived as highly contentious. Every action was invested with political significance. These pressures were of course exacerbated by my living in the constituency and having a phone number in the local directory. Gill used to say she dared not go to the local shops without making herself look presentable. One could hardly walk down the street without being involved in some sort of political controversy.

We were nevertheless very happy in Southampton. We had a wide circle of friends, many of them involved with the university. Many had children of about the same age as our own and we had a lot of fun. Every year, for example, on Boxing Day, we would have a huge game of football, involving twenty or more families, and players of all ages. We spent a great deal of time in each other's houses. Our friends did much to ease and distract us from the pressures of political life.

Gill had agreed to act as my secretary, although she was of course unable to come to London very often. I would travel up by train in the morning and get home if I could at night. Increasingly, however, I found it impossible to come home during the week. There were many late-night sittings and I soon found it essential to find some permanent accommodation in London.

We eventually bought a flat in Clapham, in a block called High Trees House, a name well-known to every law student, since the block featured in a famous post-war case which demonstrates an important principle of equity law. Our flat was in the basement, where there was also a swimming pool, in which I could swim before breakfast every morning when I stayed there.

I would dictate each day into a dictating machine and send the tape, with the relevant correspondence, to Gill for typing. She would in turn send the typed letters back to me by post for signature and despatch. Although we thought we were terribly busy, the volume of mail we had to deal with in this relatively cumbersome way was only a trickle by comparison with the torrent we had to cope with in later years.

My parents came to visit us shortly after we had moved into Furzedown road. They had not realised that we were living on a building site, but bore the experience with remarkably good grace. The visit was a success, marking a further improvement in my relations with my mother, in particular. I still found her overbearing, but she was mellowing a little as she grew older, and she was becoming increasingly fond of Gill and the children.

My parents were fascinated by my political activities, although they were still of course perplexed by my Labour allegiance. I think they found this easier to bear in Britain than to explain to their friends in New Zealand. One issue on which they did find common ground with me, however, was the Common Market.

The issue became dominant in British politics when the Wilson goverment decided to offer a referendum on the subject to the British people. I became involved in the No campaign in a small way. Somewhat to my disappointment, I found that its more senior reaches were firmly in the hands of longer-established figures, and there was little chance for me to play anything other than a local or regional role. The campaign nevertheless brought me into touch with senior Labour anti-marketeers, people like Barbara Castle, Michael Foot, John Silkin, and, in particular, Peter Shore. I found myself, on this issue at least, in almost total agreement with Peter's views. I also remember a remarkable speech by Michael Foot at a special conference on the Common Market, which he concluded by crying out, 'Don't be afraid. Don't be afraid!' He was right, of course, to identify this issue. The British people were afraid, and it was that fear which dictated the result of the referendum.

They were afraid because they had by this time been abandoned by their leaders. They had heard for a generation the insidious message that Britain was no longer viable on its own, and would have to sue for whatever terms we could get. The campaigns were in fact exercises in rival pessimisms. The No campaign warned, with justice and accuracy, that membership on the terms available (even after the so-called 're-negotiation') would harm our economy and damage our national standing. The Yes campaign replied by saying, in effect, that we were so weak it would be even worse on the outside.

This meant that the debate followed a course in Britain which was very different from that in any other member country. Elsewhere the question of membership was always put in terms of comparative advantage. It was always accepted as axiomatic that the idealism of European unity could be comfortably combined with a hard-headed assertion of the national interest. Britain, of all countries, with its unparalleled network of trading and other relationships around the world, and its continuing, though dwindling prestige as a world war victor, was being told by its leaders that in effect we were all washed up and had nowhere to go. Once again, Britain's leaders seemed incapable of grasping that the task of simply governing Britain and becoming a modern, democratic, efficient and successful country was quite enough to be going on with. There was no other country in the world, not the newest, smallest or poorest, whose leaders told their people that its only future lay in subsuming itself in some greater whole.

The campaign was fought with a considerable disparity of resources available to the opposing sides. Most important, however, was a growing public perception, carefully fostered by the media, that all good, decent and responsible people were in favour of a Yes vote and only extremists from either end of the political spectrum would urge a No vote. My impression, too, was that most of the Labour anti-marketeers at Cabinet level were inhibited, despite the dispensation which allowed them to campaign against the government's official line, by the realisation that they would again have to work with the Prime Minister and other colleagues after the referendum.

I appeared on one occasion in a debate on regional television and spoke at a number of public meetings. On the eve of the referendum itself, a large meeting was held in Southampton. I was on the platform with, among others, Eric Heffer and Clive Jenkins. The meeting concluded with a torchlit procession through the streets of the city. My parents joined in with a will and thoroughly enjoyed themselves.

Immediately after the referendum, I found myself called upon to play a much more prominent part in the No campaign. Senior figures on either side of the party divide were anxious to hand their torches on to someone new. Labour Cabinet ministers were of course bound again by collective responsibility and could play no active part. Leading Tory anti-marketeers, even moderate and well-liked figures like Neil Marten, were perceived as potentially problematic by party chiefs since it was generally assumed that the No campaign was supported mainly by Labour opinion.

I had come to the notice of many people, partly as a result of the referendum campaign, but more particularly because of my speeches and activities in the House. I had become a member of the Scrutiny Committee, the select committee which looked at the vast flood of regulations and directives coming out of Brussels and rang the alarm bell if our interests were substantially affected by this new form of non-parliamentary legislation. I also spoke in most of the quite frequent debates on European affairs.

I was accordingly asked if I would take over the leadership of the all-party anti-market body, which we decided to call the Safeguard Britain Campaign. The name itself signalled a tension within the ranks, between those who wanted a campaign for immediate with-drawal from the Common Market and those who more prudently wanted to exploit the less specific demands and concerns of that wider body of opinion which was critical of our membership.

Chairing the SBC gave me valuable political experience and brought me into contact with a number of leading figures, including Enoch Powell. I found Powell a fascinating figure; he was personally very charming and gave the impression of great intellectual rigour. He was, however, essentially a romantic, and his romanticism sometimes led him astray, in the sense that he occasionally allowed his own passionate wish that something would happen to convince him that it was certain to do so.

I remained chair of the SBC for only a year. I decided to give it up because I realised that I was becoming too closely identified with a single issue, whereas my actual range of political interests was much wider. I also found it disagreeable to be targeted by conflicting pressure groups from within the anti-Market campaign (a sign, I suppose, of my political immaturity) and I was always concerned at the need to work with uncomfortable political bedfellows.

The most significant political event of 1976 was of course the resignation of Harold Wilson. I was serving on a standing committee at the time, the one which was dealing with the bill to take into public ownership the aircraft and shipbuilding industries. I vividly remember the morning when Roger Stott came into the committee room with the incredible news that the Prime Minister was to go. Like virtually everyone, I was taken totally by surprise by the news. There was of course a great deal of speculation about his reasons for going, but this was rapidly overtaken – at Westminster, at least – by the frenetic activity involved in electing his successor. For me, as for many others, Wilson's departure was a watershed of sorts. The Labour Party I had joined had always been Wilson's Labour Party. It was hard to imagine a political landscape which was not dominated by his presence. Yet, within a few months, I remember seeing a curiously shrunken Wilson mooching down a long and lonely Westminster corridor, totally ignored and all but forgotten.

As a junior backbencher, I played no significant part in the leadership contest. I decided to vote for Michael Foot on the first ballot, because I wanted to ensure that he got a good vote. I had made up my mind, however, that Jim Callaghan would get my vote in any second ballot.

On the day after the election, I found myself standing beside Harold Wilson in the Members' urinal off the library corridor. 'You were going to be my next ministerial appointment,' Harold told me. 'I have told Jim that that was my intention and I hope he will act accordingly.' I resisted the temptation to say that I bet he said that to all the boys. He seemed perfectly genuine. No call came from Jim Callaghan, however. I think that he regarded me as a troublemaker, because of my anti-Market activities, and an intellectual, which was almost as bad.

A little earlier than this, Peter Shore asked me to become his parliamentary private secretary. The post had been held up to that point, rather improbably, by John Prescott, but John had decided to join the delegation to the European Assembly. Peter, who was at that time Trade and Industry Secretary, was looking for a sympathetic colleague to fill the gap. I readily agreed.

The post of PPS is a rather anomalous one. The holder is not a minister and is not paid as such. It is a personal appointment by the senior minister, although it must have Prime Ministerial approval. It is often regarded, in cases where the appointee is a junior backbencher, as the first step in a ministerial career.

The actual content of the job varies enormously and depends on the particular relationship between minister and PPS. Inexperienced as I was, I don't think I made the most of the opportunity, although it did provide me with a useful insight into the work of a senior minister. After a few months, there was a Cabinet reshuffle and Peter became Secretary for State for the Environment. I duly followed him to his new department.

I did the job for about a year, during which Peter and I became firm friends. Gill and I were frequent guests at the Shores' Putney house, where Peter's wife Liz was always a charming hostess. We met many interesting political figures around the Shores' dinner table.

The post came to an end rather abruptly. There had been a revolt over the defence estimates, in which a number of PPSs (though not I) had participated. The matter had apparently been raised with Jim Callaghan at his weekly press conference by Tony Bevins, the aggressive reporter from the *Daily Mail*. He had demanded to know what the Prime Minster was going to do to restore discipline, and had extracted the assurance that any further breach of a three-line whip by a PPS would be rewarded with dismissal.

A few days earlier, I had tabled a motion to oppose a government measure which would have imposed a 20 per cent import duty on a range of imported food, including New Zealand lamb. The fact that a New Zealand product was involved was purely incidental; my objection was to the principle of putting taxes on food.

I was aware of the new ruling, but I felt that to remove my name from the motion which had already appeared on the order paper would show an unattractive cowardice and readiness to abandon principle. The matter came up for debate at about 3 a.m. one Tuesday morning. I duly spoke, moved the motion, and with a handful of others, voted against the government.

Tony Bevins spoke to me on the Wednesday. He was an assiduous reader of Hansard and had realised what had happened. 'You voted against the government the other night, didn't you?' he demanded. When I agreed that I had, he said, 'I'm going to get you sacked.' He raised the matter with the Prime Minister at the Thursday press briefing and I was duly sent a telephone message in my constituency on the Friday to say that I had been fired.

I bore Tony no ill will. He was doing his job as a good political reporter. I reacted quite philosophically to the setback. I did feel, however, that an issue of principle was involved. The so-called 'payroll' vote (those who, because they were paid as ministers, were obliged to vote for the government) already totalled about 100. If the 30-odd PPSs were to be added to that number, the power of backbenchers and of Parliament as a whole would be severely reduced. 'If Jim wants me to join the payroll vote, he'd better put me on the payroll,' I told my friends.

The most interesting reaction was from Peter Shore. He was powerless to defend me, since the removal of the Prime Minister's approval meant that I had to be dismissed. He registered his own disapproval of the decision, however, by refusing to appoint a successor, and soldiered on for the rest of that government without a PPS. I was very appreciative of his loyalty.

I was beginning at this stage to focus on the issues which I thought were important. A great deal of time was naturally taken up with my constituency work. The Social Security Advice Centre continued to function, but with the help of others. My surgery on Saturday mornings was always booked up. In addition, I paid a large number of calls on constituents who for one reason or another could not come to see me. And there was always the post bag, bringing in hundreds of letters a week.

In the House of Commons, I had expected, I suppose, to concentrate on home affairs and foreign affairs, by virtue of my legal training and experience in the Foreign Office. I came to the realisation, however, that economic policy was at the heart of many of the questions which seemed to me to be politically the most important. I tended to think of politics as comprising two sorts of questions – those which arose out of the blue, often short-term issues involving the actions or personalities of particular individuals, and those which had a longer-term significance, underlying and shaping the development of our politics as a whole.

It was these latter issues which fascinated me. They were often out of the news for some time but their significance was such that they necessarily dictated the outcome of many other issues. The most important of these underlying issues was the whole business of managing the economy. If the economy was well run, then many other things became possible and the whole political landscape would change. If it was run badly, then government was an arduous business, always involving hard choices and disappointed expectations.

I began to realise that, despite my study of economics at university, I knew very little about the subject and was almost entirely dependent on the views of others. Worse than that, I had no means of making a proper judgement as to which view should be preferred. My predicament was common among MPs. Virtually none had enough expertise to enable them to make independent judgements. We were all suckers for the prejudices of the City analysts and academic economists with whose views we were daily regaled in the media.

The level of parliamentary ignorance about economics was at times quite astonishing. I remember one meeting of the Parlimentary Labour Party at which a bright backbencher made a speech in which it gradually became apparent, to me at least, that he was totally confusing the public sector deficit with the balance of payments deficit. In that instance, he was saved by the bell. The division bell rang, we all trooped off to vote, someone told him where he was going wrong and he was able to resume his speech and correct his mistake.

My unease at my ignorance in this field began to focus on the question of the exchange rate. Throughout 1976, the exchange rate was in the news. Inflation had been very high and there was a good deal of anxiety about the level of the pound, which began to fall steadily. We backbenchers were kept entirely in the dark as to what was happening. It was impossible to ask questions about exchange rate policy (they were simply ruled out of order at the Table Office) and ministers conducted policy in conditions of absolute secrecy.

As I became more and more interested in the subject, I flirted with a number of ideas. I was unhappy at the fall in the pound, which seemed to me to undermine both the government's standing and its prospects of putting the economy right. A falling pound was not only a sign, but also a cause, of weakness. Moreover, it seemed to involve us in a never-ending downward spiral. If the pound was falling because our inflation rate was high, wouldn't a lower pound simply stimulate more inflation and make the problem worse? And if the pound was weak because our balance of payments was in deficit, wouldn't a devaluation mean that we were paid less for our exports and had to pay more for our imports?

I was tempted therefore by the idea floated by some commentators that the pound should actually be raised in value, although by what means I was not at that point sure. This seemed to offer the advantage of breaking out of the cycle of decline. A higher pound would help our balance of payments, by increasing the value of our export earnings, and would also damp down inflation by reducing import prices.

I had reached this point in my thinking when I went off to Mauritius as a member of the British delegation to the annual conference of the Commonwealth Parliamentary Association. I was a keen member of the CPA and had been elected, on a vote of all MPs, to the executive of the UK branch.

Gill was allowed to come at my expense and we had a wonderful time. I took full advantage of the chance to meet parliamentarians from all over the Commonwealth. The only news we received at our hotel resort was by means of a duplicated sheet. Day after day, the news from Britain concerned the turmoil in the foreign exchange markets and the downward pressure on sterling.

This naturally excited a good deal of comment from my Commonwealth colleagues. I was constantly being asked for my view on why this was happening. I replied with the standard government line: there was no rational reason for the weakness of sterling, the fundamentals of the economy warranted a much higher rate and the problem was all the fault of the speculators.

Even I realised, however, that these arguments lacked something in conviction. If sterling was in all these respects no different from any other currency, why were the speculators able to drive the pound down when other currencies seemed problem-free? I resolved that when I returned to London, I would look into the matter further, and try to establish the real reasons for the government's – and my – embarrassment.

First of all I contacted the National Westminster Bank and arranged to visit the foreign exchange dealing room. I found this interesting but not enlightening. The dealers were clearly expert at what they did, but they were entirely concerned with the short-term fluctuations in the currency's value and had no more idea than I did of why it moved in any particular direction in the long term.

I was having little success in getting to the bottom of the mystery when I happened to mention my interest to a couple of colleagues whom I had met through the Labour Common Market Safeguards Campaign, Shaun Stewart and John Mills. Shaun was a war hero and ex-civil servant who had taken early retirement. He had been in the Board of Trade, where he had become an expert in the statistics of foreign trade and had developed a considerable interest in the role of the exchange rate and its impact on trade. During the 1960s, he had been awarded a Harkness Fellowship which had taken him to the United States for a year – a year he had used to study economic history and in particular the variations in our own and other countries' trade performance.

Shaun was a remarkable man. He had a huge capacity for concentrated work and he had made himself more knowledgeable on his chosen subjects than anyone else in the country. His one failing was that he lacked political judgement and was not very good at handling people. He was not therefore the most effective advocate of his own cause.

John Mills was a man of about my own age. He was a prominent London councillor who at that stage must have harboured ambitions of a parliamentary career. He ran his own business which involved importing goods from all over the world. He was therefore intimately aware of price movements as between home and imported goods. In addition, as a post-graduate student he had written an excellent study of the ways in which the benefits from foreign trade could be maximised.

My conversations with these two convinced me that, far from being an inexplicable mystery or the product of a wicked conspiracy by speculators against the Labour government, the fall of sterling was an inevitable response to pre-existing economic factors, principally the high rate of inflation we had suffered. Moreover, not only was it inevitable, but any sustained attempt to obstruct it would be not only unsuccessful, but actually counter-productive.

I became very interested in these ideas, and had considerable sympathy for the then chancellor, Denis Healey, who was having to contend with both an unsympathetic press and an uncomprehending public. My assumption was that Healey, who was a most impressive Labour minister, well understood the realities of the situation but was having to try to massage press and public opinion so that they would accept the inevitability of sterling's decline. Healey had had a terrible time at the 1976 Labour Party Conference over this issue.

One Sunday in October, a report appeared in the *Sunday Times*. Malcolm Crawford, the Business Editor, wrote an authoritative-sounding account of an agreement apparently reached between the British and American governments whose central element was that the pound should be allowed to fall to $1.50. I realised that this news, if true, would provoke a storm of protest. I was more than ready to believe that Healey had indeed recognised the realities of the situation. I was therefore concerned that there should be at least some understanding of why this policy deserved support.

I accordingly drafted a short statement to the effect that a fall in sterling's value to $1.50 was not only inevitable but desirable. It would free the government from a burden which had crippled the Wilson administration and would allow an expansion of economic activity which would be good for jobs, living standards and profits – in fact, good for everyone if they only had the wit to recognise it. Healey, I said, was to be supported and congratulated. I put out the statement to the Press Association.

By Monday morning, however, an outraged Healey had angrily

rejected the Crawford report and emphasised his determination to prevent the sterling rate from falling any further. I was disappointed, both in the policy and in the man, but I was only a bit player in the drama. I metaphorically shrugged my shoulders and thought little more about it. My press statement, for obvious reasons, had got nowhere and had disappeared without trace.

Later in the week, however, for some mysterious reason, an account of my statement surfaced in New York. I have never established whether this was simply an accident or whether some malign influence, intent on causing trouble for the Labour government, was at work. The New York foreign exchange markets were told that an 'influential' government backbencher had asserted that sterling should fall to $1.50. The news was enough to knock nearly two cents off sterling's value.

Denis Healey was naturally furious and lost no opportunity, both in private and on the floor of the House, to tell me so. I was the butt of many jibes, from both Healey and the Opposition, about the 'Gould standard'.

Almost immediately after this episode, Southern Television invited me to go to the United States to help make a film about the congressional elections. Gill and I had a wonderful week in New York, following the campaign of Hamilton Fish, Jnr. When I returned, I resolved to pursue my interest in the exchange rate, which I was increasingly convinced was the key to the solution of our economic problems.

This was of course the time of Britain's famous recourse to the International Monetary Fund, and the debate within Cabinet about whether or not it was necessary. Little of the detail of this argument surfaced at the time in public, and I, in common with most commentators and backbenchers, had only the haziest idea of what was going on.

The episode was much misunderstood, both at the time and, even more, subsequently. The general view, much fostered by the Tory party and press, is that a profligate Labour government, having exhausted all its money on an extravagant programme of public spending, was then forced to accept savage cuts as the price it had to pay for a loan from the IMF.

The truth was rather different. While it is true that Healey's commendable efforts to maintain the economy at a reasonable level of activity did little to commend him to the foreign exchange markets, it was not government spending which precipitated the crisis. It was instead the familiar booby trap into which so many Labour Governments had fallen – the decision to defend a particular parity for the pound – which did the damage.

Only when Healey had exhausted the reserves in a vain attempt to ward off the speculators was he forced to go cap in hand to the IMF. In my opinion, if he had accepted the judgement of the markets, allowed the pound to fall and prudently sat on his foreign exchange reserves, no recourse to the IMF would have been necessary.

The exact nature of the deal with the IMF has also been widely misunderstood. Popular mythology has it that the IMF exacted from the Labour government a savage programme of spending cuts. The truth is that the IMF proposed two conditions only: one, that sterling should be managed so as to maintain the competitiveness of British industry; and two, that monetary policy should be managed in terms of a measurement called Domestic Credit Expansion. The accuracy of this contention can be established by referring to the terms of the letter of intent published by the government in December 1976.

The purpose of these two conditions was to allow the British economy to take advantage of the fall in sterling which had preceded the crisis. A competitive exchange rate would have brought with it a solution to the balance of payments problem, and the expansion it made possible would have been accommodated by a monetary policy which concentrated on restricting a potentially inflationary growth in the levels of domestic credit but at the same time allowed unlimited growth in the economy, provided that it was achieved through exports.

Little of this was understood at the time, and most of it has subsequently been shrouded in the mists of incomprehension, political propaganda and self-serving accounts of what happened from some of the principal protagonists. The passage of events, and the account of them given subsequently, was also greatly influenced by the growing fashion for monetarism.

The writings of Milton Friedman were arousing a great deal of interest at this time, offering as they did an apparently simple and painless means of controlling inflation and, more importantly, of removing government from large parts of economic policy. In my view, Friedman was to be listened to more for his political message than for what he had to say on the economy. Many people who had not a clue about economics embraced his writings enthusiastically on political grounds. Friedman must be read very much in the context established by Hayek and Nozick.

The Times had taken up Friedman's ideas and led the campaign for their acceptance. I recall one leading article which proclaimed that monetary policy dictated the level of prices as surely as the flow of water from a tap controlled the volume of water emerging at the end of a hosepipe. Not only could this relationship be exactly established, even the length of the hosepipe could be determined.

In the view of *The Times*, the hosepipe was exactly two years long. This was established by taking a period in the early 1970s when monetary growth (however measured) was 9.2 per cent, and showing that exactly two years later the rate of growth in prices was – hey presto! – 9.2 per cent. Such ludicrous simple-mindedness was typical of the claims being made by monetarists at the time.

As usual, the politicians were completely at sea in the face of the conflicting views of their advisers and the commentators. It is easy to feel sorry for those required to take policy decisions on the basis of almost total ignorance as they are necessarily prey to fashion or consensus.

Prime Minister Jim Callaghan was at this time being advised by, among others, his son-in-law Peter Jay. At the 1976 Labour Party Conference, Callaghan told the party, on Jay's advice, that 'you can't spend your way out of a recession' – a signal that the country could no longer look to government to manage the economy so as to secure a stable level of demand and full employment. This rejection of Keynesian economics was understandable – the inflationary pressures generated by the oil-price shock made it seem very dangerous to reflate the economy – but it was a significant portent of the loss of confidence which in effect opened the door to monetarism.

I think I can claim to have been one of the first politicians to recognise the implications of monetarism and to warn of its dangers. I have developed and refined my views since, but I realised even then that monetarism was not a new doctrine but merely a re-statement of one side of an argument which has dominated political debate for the past two hundred years.

There have always been those who have argued that there is nothing that governments can or should do to manage the economy beyond maintaining a stable value for assets and particularly for the currency. Anything else, they argue, is not only futile but positively damaging. In conditions of monetary stability, the economy will look after itself and prosper. The task of establishing monetary stability is, they believe, a relatively simple one – so simple indeed, that it should be removed from the hands of politicians, who will always mess it up, and entrusted to the bankers, who can be relied upon to carry it out without the distractions of political pressures.

The contrary view is that the managment of the economy is the most important function of government and that to sub-contract it to the bankers, who will always have their own sectional interest to advance, is a complete denial of democracy. The bankers will always opt for price stability and a stable value for assets, whatever the cost in terms of jobs and living standards for ordinary people. That cost will be high, since an obsession with stability and monetary policity will inevitably lead to inadequate demand, recession and unemployment.

According to this view, the responsibility of government is to intervene in the management of the economy, using all the instruments of macro-economic policy – interest rates, exchange rates, public spending, fiscal policy – to maintain a stable level of demand so that the economy's resources, including labour, can be fully used. It was this view which had usually been taken by the left, and which had been the basis of the whole post-war economic achievement.

As I developed my views on the exchange rate, I was able to link them to a critique of monetarism. I took the position that a commitment to holding the exchange rate as high as possible was a classic expression of the monetarist view that the value of currency should be the essential pre-occupation of government. It was also a brutally clear statement of the priority given to the interests of asset-holders over those who had to make their living by making and selling things in the real economy.

I was dismayed, therefore, when in early 1977 Healey departed from the course mapped out for him by the IMF, a course which would have produced sustainable expansion based on a competitive exchange rate and export-led growth. His increasingly monetarist advisers told him that the pound was too low, that the 'hot money' which would therefore be attracted could not be insulated from the domestic money supply and that the overall effect would be inflationary.

Healey accordingly 'uncappped' sterling, allowing the pound to rise and setting his monetary policy in terms of various domestic monetary measures of which sterling M3 became the most important. The result was that the economy grew more slowly and unemployment remained more stubbornly entrenched than they would otherwise have done. Great reliance had to be placed on a wages policy, since, in the absence of expansion, the unions were naturally inclined to seek increases through their pay packets. It was the decision which, in my view, had the greatest bearing on the outcome of the 1979 general election.

The appreciation of the pound was a cardinal element in the monetarist policy being advanced by Healey's advisers. According to their view, which was sometimes called 'international monetarism', an appreciating currency was the essential 'transmission mechanism' by which monetary control exercised its discipline over domestic prices. Tight money would force up the value of assets, including the pound, a higher pound would reduce import prices, and domestic prices would then fall into line with those import prices.

During this early stage in the debate on monetarism, I concentrated on the question of how the money supply was to be controlled. Advocates of monetarism tended to assume that controlling the money supply was a simple matter – a technical task which the technicians could, if left to their own devices, handle easily.

The reality quickly became clear. Critics of monetarism were easily able to embarrass monetarist enthusiasts by pointing to the difficulty they had in settling on a proper definition of money and then in identifying effective methods of controlling its supply. With my colleagues Shaun Stewart and John Mills, I wrote a series of Fabian pamphlets which explored these issues and attempted to alert the Labour movement and the country in general to the dangers we were running.

Over the next couple of years, I tabled thousands of questions to Treasury and other ministers in an attempt to demonstrate that so-called monetary discipline and an appreciating pound would do great damage to economic output and employment. I made speeches in the House and wrote numerous articles in a range of publications, including most of the quality daily newspapers. I also spoke at meetings of the Parliamentary Labour Party.

These activities all helped, I think, to raise my own profile and to establish for me a degree of respect as someone who seemed to know what he was talking about. I do not honestly think, however, that I made many converts. There were many who were critical of the government's policies who saluted me as someone with the courage to try and rationalise that criticism in terms of policy analysis. As always, though, however careful my explanations, the issues were regarded by most people as simply beyond them. They remained lost in a wilderness for which they had no map. They were, in the main, obliged to follow their leaders because they knew no other route.

There were a few exceptions. Some, like Peter Shore and Robert Sheldon, had reached somewhat similar conclusions to my own, but they were locked into government and unable to express their views openly. Others on·the hard left were equally vociferous in their criticism of the Healey strategy, but their criticism seemed to stem from support of what was at that time described as the 'alternative economic strategy' – a strategy which relied heavily on import controls and which was weak on the analysis of monetarism or the role of the exchange rate.

Others were generally supportive of the arguments I advanced, not because they necessarily understood them, but because they agreed with me on other issues like Europe and were therefore inclined to trust my judgement on economic policy as well. And there was the occasional recruit like Austin Mitchell, elected in a by-election in 1977 following the death of Anthony Crosland, who became a close colleague of Shaun Stewart and myself.

I enjoyed my work over this period very much. I was learning rapidly. I found that, having become quite knowledgeable in a particular area, I was then able to extend that knowledge into neighbouring fields as well. I became quite confident in my handling of issues across the whole range of macro-economic policy. There were virtually no trained economists in the House (in contrast to the situation during, say, the Attlee government) and the outside economic experts on whom those MPs with economic interests tended to rely were generally very narrowly based, both in the range of their own expertise and in the viewpoints they represented. I was one of the few active politicians who felt able to take on macro-economic arguments, something I relished and was always ready to do.

Life was equally agreeable in domestic terms. The children were growing up and enjoying their school days. Gill was working harder and harder as my secretary but she was still committed to staying at home because of the children. We both liked Southampton and were delighted with our circle of friends. My parents had again visited us, this time during the long hot summer of 1976, and had brought with them our niece Karen. We had a wonderful camping holiday that summer in north Devon with our friends Aileen and Anthony Booth.

By now, I had settled in well to the pressures of parliamentary life. I can remember in the first year or so feeling very tired at the end of each week, and lying around the house throughout the weekend in a grimly determined effort to rest and relax. I usually felt worse at the end of the weekend than I had at its start. Gradually, though, I learnt that the best way to relax was to do something different. We made many enjoyable excursions into the New Forest and I continued to develop my interests in food and wine.

In Parliament, I was becoming increasingly frustrated by the difficulties I faced in trying to gain a wider acceptance of my views. I had long since given up any idea of being promoted on to the front bench by Jim Callaghan. I was too clearly identified as a critic and a trouble-maker. I confess that I was surprised to find myself in this role. I had always regarded myself as being by temperament a team player, naturally cautious and conventional.

On the other hand, I had always been attracted by those issues on which I felt I had something distinctive to contribute. I could never see the point of simply saying 'me too'. I was also rather scornful (in private) of those who concentrated on what I called 'soft issues' – those issues usually arising in distant countries, whose remoteness from our own central concerns allowed some colleagues to parade their consciences without having to know very much.

Life was hard in Westminster over this period. The government had lost its majority and was dependent on the Lib–Lab pact and the support of small groups like Gerry Fitt and the SDLP. Party discipline (at least in terms of not missing votes) was strict, which meant we were frequently up very late. Quite often, we sat throughout the night. I remember, for example, serving on the committee stage of the Community Land Bill (an obscure and complicated measure which I never fully understood and which was virtually a dead letter as soon as it became law) and in one week getting to bed on only every second night.

The political situation became even more tense as the likelihood of a general election came ever closer. In his budget of 1978, Denis Healey attempted a mildly reflationary package which would have created a slightly more favourable economic context in which to fight an election campaign. He came unstuck, however, over his apparent concession that the arbiter of his policy was a monetary measure called sterling M3. It is hard to believe now, when the figure for sterling M3 is not even kept, that the monthly sterling M3 was headline news in the quality papers. At that time, if the figure rose, it was accepted as axiomatic that monetary policy would have to be tightened.

The City liked sterling M3 because it was a figure which was entirely under their control. If they chose to buy gilts, the figure would be low. If they chose not to, the figure would rise and would signal the need to tighten monetary policy. The money markets therefore exercised total control over economic policy on a month-by-month basis.

The City decided that the 1978 budget was a bit too expansionary for their liking and that they would need higher rates of interest before they would buy gilts. When they therefore held off for a month and the sterling M3 figure duly rose, Healey had no option but to raise interest rates, thereby choking off the modest expansion he had planned. This setback had a major influence on the remaining life of the Labour government and fatally undermined its chances of re-election.

Denis Healey was, in my view, a great disappointment as Chancellor. He was a politician of many gifts – intellect, force of personality, charm and wit. He should have been the most effective and forceful of chancellors. Yet, despite the bluster, I would place him among the most craven. He handed over economic policy, in effect, to the money markets. He always reminded me of a great heavyweight boxer who had suffered a terrible beating (the 1976 sterling crisis) and who thereafter, although looking as big, strong and fit as ever, was never as good in the ring again.

In mid-1978, I was asked to represent the government at the annual conference in Geneva to receive the report of the UN High Commissioner for Refugees. It was a subject in which I had taken some interest, and for which my legal and foreign affairs background fitted me quite well. Gill came with me and, despite the high cost of buying even a cup of coffee in Geneva, we spent an enjoyable few days there. The conference itself was quite absorbing.

In late 1978, I was approached at short notice to see whether I would join a parliamentary delegation to China. It would be the first such visit for a long time, certainly since the fall of the Gang of Four. The delegation was to be led by Hervey Rhodes, an elderly Labour peer and cotton magnate who had maintained good relations with the Chinese throughout the post-war period and had done a great deal to help their textile industry.

I was delighted to go. We flew to Hong Kong first, and I found the contrast between the capitalist glitter of the colony and the communist drabness of mainland China quite overwhelming. The visit was perhaps the most interesting fortnight I have spent in my life. Quite apart from the joys of China as a tourist destination – the food, the scenery, the culture and the people – it was also fascinating, to a student of politics, as a vast political experiment.

Here was a society which simply did not operate according to the usual human motivations with which we were so familiar. The state not only dominated all activity but it also supplied the motivation for people who would otherwise have been denied all ambition to perform well. As a result, a huge propaganda effort was necessary, to exhort people to work harder. It was impossible to travel in a train, walk in a street or work in a field without hearing the propaganda messages (incomprehensible to us, of course) blaring out from loudspeakers rigged up in every conceivable location.

I got to know and like Hervey Rhodes very well. There were a number of other people in the delegation with whom I also became friendly – in particular, John Biffen, who at that time was very much out of favour with his own party on account of his right-wing views on the economy. He was, despite these views (which I discovered to be based on a pretty tenuous grasp of economic theory), a gentle and agreeable man, with a sharp mind and a kindly wit.

By the end of 1978, Jim Callaghan had made his fateful decision to defer a general election until the last possible moment. This meant that the government had to soldier on with a new round of a pay policy which was being met with increasing resistance from the unions. Callaghan and Healey had, however, persuaded themselves that the unions had no option but to accept it, given the imminence of a general election.

The pay norm was for a maximum of 5 per cent. Inflation was running at 8 per cent. The pay policy meant, therefore, not only restraint, but an actual cut in living standards, particularly for some of the lowest-paid workers in the public sector. I knew the policy was in trouble when I spoke to a meeting of some three hundred electricians and other skilled men at the local ship repair yard in Woolston, Vosper Thornycroft. Despite my efforts to explain the policy, the men would have none of it. At this point, I privately resigned myself to the probability that I would lose my seat and that Labour would lose the election.

At about this time, Roy Jenkins, as president of the European Commission, had developed his proposals for a European Monetary System. There was a good deal of debate as to whether Britain should participate. Very few understood the issues. Jim Callaghan stopped me on one occasion as we were about to go into a meeting of the PLP to ask me what I thought. I replied that joining would be dangerous for us, particularly if we locked ourselves into the wrong rate. He nodded thoughtfully and commented that Helmut took the same view.

I wrote a short memorandum on the subject which I circulated to members of the National Executive Committee. I had an appreciative note from Neil Kinnock in reply. Neil was at this point an assiduous cultivator of friends, but I have no doubt that this endorsement of my critique was genuine.

As the prospect of a general election, and a Labour defeat, came closer, I was approached by Michael Meacher and one or two others about the establishment of a left-of-centre campaigning group which would attempt to return the party to a more radical policy line when in opposition. The Rowntree Trust had agreed to finance such a group. Following a series of meetings, we agreed to name the new organisation the Labour Co-ordinating Committee.

I had not joined any group until this point. I had often found myself in sympathy with members of the Tribune Group, but I always argued that I had enough difficulty in complying with the Labour whip without accepting another one as well. I was wary of the Labour Co-ordinating Committee, in case it turned out to be a Bennite front. I liked a good deal of what Tony had to say but mistrusted his judgement.

The last few months of the Labour government were full of tension. Ministers were visibly under strain. One of the few who helped to maintain morale, by virtue of his sparkling parliamentary perform-ances, however, was Michael Foot. I recall one speech in which he wound up a tense debate and – apparently off the cuff – picked off the Tory front bench one by one with a series of amusing but wounding jibes and sallies. We piled into the division lobby in high good humour, although in reality the grimness of our political situation had not changed.

The end of the government came on a long day of rumour and intrigue, 28 March 1979. It was clear that it was a government in trouble. The smaller parties, like the Nationalists, who had generally supported it, had decided to desert now because of the failure of the devolution proposals. All turned on the votes of a handful of votes from the SDLP. Rumours flew back and forth all day and into the night as to how they intended to vote, and about the efforts being made to persuade them to stay on side.

As the vote took place, I felt almost sick with tension, not on my own account – I had long since resigned myself to my fate – but that of the government. We lost. I will never forget the way excited journalists fawned over the triumphant Tories. They knew that there was going to be a change of government.

The election campaign was a curious experience. It was clear that we were behind in the polls and that we should expect to lose. Yet, as always, hope intruded. Jim Callaghan fought an effective and dignified campaign, visiting Southampton in the opening stages and making a very good impression. Our canvassing went well. I had established a pretty good reputation as a constituency MP. It was easy to persuade my party workers and ultimately myself that we were in with a real chance.

Our canvass results showed that our vote was holding up well. The results were accurate enough, I think, but in retrospect they were misleading for at least two reasons. First, our daytime canvassing did not pick up the many young married women who were at work and who were, I believe, archetypally the voters most fed up with Labour and attracted to Mrs Thatcher and her promise that they could earn more, keep a higher percentage of what they earned and buy their own homes. Secondly, our canvassing told us of course nothing about what was happening to the Liberal vote which, in the event, went solidly to the Tories.

As always, I worked hard. I can't say that I enjoy election campaigns, as some of my colleagues profess to do, but I respond well to the flow of adrenalin. I particularly enjoy the public meetings and the debates attended by all three candidates. My Liberal opponent this time was a young man called David Hughes. We got on well and both took some pleasure in what we regarded as the bumbling incompetence of James Hill, the Tory, who, rather ridiculously, seemed to regard his 1974 defeat at my hands as some sort of personal affront and was accordingly hostile.

The high point of the campaign for me was a debate organised by the *Panorama* programme and chaired by Robin Day. The idea was that a senior figure from one party should introduce that party's manifesto and then be interrogated on it by two backbenchers from the other main party. The Tory was to be Francis Pym and the programme makers selected Joe Ashton and myself as his two Labour interrogators. This was a nice combination. Joe was an effective television performer who had a nice line as the man of bluff common sense. Mine were the more forensic skills and I enjoyed the cut and thrust of debate.

It turned out that Francis Pym, for all his political skills and personal likeableness, was not well equipped to defend the Tory case. Having spent a good deal of time as Chief Whip, he was unused to quick-speed debate, certainly on television. Moreover, he appeared to have no overall grasp of what was actually in the Tory manifesto. He bumbled and stumbled his way through an agonising hour and we cut him to pieces.

The Economist commented that it was the worst moment – perhaps the only bad moment – for the Tories throughout the campaign. It almost certainly cost Francis Pym the foreign secretaryship which he had coveted. For years afterwards, I would find myself reminded, often by Tories, of my performance on that programme.

This personal triumph did nothing to deflect the progress of nemesis. The night of the vote count was agony as usual. My supporters were full of apprehension but also irrational optimism. They knew we had fought a good campaign and they pinned a great deal of hope on what they had seen of the personal reception I had received from my constituents.

The later stages of the count went in a blur. The clearest and most painful memory I have is of grown men amongst my supporters coming up to me in tears after the result had been announced. It had been a brilliant result. I had put up my vote, my share of the vote had increased, and I had the lowest swing against Labour in the south of England. None of this obscured one simple fact. I had lost.

Bravely but foolishly, I agreed to do a number of television interviews as the night went on. By the time Gill and I finally limped home to bed and the comfort of sleep, the new day had started. My young daughter Helen heard us come home and sleepily came downstairs. 'Did Daddy win?' she asked. On hearing the answer 'No', she burst into tears.

SEVEN

Thames Television
1979–83

MY COLLEAGUES HAD always warned me that losing one's seat was a terrible experience. They said that some people never recovered from the feelings of rejection and humiliation they suffered. They could not bear, for example, to hear reports of parliamentary proceedings or to set foot in the Palace of Westminster.

I am glad to say that I felt none of this. I suppose my main reaction was to feel a bit nonplussed. Although I had recognised from a long way back that my wafer-thin majority was unlikely to survive even a tiny anti-Labour swing, I had not really thought about what I might do if I lost.

I was, however, much helped by the positive response of some of my friends. On the day after the election, I was telephoned by Professor Jim Gower, Vice-Chancellor of Southampton University, with the offer of a job in the law department. It was a typically thoughtful and generous gesture. I was even more pleased by suggestions by other university friends that I might teach economics or politics.

I was comforted by these offers but I was rather reluctant to take them up, since I did not particularly want to retrace my steps and return to academic life. My musings were cut short, however, by a telephone call from someone called Jack Saltman, who worked for Thames Television on a programme called *TV Eye*.

He said that he was calling at the suggestion of Bryan Cowgill, Thames' managing director, who had apparently seen the *Panorama* programme during the election campaign. Would I be interested in a job in television?

I said I would. It did not occur to me to doubt my ability to do the job or to wonder what television careerists might think of a totally untried newcomer muscling in on their domain. I had always enjoyed being interviewed on television and there didn't seem much to it. I accepted as the most natural thing in the world that I should take the new job in my stride. When Gill's mother heard that I was contemplating working on a weekly half-hour television show, she enquired as to what I would do for the rest of the week.

There followed interviews with Peter Pagnamenta, who was responsible for Thames' current affairs output, and Mike Townson, the editor of *TV Eye*. They could hardly have been more different. Pagnamenta was tall, thin, austere and intellectual. Townson was short, round, populist and anti-intellectual. His conversation was conducted in shrouds of cigarette smoke and punctuated by belches and farts.

I was offered the job and discovered to my pleasure that, for the first time in my life, I was to be paid some real money. Even more remarkable, the first three months of being paid this substantial salary required me to do nothing at all, since Thames Television were in the throes of a long strike.

Gill and I decided that we would have to move from Southampton so as to be nearer to my job in London. We sold our house to friends and left with many regrets. Southampton had been very good to us.

We also sold our London flat and looked for a house in or near London. In the end, we could not bear to live in London (at least, in the sort of house we could afford), so we bought a house in the Chilterns, in a small hamlet called Russell's Water. The house was called Marymead. It was a white painted brick building which had originally been a small cottage but had been extended substantially in an architecturally somewhat inconsistent manner. It offered, however, large and well-planned family accommodation, a charming garden and wonderful views over distant hills and valleys.

The house was, though, a mess. It had been let, and allowed to run down. When we moved in, it looked very sad and Gill burst into tears as we contemplated the empty rooms. My three months off work, however, gave me the time to get a great deal done. We spent every penny we could raise, and more, on putting in a new kitchen and re-decorating. It turned out to be a wonderful family home.

Southern Television suggested at about this time that they would like to make a documentary about me and my colleague, Frank Judd, whose Portsmouth seat had also been lost in the general election. The theme of the film was to be how we had responded to election defeat. The film-makers came to our home. They played all sorts of tricks on us. They filmed through our sitting-room window, for example, a white horse grazing in a neighbouring paddock and persuaded us to walk cross-country so as to convey the impression that we owned many rolling acres. The thesis was that the former Labour MP had sold out to the television millions. Frank Judd was traduced in a different but equally unfair way. One of my friends from Southern Television, Alastair Stewart, who had been asked to record the commentary, refused to do so. Gill and I were horrified when we saw the film.

When the strike at Thames ended, I found myself making my first film for *TV Eye*. It was a short report about the closure of the Singer sewing machine factory just outside Glasgow. My producer was Linda McDougall, a New Zealander married to Austin Mitchell. Linda was great fun to be with and a dynamic operator. The Singer management were naturally reluctant to allow television cameras into the premises and initially refused us access. Linda, however, with a combination of charm, threats, duplicity and bluster, managed to get us in.

It was instructive to see the operation from the other side of the camera. My experience in television confirmed for me a lesson I have never forgotten: that, as with newspapers, the interests of the pro-gramme-maker and the subject of the programme are almost always at odds. It is best if everyone understands this from the outset.

I found working in television much more demanding and stimulat-ing that I had expected. The business of keeping a viewing audience of millions hooked for half an hour while getting across to them a serious message is a real intellectual challenge. I enjoyed most aspects of the work – the search for the story, the research, the structuring of the film, the editing, the writing of the script. Oddly enough, the least interesting part of the job was the filming itself.

However, although I enjoyed television, I still found it less satisfying than politics. 'How amazing,' friends would say to me, 'that after years of obscurity on the back benches, you are now able to reach ten million people with one programme. How much more influential you are as a television reporter than you were as an MP.'

I begged to differ. Television is intrinsically transient in its impact on any given topic. The appetite of the medium is so voracious that, by definition, today's message – however striking – will be replaced by a different one tomorrow. There is little opportunity to pursue a theme. The television reporter is a cork swept along on the tide of events. The real significance of television lies not in any particular programme but in its overall output. It is the capacity of television to hold up a mirror to the whole of society over a long period which gives it its special power to influence the way society thinks about itself.

As an MP, however, it is possible to pursue particular issues and to try to change parliamentary and eventually public opinion. In the end, television is entertainment, however seriously and well it is done. Politics remains the proper means of changing policy.

I was nevertheless proud of much of what I was able to do in television. I made a number of programmes about the economy, trying to explain to ordinary viewers what was happening – why they were losing their jobs and why Britain was falling behind. I found particularly stimulating a film I made about the extreme right-wing group the British Movement. There was a moment during its making when I thought I was going to be hit on television. We were shooting at a rally organised by the BM when I recognised a man called Albert Chambers, an EastEnder who was the leader of the Movement's 'Leaderguard' and a rather frightening-looking figure. I pursued him through the crowd, with a cameraman following me. He finally turned to face me, with such a threatening gesture that I remember thinking,

'I'm going to get hit, and I must not flinch.' Fortunately, Chambers thought better of it.

I made a number of films with Linda McDougall, and even more with another producer named Anne Tyerman. A very intelligent and talented producer, Anne was an Oxford graduate who had worked for the BBC and who proved to be a natural partner for my somewhat academic approach to television. In my humble opinion, we made some excellent programmes together.

I generally found the producers more interesting people than my fellow reporters. I particularly remember Alan Stewart, a young, enthusiastic Cambridge graduate with a great passion for television who was tragically killed a couple of years later when his vehicle hit a landmine while he was filming in Africa.

In one particular respect, the job was very demanding and disruptive of family life. I was likely to be sent off at short notice on a filming expedition and I could be away from home for two or three weeks at a time. Gill found this hard, especially since she was faced with the additional burdens of bringing up two lively children who were approaching their teenage years. She was one person who was glad when my television days were over.

I only occasionally had the chance to deploy my political skills in live interviews with political figures. This was partly because the job of main political interviewer was jealously guarded by Llew Gardiner, who was naturally apprehensive that my arrival meant curtains for his career, which was in any case rapidly entering its twilight zone. I remember doing one interview with Denis Healey, and there were some others, but I was generally restricted to film reporting.

The salary paid to me in my television job did, however, allow me to realise a long-held dream. I was at last able to afford to take Gill and the children back to New Zealand for a holiday. We went back in April of 1980. It was an odd experience in some ways. My mother, always so competent, had aged considerably and had difficulty coping with so many visitors. She found this particularly galling, I think, because she had invested so many hopes in the possibility that Gill and the children would fall in love with New Zealand, and that we would all return to settle there.

The children loved the excitement of travel and especially enjoyed meeting all their cousins. The sense of belonging to a large family of aunts and uncles, cousins and second cousins, was new to them. Gill, too, enjoyed herself, but she found the country remote and empty – a common reaction among Europeans visiting New Zealand for the first time.

As for me, my return to New Zealand after a 16-year absence was like travelling in time as well as space. It was as though I were re-visiting my childhood. Everything was familiar, though not quite as I remembered it. We visited each of the places I had grown up in. In Hawera, we were invited in by the people who were then living in the house in which my mother had raised us during the war years. As we walked away, past the house two doors away, I mentioned to Gill that some people called Brown had lived there. To my astonishment, the name on the letterbox still read 'Brown' – and the person who answered my tentative knock on the door was indeed Georgie Brown, my mother's war-time friend.

I remember on one occasion going into a smart department store in Hamilton, where my parents now lived, and encountering a Frenchwoman who was working there as a shop assistant. We enthusi-astically exchanged our impressions of New Zealand from the view-point of European visitors. 'I have become a European,' I thought to myself, with some surprise.

Throughout this period, I kept alive my hopes of a political comeback. There were moments when I thought it would never happen. There is nothing more 'ex' than an ex-MP. I dreamt of returning to the House of Commons and I lived for the moment when the phone would ring and someone would offer me a safe seat.

There were occasional calls from friends suggesting that I might be interested in this or that seat, but none came to anything. The closest I got to real political involvement was when Jim Callaghan resigned in October 1979 and I helped Peter Shore in his bid for the leadership.

Peter was not a natural campaigner and organising support did not come easily to him. He was nevertheless regarded as a strong candidate, particularly in the light of the expectation that Michael Foot would not stand. In that case, it was reckoned, Peter had a good chance of emerging as the left's candidate who would survive to face Denis Healey from the right in the final ballot. Many good judges thought Peter might have the beating of Denis.

I remember sitting with Peter in his tiny office on the Shadow Cabinet corridor one evening. Messages about the leadership contest were being passed backwards and forwards from Michael Foot's office just along the corridor. As it happened, Austin Mitchell and I had written a pamphlet entitled 'Yes, Maggie, There is an Alternative' which was to be published the following day. Peter had kindly agreed to chair the press conference for us and it was settled that he would use the occasion to announce his candidature. It was also agreed that Michael would announce, a little earlier in the morning, that he would not be a candidate and would urge his supporters to vote for Peter.

In the event, Michael was persuaded overnight to change his mind and his announcement, when it came, was to the effect that he would stand for the leadership. Peter soldiered on, but his campaign was doomed from that moment. I have to concede that this account of events is somewhat at variance with those recorded elsewhere, but I can only say that my recollection is quite clear.

I maintained my collaboration with Shaun Stewart and John Mills over this period. Macmillan had contracted us to write a book, which we had decided to call *Monetarism or Prosperity?* It took a huge amount of work. Shaun wrote a good deal of the first draft. I wrote the introductory and concluding chapters and substantially rewrote most of the rest. In the days before word processors, it was a laborious business. Poor Gill had to type out innumerable re-drafts which we would then circulate amongst the three of us for further comment.

The finished book was, however, more or less as we wanted it. It made a powerful case against monetarism on both theoretical and practical grounds. Even today, the argument stands up well. The book sold well, I understand, but mainly to libraries and universities. Very few of the policy makers, the people for whom it was really intended, actually read it.

My interest in returning to Westminster was suddenly fanned into flames by the prospect of a by-election in Warrington in early 1981. The SDP had been launched and threatened briefly to re-shape the political landscape. I was never in any doubt that it would fail to do so, although there were those who did not know me well who seemed to think that I might be a natural convert to the new cause. I regarded the SDP as an unwelcome attempt to prolong a post-war consensus which had broken down – a view which I held even more strongly when I attended, as a television reporter, one of the launch meetings in the West Country and briefly interviewed David Owen for *TV Eye*.

It was clear that Roy Jenkins would stand as SDP leader in the first by-election that came along, and that Warrington would accordingly be a major political event.

I had no connections with Warrington and I was filming at the crucial time. I nevertheless threw my hat into the ring and was encouraged by a couple of invitations to ward meetings. I was alarmed to discover, though, how out of practice I was. It was also a blow to hear that I lost one nomination on the grounds that I was thought to be a bit undecided over the Common Market! So much for the reputation I thought I had developed.

I failed to get a nomination and for the first time began to face up to the prospect that I might never get back into Westminster. I had little idea of what else I might do. I was enjoying television, but I did not really see it as a career. I thought about going to the Bar, but that would require sitting the professional Bar finals examinations – papers that, as a don, I had once set and marked, but which I had never actually passed myself.

It was a few months later that I was telephoned by some old friends from Southampton. Bob Mitchell had telephoned to alert me to his intention to stand at the next election as an SDP candidate. I was sad about this, since Bob and his wife Doreen had spent all their lives in the Labour movement. I was not surprised, however, since Bob had always been very close to Shirley Williams, whose PPS he had once been, and who had also once contested the seat of Southampton Test. Bob's decision, however, meant that a new Labour candidate for Southampton Itchen was needed.

My friends urged me to seek the nomination in Bob's seat. Only I, they said, with my high profile in Southampton, could save the seat for Labour. I was reluctant to enter the fray. I was not keen to fight an old friend, and I knew that battles between erstwhile colleagues are often the most bitter. I was by no means confident, either, despite the urgings of my friends, that the seat was winnable for Labour. Bob would almost certainly not win the seat but he would do well enough to split the vote to the Tory advantage.

I was, however, eventually persuaded. I calculated that, in an uncertain political world, I might as well take my slim chances in a city where I started with an advantage. I accordingly allowed my name to go forward.

I did the circuit of ward parties and secured every nomination bar one. I was aware that a young activist named John Denham was also seeking the nomination. I knew from the occasions on which we had met that he was pursuing an argument to the effect that the party should not trust someone who had already had a spell at Westminster. I took the point seriously, and put the contrary view, but I confess that I was relieved that the argument seemed to cut little ice with party members.

There were three contestants at the selection conference – myself, John and another person who had secured just one trade union nomination and who was otherwise totally unknown. I spoke well and answered questions effectively. When the vote was taken, I was defeated by John Denham. The general management committee was dominated by the Militant Tendency and their allies, and they had clearly voted against the wishes of the branches which had sent them to the conference. The Militant delegates were jubilant. I was devastated. At the time, I did not comprehend, naturally enough, what a good turn I had been done.

In January 1982, I was sent to Japan to make an hour-long documentary about some aspect of Japanese life. My producer was

Anne Tyerman again. I went out about a week ahead of the film crew, fixed up an interpreter and made arrangements to interview some of Tokyo's leading businessmen. I found Tokyo a perplexing place; it was an odd experience trying to find my way around a city where there were no recognisable signs. It was also a shock to discover that a people famed for their aesthetic sensibilities had created an urban environment which was so unremittingly ugly.

Before I left, I had seen a notice in *Labour Weekly* to the effect that the Dagenham party was about to select a candidate to replace John Parker, the Father of the House, who was due to retire at the next general election. I had phoned the secretary, Harry Kay, and had been told that there was only one ward, Village Ward, which had not yet nominated. I managed to get an invitation to the ward selection meeting. There was a deluge on the night the meeting was held and I nearly didn't go. In the event, I won the nomination, but I was still doubtful that one nomination would get me on to the short list. My doubts were increased by the fact that I would be away in Japan in the run-up to the selection conference; nor could I be sure that, even if invited, I could get back in time.

I returned from Japan with a couple of days to spare. I had been shortlisted, along with six others, including a prominent local council-lor, George Brooker, who was clearly the front runner.

I had re-entered the country with a bad case of flu. This, coupled with jet lag and the sense of dislocation which comes from travelling halfway round the world, meant that I was in no shape to face a selection conference. My only chance was to gee myself up by speaking entirely without notes – the first time I had tried this on an important occasion.

My speech went well. I won the nomination on the second ballot. George Brooker was naturally disappointed, but he went on to a distinguished career as a council leader and became one of my closest political friends. Harry Kay and his wife Gladys took me under their wing and became my political mentors. My selection as Labour candidate for Dagenham was the best thing that happened to me in politics.

Shortly after my selection was my 43rd birthday, for which Gill's mother gave me a five-year diary. It allowed for each day of the year just a few lines to record the day's doings. I have kept such a diary every day since. It records no great political perceptions but it jogs the memory as to what happened from day to day. Thus, the entry for 13 February 1982 reads, 'Went into Henley with Gill – bought a present for her mother and some shoes for me – watched *Grandstand* – Booths came for supper, with a bottle of champagne to add to our own – celebrated Dagenham, my 43rd, etc – very agreeable.'

Shortly after my selection, Mrs Thatcher's fortunes were suddenly transformed by the Falklands War. As the war came to an end, I remember saying to Peter Shore that she was now a certain winner of the next election. She would be able to say that the virtues of courage and resolution which had triumphed in the Falklands would produce an equally acceptable outcome on the domestic front.

General Galtieri, as many people have said subsequently, must have been a Tory. The war transformed a politician who had been a not very impressive Leader of the Opposition and was deservedly unpopular as Prime Minister into a figure of glamour and international standing. It reinforced her self-confidence and gave her an ascendancy in British politics which lasted for the rest of the decade.

I threw myself into Dagenham with great enthusiasm. The Labour Party there had been used to running the borough since time immemorial. It was full of good people, who naturally saw the Labour Party as the vehicle by which they could render service to the community. It reminded me of the Labour Party I had joined, or thought I had joined, nearly twenty years earlier.

The only problem with the local party was that it was very elderly and in danger of dying out. John Parker, my predecessor, had been its MP for 47 years. The party desperately needed new blood. I did what I could to breathe new life into it and my diary shows that – even with the demands of television filming – I was able to get to Dagenham pretty frequently.

I made some very good friends over this period. In addition to George Brooker and Harry Kay, I became friendly with many of the leading councillors, two of whom, Len Collins and Fred Jones, became stalwarts of my advice surgery.

Dagenham was a fascinating community. A huge public housing estate had been built here before the war to accommodate an overspill from the East End of London and to attract workers to the newly built Ford factory. It was a one-class, extremely stable community which enjoyed guaranteed housing and employment. Dagenham people were working class, but they had no hang-ups about their ability to run their own affairs. It was in many ways a haven from the wretched British class system, although even then I would tear my hair out when I heard people say things like, 'Oh, going on to university? That's not for the likes of us.'

The confidence the Dagenham electorate felt in its own identity and abilities enabled it to welcome me without, as would have been true in most other parts of Britain, agonising over the fact that I was in most senses a middle-class intellectual. My New Zealand origins and lack of concern for class difference may have helped, but the people of Dagenham essentially recognised that my willingness to put my education and abilities at their service was all that really mattered.

I kept up a wide range of political activity over this period, in addition to my campaigning work in the constituency. I wrote articles for the newspapers and frequently attended meetings in the House of Commons. In the constituency, in addition to regular public meetings and canvassing, I helped launch a publication called the *Dagenham Herald*. My employers at Thames Television were remarkably tolerant of these activities.

Some aspects of my television work I occasionally found distasteful. The attack on HMS *Sheffield* in May 1982 in the Falklands War created a sensation. I was sent to Portsmouth with a television crew with instructions to interview the grieving widows who had learnt of their husbands' deaths just the night before. We were supplied with their addresses and the idea was that I should march up to their front doors, a cameraman behind me with camera running, and ask them how they felt. If they cried on television, so much the better.

When it came to it, I could not do it. We filmed a few days later at the memorial service in Portsmouth cathedral, but there were no weeping widows in my film. In that sense, I was not cut out to be a reporter.

At home, my life had been transformed by the installation of a swimming pool in our garden. Our house was about seven miles from the children's school in Henley and there was a danger that they would never see their school friends after school. We conceived the idea of a swimming pool as a means of attracting their friends to visit them. We accordingly extended our mortgage and had a pool installed. It was a great success. The children and their friends made constant use of it and I swam most days. I found that, when I returned from London feeling hot and tired, the day's cares would dissolve immediately I plunged into the pool.

The pool caused some raised eyebrows, however. It was somehow thought to be inconsistent with the principles of a professed socialist. I owned no property other than the house we lived in, I had no shareholdings or other investments and I did not drive an expensive foreign car. My children went to the local comprehensive school and we had no private health insurance. I indulged no esoteric hobbies. Yet there was something about a hole in the ground with water in it, financed on mortgage, which persuaded otherwise rational people that I was some sort of Hollywood plutocrat.

My political activities reached a new level of intensity as the likelihood of a general election increased. I wrote frequent articles, getting published in the *Guardian*, *The Times*, the *Observer* and the *Financial Times*. One piece in the *Guardian*, published in July 1982, was particularly significant. In it I declared that the Labour Party could no longer tolerate the 'entryist' tactics of Militant Tendency, the undemocratic far left sect, and that the party must protect itself against this unwelcome parasite. Only when the party could be sure of its own internal health could we look to the outside world with any confidence.

The issue was a difficult one for the Labour Party and my message was unpopular in many quarters. The danger was, however, in my view very real. There were some areas of the country where the party was already under the control of Militant and run in such a way as to deter ordinary Labour supporters from joining. Yet many of those who saw themselves as being on the left of the party were unwilling to indulge in what they saw as a witch-hunt against comrades who professed to be nothing more than 'good left-wingers'. Yet others, including many on the right, were terrified of Militant and their voting power at selection (and de-selection) conferences, and opted for a quiet life.

I was convinced, however, that there was a separate organisation at work, the Revolutionary Communist League, which had decided to conceal its true identity in order to seek through the Labour Party a political influence it could never hope to gain in its own right. I emphasised that party members could not be expected to work with those who had lied to them about their true identity and purpose. The tide of opinion within the party gradually turned as these truths became evident, but I was regarded as an enemy for a long time by a significant section of non-Militant left-wing opinion.

In addition to my public utterances around this time, I wrote another Fabian pamphlet on economic policy. I was also invited to submit a substantial memorandum on the case against our membership of the European Exchange Rate Mechanism to the Treasury select committee. I had regular meetings with Peter Shore and his economic policy advisers.

I was very hopeful that this time an incoming Labour government would avoid the mistakes which had dogged so many of its predecessors. Peter himself, as Shadow Chancellor, had a good grasp of the importance of not prostrating himself before the City, and of refusing to succumb to the inevitable pressure to defend some monetary measure at the expense of Labour's programme. There was an unusual degree of understanding within the party of the significance of the exchange rate and of the damage which over-valuation could do. Twenty per cent of British manufacturing capacity had, after all, been wiped out and Labour opinion had little difficulty in recognising the causal connection between the recession and unemployment on the one hand and the government's monetary and exchange rate policies on the other.

I was confident that, having seen the outcome of having the wrong exchange rate, people would understand the importance of getting the optimum rate. By now, I had shifted away from a straightforward endorsement of devaluation towards the view that the economy should be run so as to secure a reasonable rate of growth and the full use of our resources (including full employment), and that the exchange rate should then be encouraged to balance our trade by performing its proper role as a market-clearing mechanism. This was a more easily defended position than my previous one and had the merit of locating my views on the exchange rate in the context of a more general critique of monetarism.

At about this time, I had also become interested in issues of political philosophy. With the aid of the Fabian Society I helped form a socialist philosophy group, which brought together a number of academics on the left and met regularly on Friday evenings to discuss papers submitted by members. I was keen to discuss with them some ideas I had developed on the meaning of socialism and its relationship with other concepts like freedom and equality. I had begun to read widely in the area – Rawls, Nozick, Hayek, Berlin – and conceived the idea of a book on the subject.

I had by this time acquired a literary agent, Anne McDermid, who was not only good at her job but was a good personal friend as well. We negotiated a contract with Macmillan, who had published *Monetarism or Prosperity?*, for a new book, to be called *Socialism and Freedom*. Thinking about it, and then writing it, took up a great deal of my time, but I very much enjoyed the intellectual challenge.

As the election came closer, my excitement grew. I had trouble maintaining my interest in my television work and it was a relief when the election was finally declared for 9 June 1983. Back in April I had been asked by Dick Clements, Michael Foot's campaign manager, to join his campaign team. It was, however, somehow symptomatic of the way the campaign was run that, as far as I recall, I attended very few meetings, apart from one or two gatherings which were more like election rallies than attempts to organise the campaign.

When the election was called, I immediately ceased my work in television. This caused something of a financial hiccup as I then found that I was entirely without income for the four weeks of the campaign. I still had a substantial mortgage to pay and I had just spent £3,000 on a computer, printer and word-processing package.

The campaign itself was, for me, a mixed experience. It went well locally and everyone felt very cheerful and confident. Campaigning in Dagenham lacked the intensity and tension of the campaigns I had fought in Southampton. Everyone simply took it for granted that I would win, and while we went through the motions of canvassing, public meetings, and so on, no one could really see the point of working too hard. This was the seat, after all, where John Parker (admittedly when the electorate was much larger) had in one post-war election campaigned on the slogan 'Give him a 40,000 majority' – and had only narrowly failed to achieve just that.

On the other hand, the news from the national campaign was gloomy, and getting worse. We had started the campaign, as one always does, believing that the campaign itself would make all the difference to Labour's fortunes. We talked confidently of victory. I remember Peter and Liz Shore coming to dinner in its early days and Peter telling me he wanted me to join the Treasury team in the new Labour government.

Our optimism did not last long. As the campaign developed, it became painfully clear that we had no chance of winning. We would come in from an evening's canvassing feeling quite cheerful and switch on the television to find our hopes dashed by the latest news of un-favourable opinion polls and concern about Michael Foot's leadership.

Nor could we insulate ourselves entirely against national develop-ments. Our Dagenham friends tended to laugh at our fears, but Gill and I had fought so many campaigns in marginal seats that we were particularly sensitive to small trends. There was no doubt that Mrs Thatcher was making a big appeal to many working-class voters who found her policies on issues like the sale of council houses especially attractive. By the time we came to the count, Gill and I were both convinced that even in Dagenham the result could not be taken for granted.

The night of the count offered the familiar sensations of exhaustion and stomach-wrenching tension. The only difference from our earlier experiences of such occasions was the cheerful confidence of our supporters. Even they, however, were somewhat downcast by the size of my majority which, in line with results elsewhere, had been cut to just under 3,000. I had won. I was the new MP for Dagenham. More importantly, though, Mrs Thatcher had been returned with a hugely increased majority.

EIGHT

A Westminster Retread
1983–86

I RETURNED TO the House of Commons in 1983 a more mature person than the one elected in 1974. Now 43, I remember thinking on my fortieth birthday that I was no longer a young man of promise. If I was going to do it at all, I had to do it now.

I was an experienced parliamentarian with a small but established reputation among the political *cognoscenti*. Mine was a comparatively safe seat which promised an extended period in the House. Most of all, I knew what I wanted to do and what I considered most important politically.

This latter point was both a benefit and a handicap. My very focused views on economic policy – its central importance and the direction it should take – meant that I could develop an expertise which few others could match. I was for ever involved in argument, not least with some of my own colleagues who did not naturally take the same view as I did. If I had not held such decided opinions, life and politics would have been much easier. If I had relied solely on my by now well-developed presentational and debating skills, I believe my political career would have proceeded fairly effortlessly and in some senses more successfully.

I have no regrets, however, about my espousal of decided views. That, after all, was what I was in politics for. I have little time for those who pursue what I call the 'ra' style of politics, in which the only thing that matters is that your team wins. If that is what concerns you, then go and support Manchester United and get your kicks that way.

To me politics is all about what you do with power, not just about winning it.

None of this dimmed my enthusiasm, however, as I came back to Westminster as a 'retread'. I launched into my resumed career with gusto. I had reached some clear conclusions about the state of the party which I took the first opportunity of expressing when I spoke at the first meeting of the new session of the Parliamentary Labour Party. I was flattered to be the first backbencher to be called.

I said in that speech that Labour could not hope to be re-elected if we allowed ourselves to be seen as a party which stopped people from doing things, which prevented them from realising their aspirations. Mrs Thatcher had succeeded because paradoxically she, and not Labour, was seen as the liberator of working-class ambitions.

I singled out housing as a prime example of where we had gone wrong. We had opposed the sale of council houses because we saw that, unless, those sold were replaced, there would be a shortage of affordable housing. But instead of concentrating on the real issue – the need to build more houses – we had got ourselves hooked ideologically on a lawyer's distinction between different forms of tenancies, as though this was the essence of socialism. As a result, we were intent on imposing a form of apartheid in housing which was completely at odds with what we were saying in health or education and which denied to working-class people the benefits of home ownership which were seen as a birthright by everyone else.

I developed these ideas in a series of articles for *The Times* and the *Guardian*. I was also making good progress with my book on socialism and freedom and was active in debates and at question time on the floor of the House. Just a month after the State Opening of Parliament, I had a bitter row with John Selwyn Gummer, then the junior employment Minister, over the number of accidents suffered by young people employed on YT schemes. The exchange culminated in Gummer calling me a 'disgrace' – a charge I bore with equanimity.

Gill had been working part-time at the perinatal unit at the John Radcliffe Hospital in Oxford for a couple of years before the election. Now we decided that she would revert to working as my secretary.

This time, however, with the children so much older, she would be able to spend more time in London. We decided to keep our house in Russell's Water, which was very much a family home, and to rent a flat in London, using the parliamentary allowance to pay the rent. We rented first in Judd Street, near St Pancras, and then, more conveniently, in Abbey Orchard Street, just five minutes' walk from the House.

Our main political preoccupation at this time was the contest for the Labour Party leadership. Michael Foot had announced soon after the election that he was standing down. Peter Shore had always intended to try again, but he stood little chance. The contest was over before it had begun. Michael had made his decision in consultation with some close friends – friends who had decided that his successor should be Neil Kinnock. Neil's candidature, and the support he enjoyed from some leading trade unionists, were both announced within a few hours of Michael's resignation.

Neil was an attractive candidate for whom I had always had a high regard. Of all my political contemporaries he and Robin Cook were the two for whom I had the greatest respect. Neil was bright and open to ideas. The subsequent portrayal of him as some sort of intellectual second-rater was entirely wide of the mark. He was, perhaps, not an intellectual in its purest sense, but he was a good deal more intelligent than most Prime Ministers. The attacks made on him on intellectual grounds were based in most cases in an Oxbridge snobbishness which could not come to terms with Neil's Welsh working-class origins.

In other circumstances, I would almost certainly have backed Neil for the leadership. Believing as I did in the value of loyalty, however, I was committed to supporting Peter Shore, despite the hopelessness of his cause. Peter soldiered on bravely, but the campaign, such as it was, was merely a matter of going through the motions. I remember attending a televised Fabian debate between the candidates and, as an acknowledged Shore supporter, asking a question of each of them.

At one point during the campaign, Robin Cook, who was Neil's campaign manager, told me that Neil would like to see me. I agreed, feeling slightly surprised that so certain a winner would bother to spend time on someone who was so clearly committed to another candidate. I had an agreeable meeting with Neil who assured me that on issues like the economy and Europe he was very much of my view. I expressed my satisfaction that this was the case.

The campaign moved to its inevitable climax. Neil scored an overwhelming victory and made an inspiring speech at an excited and memorable conference. Roy Hattersley, who had also contested the leadership, was elected as deputy leader.

Much to Peter Shore's disappointment and resentment the new deputy leader claimed as his due the job of Shadow Chancellor as well. Peter was demoted to Shadow Secretary for Trade and Industry but was compensated by also acting as Shadow Leader of the House. I went to Strasbourg for a few days at the end of October to complete work on an article I was writing jointly with John Prescott and Stuart Holland. Peter told me on my return that he would like me to join his front bench team.

I was delighted at the promotion. I was at last on the front bench and my career was now pointing in the right direction. I was working for someone with whom I largely agreed – at least on the central issues – and the party leader seemed as if he would encourage the sort of new thinking which I was keen to promote.

I had myself stood for the Shadow Cabinet, with no hope of getting elected but as a signal of my intention of being taken seriously. I had obtained 25 votes which, for a first-timer who was not on any 'slate', was not a bad effort. I felt sufficiently encouraged to expect that I might get elected during the lifetime of this Parliament. It now became my conscious objective.

It was a great thrill to me to sit on the front bench for the first time and to speak for the Opposition in a debate on shipbuilding. It was a particular pleasure to speak at a despatch box which was inscribed with the legend 'A gift from the people of New Zealand'.

Peter had asked me to take responsibility for the City of London and financial affairs generally. Labour had few contacts – or friends – in the City, but I set about maximising those we had. I was particularly grateful to people like Peter Wills and Mark Cornwall-Jones who, while not necessarily Labour supporters, were prepared to invite me to City occasions and to introduce me to their colleagues.

I rapidly discovered that the City was a very hospitable place and that most people were more than willing to give a fair hearing to the views I expressed. In all my criticisms of the City, I have always been clear that it is the institution, and the influence which policy-makers concede to it, which should be resisted. The great majority of those who work there are quite blameless as individuals and earn their living as constructively there as they would do elsewhere in the economy.

At the end of that year, 1983, I briefly revived my television career, this time solely in the interests of the party. The Labour group at Strasbourg was anxious to make a campaign film for the forthcoming Euro-elections. They contracted Linda McDougall and me to make the film. We in turn engaged a Dutch film crew and spent an enjoyable few days filming, mainly in the north of England. We also filmed an interview with Neil and flew with him on a trip to Paris during which he met President Mitterrand.

In the New Year, I became involved in the dispute over Mrs Thatcher's role in securing for her son Mark a contract from the Sultan of Oman during her official visit to that country. It was pretty clear that she had intervened personally to secure this advantage for her son. What I found shocking was that no one seemed very surprised. The general attitude seemed to be that this was only to be expected, especially from someone like Mrs Thatcher. She was at the height of her powers and few cared to challenge her. So much for the freedom of the press! The whole episode was a sad reflection, in my view, of how far standards in public life had fallen.

Domestically, life was settling into a very agreeable pattern. Gill was enjoying her work and her considerable skills as an office manager were very valuable to me. The children, now aged 15 and 14, were asserting their independence but still liked being at home. Although I was totally absorbed in my work, it remained my greatest pleasure to get home for the occasional evening or to spend the whole weekend with my family.

My book was going well, in that I was enjoying writing it. I was also active in a number of different forums – the Fabians, the Hansard Society, the Labour Common Market Safeguards Campaign, and a dining club called XYZ. The club had been formed by Douglas Jay and others before the war and gathered regularly in a House of Commons dining room to hear a visiting speaker talk over dinner on some issue of economic policy. I even spoke to the group from time to time myself.

In January 1984 I attended a meeting in the House of Commons at which David Lange, the then leader of the Labour opposition in New Zealand, spoke. The room on the committee room corridor was crowded. I was unable to stay for the whole meeting, but I was impressed by David's fluency and evident political skills. I confess to having been somewhat surprised, however, at his response to a question on the economy. He disclaimed any knowledge of economic policy, and indicated that if he were elected he would leave all such matters to his finance minister. It was an odd stance, I thought, for a potential prime minister.

The Oman issue dragged on through the early months of 1984, but got nowhere. I found plenty, however, to keep me busy. I became interested in the question of pension funds. It struck me that these funds, which were rapidly becoming the most important source of investment finance for British industry, were essentially the organised savings of millions of ordinary people – yet they were controlled and directed by just a handful of investment managers in the City of London to whom those ordinary savers were prepared to cede control.

It seemed to me that relatively minor changes in the law – to give the beneficiaries of the funds greater control over what was done in their name and to widen the criteria according to which investment decisions could be made – would at a stroke create a powerful instrument of social ownership. The limitations of state ownership – not least its political unpopularity – were becoming painfully apparent. This did not mean, however, that other forms of social or common ownership had to be abandoned. I believed then, and remain of the view today, that the democratisation of pension funds would have meant a major step towards economic democracy.

My diary records that on 19 April 1984, I appeared on *Question Time*. As always, I enjoyed the experience. *Question Time*, in those days at least, was an important platform, because it was regarded by so many people as their most valuable source of political information. For the viewers, this was one occasion on which they saw politicians spontaneously having to face questions from ordinary people; they were therefore more inclined to draw decisive conclusions from what they saw. This was to some extent an illusion. It is not that the programme is in any sense rigged – the questions are not revealed to the panel beforehand – but experienced politicians are in most cases easily able to deal with the necessarily uncoordinated questions of members of the audience.

Easter that year was gloriously fine. Gill and I took the children on a boating holiday on the Thames. At that time, I did not know of my family connection, through my great-great-great-great-great-grandfather, with the Thames. If I had, I might well have linked that fact with the tremendous enjoyment we all gained from the holiday.

One Wednesday in May, I was woken at 5.45 in the morning at the Abbey Orchard Street flat by a phone call from Gill. She had just learnt from my sister that my mother had died. My mother had been troubled by a heart condition for some time but had not stopped doing the things she liked. She had in fact died as she would have wished – from a heart attack on the golf course.

I immediately arranged to fly out for the funeral. I stayed with my father, as did my brother Wayne, who was by this time a magistrate in Hong Kong. My sister Ngaire had made the necessary arrangements. Interestingly, although I was too upset to take much notice at the time, my mother had a humanist funeral, though whether by her own choice or not I do not know.

I kept remembering the last time I had seen her. She and my father had come out for a holiday the year before and had stayed with us in Russell's Water. It had been in many ways the happiest of all the holidays they spent with us. When I took my parents to the airport, my mother had hugged me long and hard as we said goodbye. As I drove away, I saw that she was standing with her face close to the window, staring at me intently, as if to impress on both of us the image of our parting. Now it struck me that she had believed we would not see each other again.

I owe an enormous amount to my mother. No child could have had a happier upbringing or a more secure and loving home. The fact that her virtues in some sense betrayed her in later life should not obscure the strength of the bond between us and the great debt I owe her. I still think of her often. Every day, as I drive to work, I pass the house where she lived in Hamilton and the golf course on which she died.

I stayed only for the weekend in New Zealand, but I had time to see my sister and her husband Doug in the splendid new home they had recently built. I felt very close to my family. We all realised how much my mother had done to keep us together, despite the fact that we were scattered to the four winds, and how much she would have wished us to remain in touch with each other. We have followed her wishes.

I plunged straight back into political activities on my return. I wrote regularly for the leading papers on a wide range of topics. I also spoke regularly at Wilton Park, the Foreign Office conference centre, on Europe and related matters. The Euro-elections of 1984 kept me busy. I was in demand as a speaker in constituencies throughout London and the south of England.

Neil Kinnock had by this time begun to redefine his position on Europe. In this respect, he was reflecting a growing feeling in the party. There was a tide of anti-Americanism running through it and a feeling that we could not afford to antagonise our friends in Europe at the same time as we were taking on the Americans over nuclear disarmament.

I saw Neil from time to time, usually at his invitation. For some reason, he often seemed to need reassurance that he was doing well. 'What do you think of the show so far?' he asked at one of our early meetings after his election as leader. I quite genuinely replied that I thought he was doing very well. The bad press he had received was getting to him, without doubt, and he was already showing signs of what I call the beleaguered leader's syndrome – the attitude that 'if you're not with me, you're agin me'. For the time being, he knew that I was with him. There was no disguising the fact, however, that our views on Europe, and perhaps the economy as well, were diverging somewhat.

My brother Wayne and his family visited us during the summer of 1984. It was a very happy time. We had a pretty good summer, in terms of weather, and there was a great deal of swimming, some highly competitive croquet (at which Wayne proved to be pretty good), boules, and barbeques in the evenings. It was a wonderful opportunity for our children to get to know their cousins.

The idyll was slightly marred by my discovery that I had a lump in my groin. I was initially quite frightened. It seemed to me to be quite unmistakably sinister. My doctor recommended that it be removed immediately. I went into the Royal Berkshire Hospital, had a general anaesthetic and was discharged later the same day. When I got home, I remember trying to stand up on our back lawn and suddenly having to sink to the ground before I actually collapsed.

Much to my relief, the lump was pronounced benign. To be doubly sure, however, that nothing nasty was happening, the doctors decided to remove a mole from my foot a few weeks later. This caused me even more inconvenience than the cut in my groin. I seemed to spend the whole of the summer hobbling round with a walking stick. Our summer of medical adventure continued when our son, Charles, had his appendix removed.

I worked hard over the summer on *Socialism and Freedom*. I particularly enjoyed wrestling with John Rawls and I was pleased at the way the book was shaping up.

In September I joined a party of MPs on a visit to Hong Kong. Gill and I decided that we would travel out via Sri Lanka and spend a week there beforehand as part of our annual holiday. We fell in love with that wonderfully lush and hospitable country full of cultural riches and abundant vegetation. The week in Hong Kong was a welcome chance for me to meet up with my father, sister and brother-in-law, who had flown out from New Zealand to see my brother and his family, and to learn more about a colony whose success made it in some ways one of the most exciting places in the world.

My overseas travel continued, a little less exotically, when I joined the British delegation to the Commonwealth Parliamentary Association's annual conference in the Isle of Man. The conference had a certain low-key charm. I was the senior Labour MP in the delegation and I enjoyed this slight degree of added responsibility. As always, the CPA conference provided a valuable chance to meet fellow parliamentarians from Commonwealth countries. I was always interested to meet my fellow Kiwis, and I have a vague memory of talking to a very young Simon Upton, now a New Zealand cabinet minister.

One benefit of my trip to the Isle of Man was that I missed the annual Labour Party conference in Blackpool. I have always had a love/hate attitude towards conference. On the one hand, it is exhilarating and at times rewarding – a real chance to recharge one's political batteries. But it is always exhausting and often bad-tempered. I always returned from conference feeling that I needed a rest, both physically and mentally.

I sent off the manuscript of *Socialism and Freedom* to my publishers, and looked forward with anticipation to the results of the Shadow Cabinet elections at the end of October. I had done no canvassing or made any other attempt to gather support. I simply assumed that my evident merits would attract votes from my colleagues. Again, I did not expect to be elected but I certainly hoped for some advance in my vote.

The result was a great disappointment to me. I received 25 votes – exactly the same as the year before. I was very dejected and felt miserable all day. I felt that my first year on the front bench – my first real chance to shine – had passed entirely unnoticed by my colleagues. I began to face the fact that I might not achieve my goal of getting elected to the Shadow Cabinet by the end of the parliament.

Politicians are, in my view, self-selecting on grounds of temperament. You need a particularly robust temperament to ride the roller-coaster of political fortune. It can, and does, take you to the heights and the depths – sometimes at half-hourly intervals. Anyone can enjoy the highs, but it takes considerable inner resource to recover quickly from the lows.

My disappointment did not last long. I set myself other goals and concentrated on doing my best at whatever I set my hand to. Nevertheless, the next couple of years were in many ways a frustrating period for me. I was no longer a newcomer; I felt myself to be at the height of my powers, mature both personally and politically, and ready to take on the greater responsibilities which I felt beckoned me. I was well respected and widely listened to, yet I seemed to be making little progress in any formal career sense. I often regretted my four years out of politics which, it seemed, had delivered a check to my career which would not be easily overcome.

The Shadow Cabinet results had also come as a blow to Peter Shore. His vote had slumped and Neil took the chance to replace him as Shadow Trade and Industry Secretary with John Smith. As soon as the change was announced, John got in touch with me and asked me to stay on in his team as trade spokesperson with special responsibilities for the City.

I had known John only slightly until this point. He was only a little older than me but he had come into the House much earlier and had already been a Cabinet minister in the Callaghan government. He came from a different part of the party from mine – traditional, Scottish, right-wing. His friends were on the right, and identified themselves largely by their pro-European views.

Despite these differences, John and I got on well. It would have been surprising if we had not. I always liked to think of myself as someone who made friends easily and John was the most affable of men. We also quickly developed a mutual respect for each other. I remember telling someone shortly after I began working for John that, although he was not much interested in ideas and his thinking was naturally rather cautious, he was a good operator who would deliver on a proposition once he was convinced of its merits.

For his part, I think that John was pleased to have someone in his team on whom he could rely to do a good job on a significant part of the overall brief. John was a good delegator. He rarely showed much interest in what I was doing but was content to let me get on with it. I much appreciated the freedom this gave me, and it spurred me on to greater activity.

My first major responsibility in the new team was to take charge of the Films Bill which the Government had introduced in the new session. The bill was a complex measure which in effect removed a good deal of government support from the film industry. Naturally, it attracted a good deal of opposition from within the industry.

This was my first experience of leading for the Opposition on a bill. It was an experience I enjoyed very much and is, in my view, just about the most interesting and worthwhile thing one can do in opposition. One controls all aspects of opposition strategy – the welding together of a team in committee, the allocation of responsibilities, the drafting, selection and tabling of amendments, negotiations with outside lobbying groups, deciding which amendments to press to a division, manoeuvring over the timing of particular debates and divisions, forming relations with backbenchers on the opposing side – some of whom might be potential allies on particular issues – and the virtually hand-to-hand personal contest with ministers.

The committee stage of a bill is one of the few opportunities one has to demonstrate genuine debating skills. Committee debates allow for repeated interventions and for several speeches from the same person in the same debate. It is therefore possible, in a way that does not present itself in other parliamentary contexts, to pursue a point until it is resolved. There is no more satisfying parliamentary experience than getting a minister on the ropes, then dogging him or her until the knockout blow is delivered.

All this has to be undertaken with the odds stacked heavily against one. The minister will have been intimately involved with the bill from the moment of its conception. He will have dealt with all the interested parties and will be familiar with their views and interests. He will have had a hand in the drafting of the bill. Sitting beside him in committee will be his senior and specialist civil servants, including the drafters of the bill, ready to advise him at every stage.

The Opposition leader, by comparison, is completely without

resources. There are no civil servants or drafters. There is no background of intimate familiarity with the bill's provisions. A great deal of political skill and ingenuity is needed to offset these disadvantages.

In the case of the Films Bill, my opponent was Norman Lamont. I knew Norman slightly. We had a friend in common, Mani Shankar Aiyar, the Indian diplomat whom I had met in Brussels and who had been at Cambridge with Norman. I liked Norman and found him a congenial opponent. He was bright and able but on this occasion he made the mistake of confessing to complete ignorance of the film industry. As a new minister who had inherited the bill, he did not have the usual advantages, and I was able to exploit his confession mercilessly. I learnt a lot from the experience. So, I believe, did Norman.

I was also very busy at this time with the media. My diary records frequent interviews for various radio and television programmes – *The Jimmy Young Show* (always an important political opportunity), the *Today* programme, *Channel 4 News*, *The World at One*, *Newsnight*. I was asked to do a pilot programme for a new BBC Sunday current affairs show to be called *This Week, Next Week*. I was interviewed in the role of Labour Party leader. I imagine that I was asked to do this because of my television experience, but I confess that I also flattered myself in thinking that the programme-makers exhibited a certain prescience in their choice.

Just before Christmas, Gill and I went to dinner with the Kilroy-Silks. Robert and his wife Jan were among the relatively few political colleagues with whom we mixed socially. Among the other guests were Glenys and Neil Kinnock. Neil had been to a rugby function earlier and had had a few drinks. He was entertaining and voluble, but as the evening went on, he became more and more depressed. I was dismayed at what I saw of his state of mind. It was clear that media criticism was getting to him. He talked of throwing it all in, though I believe this was very far from his mind and was done more to elicit protestations of disagreement from his friends. Glenys was visibly displeased by his performance. I was sufficiently concerned to phone Robert Kilroy-Silk the following morning to check that his reaction was the same as mine. It was. However, we were both at a loss as to what could be done about it.

The year ended on a sad note for us. We spent New Year's Eve with our friends Aileen and Anthony Booth. Our elderly West Highland White terrier, Dougal, who had been the children's constant companion, wandered off during the evening, and – virtually blind – fell into the Booths' swimming pool and drowned. Our search for him, the discovery of his body, and my unsuccessful attempts to revive him blighted the evening for us.

We decided to make good our loss with a new puppy. A tiny ten-week-old Westie duly arrived in mid-January. We called him Angus and he has been a constant pleasure to us ever since.

Later that month, I rather embarrassingly succumbed to a moment of vanity. I received a letter out of the blue from the well-known painter John Bratby. He said that he was painting a series of portraits of prominent people who particularly interested him and who he thought were likely to be of some interest to posterity. The paintings were to be exhibited together. Would I consent to be painted?

I said I would and travelled down to Brighton on the appointed day to see him. He lived in a curious, turreted house, with a large studio on the top floor. To my surprise, he made no preparatory sketches, but painted directly on to the canvas. The whole painting was completed in an hour and a half. It was, to my untutored eye, pretty good, albeit in the familiar garish Bratby reds, oranges and greens.

As I travelled back to London by train, I began to wonder what would happen to the painting after it had been exhibited. Perhaps I should offer to buy it? I resolved to write to John Bratby with that suggestion. I need not have bothered. A letter arrived from him, saying that the exhibition had not come to fruition and did I want the painting for £400? I bought it, and then discovered that quite a number of my colleagues had had the same experience. None of us was too keen to talk about it.

I also discovered that it is almost impossible to know what to do with a large brightly coloured portrait of oneself. It can't easily be hung in pride of place, as it looks rather vain; in any case, it didn't suit our decor. On the other hand, there seems little point in having an interesting and possibly valuable painting without hanging it somewhere. We have usually compromised by hanging it in decent obscurity in a back hallway somewhere.

1985 was a year of consolidation for me. My diary shows a record of perpetual activity. I was of course busy in the constituency, and becoming increasingly fond of my party colleagues and the people of Dagenham. The local party was full of good people. The Labour Party was still seen there as the natural vehicle for those who wanted to be active in public and civic affairs. People like Bob Little, the new secretary of the party, became good friends.

Early in the year, I was involved in a curious little episode with the media. For some time I had watched, with growing irritation, a popular television commercial for British Caledonian Airways, the soundtrack to which, to the tune of the Beach Boys hit, was 'I Wish They All Could be Caledonian Girls'. Simpering air hostesses dressed in kilts ministered to every whim of appreciative dark-suited businessmen.

I thought the ad was outrageously sexist and demeaning to women. I decided to complain to the Advertising Standards Authority (they were actually the wrong people to write to). My letter attracted a good deal of media attention, however. I was interviewed on *The Jimmy Young Show*, was the subject of a cartoon in the *Sun*, and was invited on to *Wogan*. I duly turned up just before seven o'clock at the Shepherds Bush studio. I asked where I would be sitting for the interview, only to be told that I was not going to be interviewed. Instead, I would chat to a group of Caledonian air hostesses who were going to march on to the set to the Beach Boys' tune.

By this time, it was 6.59 p.m. I was due on at any moment. I knew from my previous television experience that once the cameras were on me, I would lose any control of the situation. I had visions of being tickled and patted and having my hair tousled by dozens of air hostesses, with no chance of explaining my true concern. To the fury of the producer, I refused to go on and they had to abandon the whole idea.

I was also involved in more conventional parliamentary issues. I was active in the Chamber, and in committee. With the Films Bill out of the way, I was then plunged into a much longer and more complex measure, the Insolvency Bill. The issues in this piece of legislation were complex and I was immensely grateful for my training as a lawyer as I grappled with its complexities.

My opponent on this occasion was a soft-spoken Scot named Alex Fletcher. He was a competent middle-ranking minister in the Department of Trade and Industry, who worked hard and knew his stuff. I liked him very much and we remained friendly until his premature death a few years later. The Insolvency Bill was, however, a nightmare for a minister without legal training. For some reason, the department had brought the bill forward without adequate preparation and it was constantly being re-drafted as we worked our way through its provisions in committee. By the time we had finished the committee stage, more than 1,000 amendments had been tabled for the House of Lords to incorporate into the bill.

To say that I destroyed Alex Fletcher in committee may be a little melodramatic, but it is not far short of the truth. He had a very uncomfortable time. The corollary of the advantages which a minister has in handling a bill in committee is that, if he cannot make those advantages count, he looks pretty bad. The opposition leader, on the other hand, can conduct a sort of guerrilla campaign, choosing those issues on which to fight, probing relentlessly any weakness or uncertainty in the government position. It is hard work and immensely time-consuming, but it is intellectually challenging and politically rewarding.

I was at this time becoming more and more interested in the actions of the City. It was a good issue to be looking at as there was a rising tide of political interest in the question. There was the familiar rash of City scandals, and a growing realisation that some increased level of regulation was becoming necessary. The City was, however, opposed to any imposed form of regulation and suspicious of Labour's intentions in this regard.

I also pursued my long-term interest in economic policy. I continued to table large numbers of questions, to ask questions of Treasury ministers on the floor of the House, and to speak in debates on economic matters. My expertise was generally recognised, although few knew or understood any more about my views than that I was supposed to be in favour of devaluation.

My relations with John Smith continued to be good. I formed the view that he was inclined to be a little lazy and was more than a little relieved to discover that he had a lieutenant who took a good chunk of his burden off his shoulders. It suited me very well, and I gradually built up for myself something of a reputation on City issues.

I had several meetings with Neil at about this time over Europe. I was saddened to find that Neil was, in my view, succumbing to pressure. I could understand why. He was widely regarded by his senior colleagues as a lightweight. The press portrayed him as a windbag. He had few friends he could trust. He was involved in a damaging dispute with the Americans over nuclear weapons. Some of his friends on the left, who had always favoured a 'socialist United States of Europe', were trying to convince him that to be sceptical over Europe was to be a little Englander. I believe he was also influenced by his own family, especially his son Stephen, who was telling him that the younger generation had little interest in old-fashioned nationalism.

In the face of all these pressures, it was hardly to be wondered at that Neil was susceptible to the flattery of his colleagues in European parties of the left. After the sticks which belaboured him in Britain, it must have been pleasant to be offered the carrots in Europe. Here, at least, he was treated seriously, as a putative prime minister, and the more he expressed pro-European sentiments, the more gratifying was the attention he was paid.

I had decided on my return to Westminster to abandon my reluctance to align myself with political groups and to join the Tribune Group. I had realised that if I were to make any progress in the party, I needed political friends. Tribune was, however, a great disappointment. It had changed character entirely since the 1974–79 parliament, and was now merely a vehicle for careerists. Its major function was to draw up a slate for the Shadow Cabinet elections, and there were many who turned up only when that business was being discussed. I suppose I could also be accused of joining for that reason myself but I plead in mitigation that I was also genuinely interested in debating policy issues and was disappointed in the group's failure to do so.

In September, I was commissioned by the BBC to attend the Liberal conference in Dundee and to make my own radio programme for broadcast the following Saturday. I spent a pleasant, low-key week with people who seemed to belong to a different political world. They thought they were involved in politics, but they were not – at least, not politics as I knew it. The only figure I recognised as a real politician was Paddy Ashdown. I recognised him as such because he was engaged in a not very elegant withdrawal from his former espousal of nuclear disarmament.

At about this time, I finished writing a novel about a young Oxford researcher who had discovered a cure for cancer. I was happy with the writing but in the end I did not think it worked as a novel. Anne McDermid assured me that she would find a publisher for it and that someone would help me to rewrite it. I declined. I had seen too many of my colleagues publish embarrassingly bad novels.

As our own conference approached, I was tickled by a piece in the *Observer* colour magazine which speculated about a future Labour Cabinet and opined that I would be Education Secretary. My hopes for the Shadow Cabinet elections later in October were raised once again.

At about this time, Brian Walden had announced that he would give up his job as the interviewer on *Weekend World*. I was approached informally at the beginning of October to see whether I would be interested. I said no, even though it was probably the top job in current affairs television at the time and the salary was rumoured to be in six figures. My lack of interest was eventually reported in the press and I was then phoned with a formal offer of the job. I turned it down. I was convinced that a substantial political career awaited me, and I was unwilling to give up the chance.

I had obtained Tribune's permission to put my name forward for the Shadow Cabinet. Without that permission, which I was obliged to have as a member of the group, I would not have stood. In the event, I was pleased with my showing. I gained 63 votes, which represented a big increase over the previous year and meant that I was at last knocking on the door. I felt that my hard work over the year was being recognised. John Smith and I had lunch with the Governor of the Bank of England on that same day. Afterwards, John said to be, 'We'll have to get you in next year.'

At the end of the year, I faced re-selection in my Dagenham constituency. There were no other nominations. The Young Socialist delegate to the selection conference, who actually worked as a paid employee of Militant and was no doubt instructed to vote against me, arrived late (I always thought by design) and was unable to vote. I was re-selected unanimously.

By now, the City was moving up the political agenda. I was gratified to find that my views and initiatives were often being reported. The front page of the *Observer* Business News was a particularly happy hunting ground for me. There was a great deal of concern about City fraud, and my old friend Professor Jim Gower, a leading authority on company and commercial law, had been asked to write a report and make recommendations as to how the City should be regulated. Even as he did so, however, the issue of fraud was largely overtaken by the imminence of what became known as the Big Bang – the complete deregulation of financial markets. This was, in many ways, the high water mark of Thatcherism – a complete faith (which in hindsight looks completely misplaced) that free markets will always produce ideal outcomes.

The Financial Services Bill had been introduced early in 1986. John opened for the Opposition in the second reading debate and I wound up. John thankfully handed the bill over to my care at that point and never again, as far as I was aware, took any interest in it. I was grateful for his confidence in me.

The bill went straight into committee and dominated my life for several months. By this time, I was quite experienced in committee and had established a formidable reputation as a consequence of the Insolvency Bill. My opponent on this occasion was Michael Howard.

Michael was a formidable opponent, an intelligent man with a barrister's ability to master a brief. He knew his stuff and was not above putting the boot in if he thought he saw a chance to do so. But (at that stage, at least) he was politically inexperienced and was perhaps a little short of the skills one needs to handle one's own supporters and to keep them a united team. The bill was a complex measure and, even on the Tory side, there were differing views on some of the central questions. The main issue was the nature of the regulatory regime to which the City should be subjected. Most people agreed that there should be a large element of self-regulation, so that experienced practitioners could bring their expertise to bear. Opinions varied, however, as to whether there needed to be, at the heart of this structure of self-regulation, an independent body with statutory authority.

I took the view that the proposed Securities and Investments Board should be a statutory body and that without that degree of independence from City interests it would lack both authority and credibility. So, too, did many in the City. Indeed, a poll of City opinion published during the course of the bill's passage showed 70 per cent support for that view. The Government, however, in the person of Norman Tebbit – then Secretary of State – was caught in a time warp and assumed from the outset that the City would fight any form of imposed regulation tooth and nail.

In the committee, I pursued the tactic of making alliances on particular issues with potential rebels on the Tory side. I found people like Tim Smith, John Butterfill and Anthony Nelson ready on occasion to use their own experience and knowledge to defy their own front bench. This annoyed Michael Howard intensely. His reaction actually made my task easier.

I also clashed with Michael over the question of Lloyds. Many of the problems of fraud had involved Lloyds and the institution cried out for proper regulation. Such regulation fell squarely within the area that the bill would ordinarily have covered; however, Lloyds had negotiated a special exemption clause for themselves. I found it scandalous given the circumstances that many Tory MPs were 'names' at Lloyds, and their numbers included Michael Howard, the very minister who was handling the bill.

To be fair, Michael had done what he could to divest himself of his Lloyds interests when he realised the conflict of interests which would develop, but the nature of Lloyds arrangements, with accounting done two or three years in arrears, meant that he could not fully do so. It was again a sign of the decline in standards in public life that Mrs Thatcher was not forced by press and public opinion to appoint another minister to look after the bill.

I grew to like Michael and to have a healthy respect for his abilities. We both performed well in committee and improved our reputations. My standing with my colleagues rose considerably, since there was no one else in the Labour Party capable of understanding the issues and taking the fight to the Tories. The views I expressed then have, incidentally, been substantially vindicated by subsequent events.

The political scene was dominated at this time by the Westland issue, which had led to two Cabinet resignations and offered Neil for the first time a real chance to strike a damaging blow against Mrs Thatcher. In the major debate, however, Neil delivered an indifferent speech. He allowed himself to be distracted by interventions and – as often happens if a speech loses shape – he spoke for too long by way of attempted compensation. He received a very bad press. At a meeting of front benchers a few days later he apologised for his failure. I thought this was unnecessary. The speech had perhaps lacked the forensic skills which would have made it truly effective, but it was not all that bad. This was another instance, I believe, of Neil allowing the Tory press to get to him and to set the public agenda.

In the middle of the year, we moved house. Charles had done his A levels and had got a place at Cardiff University. His departure meant that, with Gill spending more and more time in London with me, Helen would be left at home alone for several days a week while she went on to her sixth-form studies. We decided that we should sell our house at Russell's Water and move to London. Helen would go to school in London and the three of us would live together in a London flat.

This worked very well. Helen started at Pimlico School, where she was very happy and did very well. We bought a flat at Vanbrugh Court in Kennington and also a small Cotswold stone cottage in Westcott Barton, Oxfordshire, in which we intended to spend our weekends. One of the greatest pleasures of moving there was to discover that we had acquired a 150-year-old cider apple orchard with it. I bought a cider press and made several gallons of very good cider.

I was very busy at that year's Labour Party conference. I spoke at a number of fringe meetings and did a number of interviews. Immediately after the conference, I featured in a party political broadcast as part of Labour's team for government. Neil made it clear to me that he hoped I would be elected to the Shadow Cabinet.

My interest in this subject was somewhat diminished by the discovery of a new lump in my groin. I saw the doctor at the House of Commons who made an immediate appointment for me at Westminster Hospital. I kept the appointment on the morning of 29 October. The doctors advised an immediate operation. I phoned Gill to tell her. She was able in turn to give me the news that I had been elected to the Shadow Cabinet with 82 votes. I had achieved my target with a year to spare. I saw Neil that afternoon. He was lavish in his congratulations. I thanked him for his support. Gill, Helen and I had a celebratory meal that evening in the House of Commons restaurant.

NINE

The General Election
1986–87

DESPITE THE EXCITEMENT of my promotion to the Shadow Cabinet, I was disappointed with the job I was actually offered. Robin Cook, who had been campaigns co-ordinator, had lost his seat in the Shadow Cabinet. Neil wanted me to take his place. I had hoped for a proper departmental brief.

For Robin, the role of campaigns co-ordinator had been a sort of non-job which had kept him from the floor of the House. It was probably this lack of exposure which had cost him his Shadow Cabinet place. Although an election was clearly imminent, no one – including myself – had really taken the job seriously in past elections and no one therefore realised its potential importance.

Neil was nevertheless persuasive and, as a newly elected member, I was in no position to argue. I agreed to do the job and was gratified when Roy Hattersley suggested that I might also act as Shadow Chief Secretary and help him with economic policy. This was a generous gesture on Roy's part. I had been a critic of Roy's policy, which I felt accepted too much of the monetarist agenda being pursued by the Tories. I had also had several public disagreements with Roy's policy adviser Doug Jones who, to my dismay, had said at a meeting that there was little difference between us and the Tories on macro-economic policy.

I deduced from Roy's interest in getting me on board that he felt the need for some different advice. Roy was not at home with economic policy. As it turned out, however, I found the campaigns job so demanding that I had little time to fulfil Roy's expectations, if that is indeed what they were.

I had been admitted to hospital for my lump on 3 November. Neil had confirmed my appointment to my two new jobs in a phone call to Gill while I was under the surgeon's knife. I left hospital the following day, but was hobbling badly. I remember being interviewed by Robin Oakley for *The Times*. He wrote a flattering piece in which he suggested that, on all sorts of grounds, I was Labour's coming man. His thesis was that I was young, bright and on the threshold of a glittering career which could well take me to the top. He would like to have said that I was fit and in good health but one look at my pathetic hobble led him to second thoughts. He contented himself with observing that I was in 'reasonable' health.

On 6 November, I sat in the Chamber for the first time as a Shadow Cabinet member to listen to the Autumn Statement and the beginning of the subsequent debate on the economy. As I sat there, a message was passed to me. Gill wanted to see me in the Central Lobby. I went out to meet her. She told me that she had just had a call from Professor Ellis at Westminster Hospital. The tumour had proved to be cancerous.

Gill was terribly upset and frightened. I, however, felt quite calm. I was quite confident that my condition was not life-threatening, since I felt so well. My confidence was scarcely shaken by my conversation later that afternoon with Professor Ellis. He told me that I had Hodgkin's Disease, a form of lymphatic cancer. I would have to go through many tests to see whether the cancer had spread from the lymph system. I would also have to have radiation treatment to follow up the surgery.

Over the next few months, I went through every conceivable test. I had blue dye injected through the soles of my feet into my lymphatic system. I had fluid removed from my spine by means of a very unpleasant lumbar puncture. I had a body scan at the Royal Marsden. I had tests on my liver. I had frequent X-rays and blood tests. After a while, I began to feel like a pincushion.

I began radiation treatment on 8 December. Lying under the

machine itself was no hardship, but I was dismayed to find that I felt very ill following the treatment and had to go back to the flat for a few hours to get over the feelings of nausea. Fortunately, I was prescribed some anti-nausea pills which helped to reduce these symptoms over the next couple of months. I went into the Westminster Hospital most days for treatment, travelling up to London for the purpose each day over the Christmas recess.

I have always been astonished that no one ever noticed my comings and goings. I was convinced that the story would eventually reach the press. Only my close family knew what was happening. Otherwise, I kept up a hectic schedule of interviews and meetings, with no one else any the wiser.

The one great consolation of all this was that, as the tests progressed, the results were favourable. Although I frequently felt tired and ill as a result of the tests and treatment, I continued to feel deep down that I was fundamentally well. Gill began gradually to feel more confident as well. We had one nasty moment when an unfortunate woman wrote to us out of the blue asking for help in setting up a fund in memory of her husband who had, she said, recently died of Hodgkin's Disease, a condition she described as invariably fatal.

For the next five years, I continued to have regular tests and X-rays. My doctors at the Westminster Hospital, particularly Dr Phillips, were marvellous. I am glad to say that I made a complete recovery and that the treatment I received – the surgery and the radiation – eliminated every last trace of the cancer from my body.

It is probably true that the demands of my new responsibilities were actually a help in getting me through this period. I had no time for introspection. I was plunged into a level of activity which demanded every moment of my waking day.

My misgivings about the campaigns co-ordinator's job were quickly set at rest. Everyone knew that a general election was going to be called and so suddenly my job became of central importance. I found myself in constant demand as a spokesperson for the party in every situation. As I proved that I could handle these situations, Neil's confidence in me grew. We rapidly reached the point where he wanted me to do everything. I remember the Shadow Cabinet meeting after Christmas, when I had been active on most days of the recess issuing press statements and doing interviews. Neil told my colleagues that I had 'played a blinder'. They listened to this encomium with as good a grace as they could muster.

I, in turn, formed a new respect for Neil. Watching him at close quarters, particularly in Shadow Cabinet meetings, I began to appreciate his tremendous courage and resolution. It cannot have been easy for him, especially when he was first elected leader. Then, he had presided over a Shadow Cabinet which was almost entirely senior to him, and of which a large majority had voted against him. Yet he nevertheless succeeded in establishing his authority over his colleagues and even in securing their grudging respect. Unfortunately for him, the respect remained in many cases more grudging than it should have done.

My own relations with my colleagues were good, although it must have been galling to them to see a newcomer attract so much attention. I was aware of this, but there was little I could do about it. I concentrated on doing my job as well as I could whilst avoiding, I hoped, treading on too many toes.

I was concerned about my relations with Robin Cook. Robin had lost his seat as I came into the Shadow Cabinet and we had in effect swapped jobs. It would not have been surprising if Robin had felt some resentment against me. There was indeed an awkward moment or two when Robin initially insisted that, not only should he remain a member of the Campaign Management Committee (it made sense, he said, to make use of his experience), but that he should actually chair it. I managed to persuade him, as gently as possible, that neither was a sensible idea.

I was always careful subsequently to pay tribute, quite genuinely, to the contribution which Robin had made to the preparations for the election campaign. Much of its structure and the organisational preparations had been put in place by the time I came along. Robin's research assistant, Nigel Stanley, whom I had known a little when he had been a student in Southampton, had played a large part in this.

Robin was commendably concerned about Nigel and the fact that, outside the Shadow Cabinet, he could no longer afford to keep him on. I agreed to take Nigel on.

It was one of the best decisions I made. Nigel was a rather reserved person whose trust took some time to earn. However, he had excellent political judgement, and worked hard, long and loyally. He worked for me for the next seven years and became over that period the doyen of research assistants. We grew to know and like each other very much.

I also got to know the other colleagues with whom I was to work through to the general election. The most important of these served on the Campaign Management Committee. I chaired the committee, which comprised Larry Whitty, the party's General Secretary, the three senior directors – Peter Mandelson (Communications), Joyce Gould (Organisation) and Geoff Bish (Research) – Neil's senior aide, Charles Clarke, and Neil's press officer, Patricia Hewitt.

It was more by good luck than good management that this committee proved, in the light of experience, to be about the right size for the job in hand. It was large enough to represent a proper range of views, interests and expertise, but small enough to be focused and coherent. It was, I think, one of my major contributions to the election campaign that I managed to get the committee working as an efficient unit.

The personalities involved were at times difficult to handle. Joyce Gould and Geoff Bish were good colleagues, but, because they tended to limit themselves to their particular responsibilities, carried perhaps less weight than the other committee members. They nevertheless provided useful ballast to the committee and injected a fair degree of good common sense.

Larry Whitty I found to be an admirable colleague. He was a self-effacing person who was nevertheless acutely aware of what the party, and particularly the trade unions, would or would not like. I always thought that he did an excellent job as general secretary of the party, which must be one of the worst jobs in the world. He laboured under the constant suspicion that he did not enjoy Neil's full confidence, a suspicion assiduously nurtured, I have no doubt, by some of his rivals.

I always felt, however, that I could rely on Larry, and he never did anything to shake my confidence in him.

Charles Clarke was a powerful figure. He undoubtedly enjoyed Neil's confidence, which gave him considerable influence. His effectiveness was limited only by the fact that he always saw issues primarily from the viewpoint of what effect they would have on Neil. This somewhat restricted him in taking the wider view of the party's interests, which was the true business of the committee. This was a minor consideration, however, and did little to reduce Charles' value to the committee, of which he was always a constructive and thoughtful member.

The best strategic mind on the committee belonged to Patricia Hewitt. I always felt that she thought hardest and saw furthest. I listened to what she had to say with particular attention. She worked hard and was well organised. Her political judgement could occasionally be questioned, but her contribution to the work of the committee was invaluable. More than anyone else, I believe, she ensured that after the debacle of the 1983 campaign, the party was well prepared in 1987.

The most interesting member of the committee was the communications director, Peter Mandelson. I had known Peter for some years, although only slightly. We had a good friend in common and, while I had been working in television, Peter had asked me for a reference which presumably helped him to get his job as a researcher on London Weekend Television's *Weekend World*. He had come straight from that job to his post as the party's director of press and public relations.

Peter had already begun, before I arrived as campaigns co-ordinator, the process of transformation which saw the party adopt the red rose and the slick presentation techniques for which he became renowned. In late 1986, when we became professional colleagues, he was already recognised as an effective operator, but his reputation had not reached the towering proportions, for good or ill, which it did in later years.

In my experience Peter was a curious mixture of strengths and weaknesses. He was among the most charming people one could wish to meet, when he wished to be, and was the most effective manipulator of people I have ever come across. He was a brilliant strategist, in the sense of securing goals of a personal nature, but he was a limited political thinker who was surprisingly wooden when it came to articulating ideas. The briefings he supplied to the committee and to the Shadow Cabinet on the political outlook were usually accurate and well-focused, but stunningly banal.

He could also be an awkward colleague, unable to hide his low opinion of some of those he had to work with, and prone to occasional sulks. It was another achievement, of which I was quite proud, that I managed to keep Peter on board as an effective member of the team. I achieved this on the basis that Peter at the time genuinely liked and respected me and was prepared to do what I asked of him in the interests of the party.

The committee met at least once a week in the run-up to the general election and then more frequently as the election became imminent. Although much attention has been paid to the 1987 campaign, insufficient weight has been given, in my opinion, to the importance of this preparatory phase. It was here that the ground work was laid. We were all driven by the memory of the 1983 chaos and were determined that, whatever else happened, we would not be found wanting this time for lack of preparation.

We attempted things which had never been tried before. For example, we drew up three months in advance a 'grid' which told us exactly where about 50 key campaigners would be during every hour of every day of the campaign; what subject they would be speaking on; what interviews they would be doing; and what television or radio studios they would be using. The task of agreeing and then co-ordinating the personal diaries of 50 prima donnas was well-nigh impossible, but we managed it. It was this hard work, attention to detail and ambition to get things right which was the real explanation of the success of that campaign.

Another key figure whom I got to know at this time was Philip Gould. We always jokingly referred to ourselves as cousins, since Philip's father was called Caleb – a name which, because of my lockkeeper forebear of that name, had considerable significance in my family. Philip was the advertising man who advised us throughout the campaign. He had a contract with the party and his partner, Deborah Mattinson, did most of our qualitative research. Our normal polling was done by Bob Worcester of MORI.

Philip brought together a 'Shadow' communications agency of volunteers from the advertising industry. They met once a week, usually early on a Tuesday morning. I would normally attend these meetings, which were often useful brainstorming sessions. Many of the ideas thrown up came to nothing, but the meetings gave us a valuable chance to see ourselves as others saw us.

The frequency and intensity of these regular campaign meetings, together with my new obligations to attend Shadow Cabinet meetings, the increase in my mail bag and the huge new demands made on me by speaking engagements and the media, all added greatly to my normal responsibilities. I found myself working, as a matter of course, a 12- or 14-hour day. Gill began to work a 70- or 80-hour week as well.

We worked at this pace and intensity for the next six or seven years. It was something we took in our stride and which seemed at the time perfectly natural. It is only in retrospect that I realise how peculiar it was. There were times, for example, when it could take me three days to respond to a telephone message asking me to phone a friend. When I did so, and explained that I had not had a moment, the friend would not of course realise that this was literally true. If your day is crammed full of engagements, at 20- or 30-minute intervals, for 12 hours at a time, if the phone is never silent for more than 30 seconds, if you are always late and literally running from one engagement to another, if your mealtimes are either non-existent or more or less indistinguishable from other business engagements, then the time available for a private social life is necessarily pretty limited.

I made my first speech as Shadow Chief Secretary in a debate which I wound up for the Opposition on 17 December 1986. The speech went very well and was described by Peter Riddell in the *Financial Times* as an 'impressive début'. I received many congratulations from colleagues. It was in many ways the best time of my political career.

Most people seemed genuinely pleased that I was doing well. The imminence of the election meant that many of the normal personal rivalries and hostilities were submerged in an overriding recognition of the need to play as a team, and I was probably too new on the scene to have made too many enemies or to be perceived as too much of a threat.

I was in any case blisfully unaware at this point of the murky waters in which senior politicians swim. When people sometimes said to me that politics was a dirty business, I would quite genuinely protest that, in my experience, this was not so. I was of course aware that my rise to prominence might cause some resentment, and I did what I could to avoid giving any provocation on this score, but it had been my experience up to this point that individual success was welcomed as contributing to the success of the team. It may be that my naïveté on this point helped me to infect others with my commitment to the wider cause.

The Shadow Cabinet met for a 24-hour strategy session at a trade union conference centre at Bishop's Stortford in early January. I made a presentation, with Peter Mandelson's help, which went very well. I did a number of media interviews, used the excuse of having to do a *Newsnight* interview to get back to London for my daily radiation treatment and returned to Bishop's Stortford the following morning.

A few days later, I went with some Dagenham colleagues to Germany to visit our twin town of Witten. It was a pleasant break but somewhat abbreviated by my having to get back to do a *Weekend World* interview on the Sunday morning. London Weekend flew me back from Düsseldorf by private plane. I was interviewed by Matthew Parris, who had taken the job I had turned down. The main issue he wished to discuss with me was an opinion poll commissioned by the programme which showed that Labour was doing badly and had little chance of winning the election. I took a pretty robust line, attacking the methodology and therefore validity of the poll. It was, though I say it myself, an effective attack and further increased, I imagine, my colleagues' confidence in my ability to handle these sorts of issues.

There was, however, worse to come for the Labour Party. The Tory press was pulling out all the stops. The Conservatives had had an excellent conference a couple of months earlier and was in fine fettle; by contrast, Neil had come under further pressure and was looking vulnerable. The heightened political atmosphere made every step we took fraught with danger.

We then had the bad luck to run into a by-election in Greenwich caused by the death of my friend Guy Barnett. Our candidate would ordinarily have handled the campaign quite adequately. The media spotlight, however, focused on her political past, as an extreme left-winger, and exploited her uncertainty in handling the press. The outcome was a humiliating loss of the seat, which was especially damaging with a general election imminent. It was a painful lesson for the Labour Party on the nature of modern by-elections.

From then on, we were up against it. I became a past master at putting a favourable gloss on unfavourable developments, and on maintaining a confident front. Neil turned to me often for advice but more particularly to undertake tasks which he feared might be too difficult for others.

A case in point was the party's jobs programme. Unemployment had been the dog which refused to bark. It had not barked for a long time. It puzzled many people that the high rate of unemployment seemed to leave the Tories unscathed. In an attempt to raise the profile of the issue, the party had somehow managed to lumber itself with a commitment to create one million jobs within two years of taking office and to spend no more than £6 billion doing so.

The pledge was always a ridiculous one. It reeked of the mechanistic approach to economic issues (so much public spending or so much on training or so much on investment will produce so many jobs) which had dogged the Labour Party's economic policymaking for so long. It showed no understanding of the fact that the only way to attack unemployment effectively was with an accommodating macro-econ-omic policy – something which, ironically, the Tories demonstrated unwittingly when the Lawson boom created far more than one million jobs in the two years after the election.

John Prescott was the party's employment spokesperson and had been working for some time on how to make good the commitment. He had consulted closely with people in local government, coming up with a highly formulaic programme for investment in local government services which would produce, at least for as long as the money kept coming, the requisite number of jobs.

Neil took one look at the draft and decided he could not allow it to go forward. It would, he thought, fail to carry credibility and, to the extent that anyone took it seriously, it would reveal the party as dangerously in hock to the public service unions.

I was brought in at the last moment to try to rescue the operation. It did not earn me many friends, especially among John Prescott's supporters. Helped by Charles Clarke and Roy Hattersley, I eventually came up with a four-part package which relied, at least to some extent, on a boost in demand. I presented the package first to the Shadow Cabinet and then to the Leader's Committee – the large group of senior party and trade union figures who met occasionally to be reassured that the campaign preparations were going well.

The package was, I think, as good an attempt as it could have been but it didn't cut much ice with the media. It wasn't much helped by the fact that the press conference – the culmination of a good deal of work by many people – was totally overshadowed in the minds of the media by a punch-up John Prescott had had in the House of Commons tea room the previous day over a disagreement he had had with Jim Callaghan and others over defence policy.

We had dinner at the Kinnocks' place in February. Glenys was an excellent hostess and a genuinely likeable person. I always felt that she had a better grasp than Neil of what made people tick. Neil was someone I liked and respected but he was not always the easiest person to get on terms with. At that time I thought he was beginning to develop another aspect of 'leader's syndrome' – a difficulty in conducting ordinary conversation. He often felt the need to dominate the conversation, with the result that others tended to fall silent.

On 19 March, my doctors gave me a clean bill of health. Although

I had to go back regularly for X-rays and check-ups, and did so for the next five years, my medical crisis was over.

Things were also happening on the domestic front. We had decided to convert the barn next to our house in Westcott Barton and to incorporate it into the house. A local builder had undertaken the work and, although progress was slow, he was making an excellent job. We were thrilled with the outcome, and with the swimming pool which we had also decided to install.

Brook House was altogether a great source of satisfaction to us. It was a Grade 11 listed cottage nestling in a small valley, with an acre of ground bounded by a small stream, the river Dorn. There was even a ford at the front gate. The only problem was that the place required a great deal of work – the garden, in particular – and we could never get there. We spent most of our time in London, living in a one-bedroomed flat in which Gill and I slept on a sofa-bed in the small sitting-room.

The Kinnocks came to lunch at Brook House one weekend in April. They were very late in arriving, and Neil began with a couple of stiff whiskies. The lunch went well, however, and we had a delightful walk around Westcott Barton in the afternoon. They left at 7 p.m., just before some other friends arrived for dinner. Their visit did not go unnoticed in the village, however, and a rumour spread like wild fire. Neil Kinnock was moving to Westcott Barton.

It is hard to convey the pace and intensity of my schedule at this time. The only saving grace of the insane hours and the number of engagements was that I actually enjoyed what I was doing. Although I was constantly tired, I was relatively young, I slept well, and generally I awoke ready to face another day.

I recall one particularly significant meeting with Neil at about this time. He had had a bruising time on a visit to Washington when he had been treated pretty roughly over our policy on unilateral nuclear disarmament. He was criticised by both domestic and European friends and critics over the same issue. He knew that it would be an electoral liability. In his heart, I believe, he had ceased to believe in it himself. He cautiously broached the subject with me and quoted

Henry of Navarre's question 'Is Paris worth a mass?' I was taken by surprise at the implications of the question and offered little comment. I believe that Neil was seeking support at that point for an abandonment of the policy.

We were by now in a fever of anticipation as to the calling of the general election. We were still behind in the polls and the Tories were hot favourites to win. There was a general feeling in the Labour camp, however, that everything would change once the whistle blew. We knew we were ready and we also sensed that Neil would hit his stride once the campaign began.

Peter Mandelson and family came to visit us for tea at Brook House on May Day Bank Holiday. Peter was at that time living with Peter Ashby, who was the father of a small boy called Joe. The two Peters saw a good deal of Joe and were both very fond of him. We were delighted to see them all and very much enjoyed their visit.

A week later, I did what was in effect a pre-election meeting at Mitcham and Morden, a London marginal seat which we would have to win in order to secure victory. The television cameras were present and what I had to say featured on the news that evening. The election was announced on the following day.

We swung into action. I was always determined to get off to a fast start. My nightmare was that we would fall behind in the early part of the campaign. If the polls showed us trailing the Alliance, we would face the danger of a squeeze on a national scale of the same sort we had faced in by-elections. The Tories were also preoccupied with the Alliance, which was doing well in the polls off the back of their Greenwich victory. Its leaders, the Davids Owen and Steel, were also attracting a lot of media attention. The Tories were convinced that we posed no threat and were in effect down and out. They had imagined that they could hold us under water with one hand, while we quietly drowned, and so concentrate on the real battle, against the Alliance – astonishing though that may seem today. It took them a good couple of weeks to realise that we were not drowning but waving.

Two days into the election campaign, I had a phone call from my sister Ngaire. My father had had a stroke and was in a coma. She did not suggest I flew out to New Zealand but merely wanted me to know. Four days later, he died. It was by this time impossible for me to abandon the campaign, so I did not even attend his funeral. I have often regretted this, although I know that I had no real alternative. My father had had a very happy holiday with us, following my mother's death, and I felt closer to him in his later years. I catch myself often now looking more and more like him as I grow older. I must admit I have a higher regard for his integrity and self-contained-ness that I ever did when he was alive.

Gill and I moved into Walworth Road when the campaign proper began. The whole of the top floor was given over to election staff. Gill and I operated from one corner of a huge room in which dozens of others also worked. My right-hand men were Jack Dromey and John Carr. The whole building was alive. A wonderful spirit developed. Everyone felt that they were involved in something worthwhile, which was going well.

Neil began the campaign with an inspiring speech at Llandudno. At his height, he was the best speaker on a public platform in Britain. As we had hoped, he threw off all his problems as soon as the campaign started. It was almost as if he knew that this was what he did best and that, whatever the media said about him, he now had the chance to show the people what he was really made of.

The campaign day started at 7 a.m. with a meeting of the campaign management committee. The committee was without Charles Clarke and Patricia Hewitt during the actual campaign, since they were out on the road with Neil. We looked at reports on the media coverage, on our polling, and from our party agents throughout the country. We decided the theme of the day's briefing to candidates, and dealt with any emergencies. I would then usually have a separate meeting with Philip Gould and Peter Mandelson to consider our advertising campaign.

I would then often do an early morning interview about the campaign and go on to Transport House for the morning press conference. Neil had decided that he would, on most days, campaign in a regional or provincial centre, and would do a daily press conference from wherever he happened to be. Naturally, he was attended by a substantial press corps, but it was recognised that many of the heavyweight political journalists would not be able to leave London, and that their needs should be met by a separate London press conference. I took that press conference each morning, except on those few days when Neil was there.

I confess that I did little by way of preparation for the press conferences. I tackled them with all the confidence of the novice. I found that I had a particular talent for giving the journalists proper answers to their questions but answers limited to what we wanted them to hear. The main aim of the press conferences was to get through them without making a mistake on which our enemies could fasten. If we could occasionally score a point, or enhance our reputations in some way, so much the better.

To my delight, the verve and élan with which we had launched the campaign intrigued the journalists. They had expected a repeat of 1983's sad performance. When it became clear that our campaign was slick and professional, that we were outgunning the lacklustre Tories and an Alliance which was threatened constantly by division and personal antipathy, the media was enchanted. The revelation that Labour was doing well, at least in terms of electioning techniques, became the story of the campaign.

I discovered an important feature of campaigns in general – that once the journalists have decided on the theme, it is very difficult to persuade them to change it. What they really want is a daily development of the theme. If the theme is in our favour, it is a marvellous situation to find ourselves in. All that has to be done to keep the theme going is to offer a new morsel each day. This is enough to shut out the opposition, who will have the greatest difficulty in getting a new theme going.

This isn't to say that our campaign was all straightforward. We were constantly trying to douse bush fires which threatened to get out of hand. Early in the campaign, the Tories thought they had their chance to knock us off our stride. They knew we would be vulnerable on defence and, in particular, on unilateral nuclear disarmament. Neil gave an unwise interview to David Frost in which he was induced into talking about guerrilla warfare if we were invaded. The Tories, and their friends in the press, leapt upon the issue with glee.

The story ran for several days, fuelled in part by the uncoordinated efforts by various party spokespeople to swat it away. The trouble was that without realising it, they would invariably employ phrases which differed in some respect from those used by their colleagues. This was enough to allow the media to keep the story going, on the basis that Labour's spokespeople kept saying different things.

In the end, I wrote out a short statement to be distributed to every campaigner. They were all instructed not to depart from the text at any cost. After two or three days without new developments, the story ran out of steam. The Tories had failed to get it established as a major campaign issue.

The other issue which dominated the opening week of the campaign was a row with Norman Tebbit, who was in charge of the Tory campaign. He had said, some months before the election, that if unemployment was still at 3 million on election day, the Government did not deserve to be re-elected. We reminded him of this assertion when it became clear that unemployment was still above that figure. Characteristically, he fought back with a robust denial that he had said any such thing. Since we had some difficulty in proving his exact words, he tried to make the issue one of our veracity while we tried to keep the focus on the unemployment total. The outcome was a draw.

I had little direct contact with Norman Tebbit through the campaign. The person I found myself dealing with most often in television studios was Cecil Parkinson. I nevertheless watched Norman closely. It struck me, despite the subsequent revelations about his travails as Tory chairman, that he had it pretty easy by comparison with my job as Labour campaigns co-ordinator.

The big difference between us was that Norman could pick up the phone whenever he wanted and launch a story, however unfounded, on the front pages of half of the nation's newspapers. Even if we could show that the story had no foundation, the mere fact that it dominated the front pages of so much of the press would compel the broadcast media and the rest of the press to follow it. So much for independent media.

We, on the other hand, had to struggle to get our themes established. We were often asked in the years following, for example, why we had not made the poll tax an issue in the 1987 campaign. The answer is that we tried three times, with three separate press conferences, to get the story launched, but the press would not touch it. Imagine how a Tory story about a similar Labour proposal would have been treated.

About halfway through the campaign, a scurrilous attack was launched by David Montgomery, then editor of the *News of the World*, against Peter Mandelson, on grounds of his homosexuality. Peter was terribly upset, not so much on his own account, since he had long ago decided to 'come out', but on behalf of Peter Ashby and little Joe. I recall being asked at a press conference held to launch a range of publicity material whether, in the light of the story, I had lost confidence in Peter. I rejected the suggestion with contempt, and pointed to the material as evidence of Peter's value to the campaign.

My party in Dagenham were tolerant of my absence for days on end from the local campaign, since they knew very well the efforts I was making in the campaign nationally. I managed nevertheless to get to the constituency quite often, and spent a good part of the Saturday before polling day on a motorcade through the constituency. I was hopeful of doing well on the strength of the hard work I had put into the constituency previously, all the thousands of constituency cases I had dealt with over the preceding four years.

By this time, we were all very tired. We had always intended to leave the last week of the campaign unplanned so that we could inject some new thinking, in response to the development of the campaign at that point. In the event, however, we were too exhausted to come up with anything. We made a particularly serious mistake, as a consequence, on the last Saturday of the campaign. For the first time, we had no press conference organised on a particular theme for the Saturday morning. We therefore left the field open for the Tories.

Nigel Lawson was in the West Country that day and launched an effective attack on our plans for tax, in particular national insurance. Our absence from the field of battle, even if only momentarily, allowed the Tories to get the issue launched. Matters were made worse when Neil and Roy, when challenged separately, gave explanations which were slightly at odds with each other. I tried to repeat the exercise which had succeeded over the defence issue, but by the time we had got control of the situation, it was too late. While the eventual result showed that we would have lost comfortably anyway, the issue certainly cost us.

One of the campaign committee's problems was that we had difficulty in keeping close touch with Neil. We saw him only rarely, and managed to communicate with him or his office not much more frequently. In the early stages of the campaign, this did not matter too much. Our preparation and our understanding of each other were so good that we knew, without the need to consult too often, pretty well what each person was meant to be doing and saying. But in the later stages, it became more important, and our deficiencies in this regard played an important part over the last week.

We had always intended that the final period of the campaign should be devoted to a last push which would sum up for the voters what was at stake. We had been buoyed up by a BBC poll on the last Monday or Tuesday which showed that we were closing the gap on the Tories. This was an important psychological boost for us, since it was consistent with the impression we had tried to give throughout the campaign: that, having started from way behind, we were catching up with the Tories and would overtake them on polling day.

However, the poll turned out to be quite misleading, at least in the light of the eventual result. Irrespective of the poll, though, I wanted Neil to make a real pitch for victory, by exploiting the uncertainties in the Alliance campaign and appealing directly to wavering voters to switch to Labour. I wanted him to use his last major press conference as an opportunity to turn directly to the television cameras and deliver a powerful appeal aimed squarely at Alliance voters.

Neil had, I believe, realised by this time that we were not going to win. He was afraid of appearing vainglorious, particularly in retrospect. The result was that the last few days of the campaign lacked focus and just drifted away from us. Neil's attitude was, I think, a sign of a political maturity which appeared to escape the notice of so many of his critics. I still believe, however, that it was worth a last effort, even if that effort was to prove futile.

By the time polling day arrived, we were all privately reconciled to defeat, although not on the scale which actually materialised. Morale in our campaign, however, remained high. There was a good deal of justifiable pride in the way we had confounded the critics and carried the fight to the Tories. There was also some secret relief that we had seen off the Alliance and had consolidated our position as the main party of opposition.

I had difficulty judging my own impact on the campaign. I had been so immersed in the press of events that I had little time for reflection. Some indication of how I was regarded by the Tories came, however, at midnight on the day before polling day. I had a phone call from Chris Moncrieff, the Press Association's chief political correspondent, just as I was going to bed, alerting me to the fact that the *Sun* newspaper had decided to launch an attack against me.

Page three of the *Sun* was notorious for carrying in every issue a photograph of a topless girl. In the polling day edition, however, probably for the first time ever, it sported no voluptuous nude. Instead, pages two and three were devoted to an attack on myself, headlined 'Mr Gouldfinger'. In place of the usual photograph was a picture of my modest home in the Cotswolds.

The gist of the piece was that I was a 'champagne socialist' who was hypocritical in my championing of the interests of the downtrodden and was somehow unfitted to represent my constituents by virtue of the fact that I had a swimming pool. The piece would have been laughable if it had not been such a deliberate attempt to unseat me. I was defending a majority of under three thousand, and statistically, I was told, my Dagenham constituents read the *Sun* in greater numbers than anywhere else in the country.

What I found particularly sickening was the perversion of the *Sun*'s usual attitudes which underlay the attack. Normally vociferous in its celebration of ostentatious wealth, the paper held up to its readers all sorts of cases of crass materialism as something to which they might aspire. It urged them on in the pursuit of the sort of goodies which Mrs Thatcher promised them. Yet on this occasion, it flip-flopped itself into wearing a hairshirt for the day in order to accuse me of hypocrisy. I had always found it wryly amusing to be accused of enjoying wealth whenever I contemplated my modest MP's salary, worth about one-fifth of what I could have earned elsewhere.

I spent polling day in the constituency. My good friend Eric Parsloe drove me round in his car and we visited every polling station, broadcasting over a loudspeaker as we went. There is no doubt that the *Sun* article had had some impact, at least in the sense that people were talking about it – naturally enough, I suppose, since there would have been many who turned to page three for their daily fix and would have been bemused by what they found.

The count took place in Barking town hall. Not only did I have to put up with the usual pressures of waiting for my own result, but I was also interviewed every half hour or so by the national media who had set up special outside broadcast facilities for the purpose. It became obvious from the first results not only that the Tories had won, but that Labour had made only the slightest of dents in the size of their majority. The night became a long exercise in putting a brave face on a disappointing defeat – all the more disappointing since our campaign had gone so well.

My own result was also a disappointment. Instead of my majority doubling, as I had expected, it fell slightly, to just 2,500. The result was in line with other results around the northern and eastern fringes of London: we actually lost two seats in this area, in Walthamstow and Thurrock. It was the part of the country where Mrs Thatcher had been most successful in eating into the working-class vote. Being part of a wider trend, however, did little to comfort me.

I got to bed at 4.30 in the morning. The following day, I and the whole staff at party headquarters gathered to welcome Neil and Glenys when they arrived at Walworth Road following a car journey from Neil's constituency. Neil and I embraced. I was in tears. He received an emotional welcome from his supporters. Everyone recognised the effort he had made and the superb campaign which he personally had fought.

I became accustomed in later years, when talking about the campaign, to describe it as successful in every sense, except that we lost. This would usually raise an ironic laugh. There were often those who would decry the campaign as an instance of presentation taking precedence over substance. For some years afterwards, I was attacked by opponents from within the party as an exponent of 'glitz and glitter', with the implication that I was somehow devoid of principle.

I have never felt any need, however, to apologise for the campaign in any sense. I could never see the point of doing badly something we had to do anyway. We owed it to our supporters to get our message across as effectively as possible. My view, on which I always tried to act both at the time and subsequently, was that good presentation was necessary, but it could never be enough. Indeed, presentation was only effective if it reflected a substance in which one had confidence and believed fervently.

The real point of the 1987 campaign was not that it failed to achieve victory but that it averted something much worse than the defeat we actually suffered. The Labour Party could have been humiliated. It could have been fatally wounded. Instead, we had fought a campaign which had restored our self-confidence and at least provided us with a platform from which we could go forward as the only party capable of offering an alternative to the Tories.

TEN

The Shadow Cabinet
1987–89

I SPOKE TO NEIL on the phone on the Saturday following the election. He was due to speak the following day at the Durham Miners' Gala. I sympathised with him, after the exhausting efforts he had made throughout the campaign, at having to speak at a major occasion so soon. He would have none of my sympathy. 'The next campaign starts now,' he said.

For most of us, however, there followed a much-needed opportunity to rest and to lick our wounds. I had emerged from the campaign as, after Neil, pretty well the most prominent Labour politician in the country – as witness the fact that my puppet featured occasionally on *Spitting Image*. It took me some little time to understand my new high profile and to come to terms with the truly remarkable extent of media interest in all that I did and said. I remember joining Neil one evening to help him entertain some visiting SPD politicians from Berlin and being introduced to them by Neil as the *de facto* deputy leader.

There was a great deal of speculation in the press as to who would get which Shadow Cabinet job. It was well known that Roy Hattersley had decided to give up the Shadow Chancellorship, and equally well known that John Smith regarded himself as the natural heir to the job. The press, however, detected a potential clash between John and me over the issue, since they well understood my long-term interest in economic policy. There were constant reports that one or other of us would get the nod.

John took this press speculation rather badly, and seemed convinced that I was somehow orchestrating a campaign on my own behalf. He was particularly incensed by a report in *The Times* to the effect that 'Gould could choose any job he wanted'. My research assistant, Nigel Stanley, reported to me that John had been very rude to him on the terrace one evening. John had had a few drinks, and was telling everyone within earshot that he was not about to be muscled out of his rightful inheritance by an upstart like Gould.

I was in fact entirely innocent of the charge. If asked, I would say that I would like to be Shadow Chancellor, which was true, but I did nothing to promote my chances. I was content to leave it to Neil, and I always assumed that my decided views on economic policy would mean that Neil would have to swallow hard before giving me the job. Nor for the first time, I would have done better to have had no views.

The Shadow Cabinet elections were held that summer, following the State Opening of Parliament on 25 June. The results were known on 8 July. I topped the poll by a wide margin. I have never done the calculations properly but I think my 163 votes, in a relatively small electorate, must have been just about the highest proportion of the Parliamentary Labour Party vote ever secured.

Neil saw me that afternoon. He congratulated me on my result, but I thought I detected just a hint of wariness in his manner. For the first time, I think, Neil saw me as a potential rival. This was no doubt helped along by advice from some of his advisers that, at that moment at least, I was very popular in both the party and the country, and that Neil had better watch me carefully. Nothing, however, was further from my mind. I was delighted by my success and hopeful, in a vague sort of way, that it might eventually lead me to the leadership, but my loyalty to Neil was never in doubt.

Neil offered me the Shadow Trade and Industry job. I was a little disappointed. I cannot remember whether I raised the possibility of the Treasury job at this point, though I rather think not. I always acted on a rather odd sense of pride which prevented me from being – as I thought – a supplicant. I felt that Neil either recognised my merits and would offer me the job, or he wouldn't. I did not wish to demean myself by asking for it.

I undertook to go away and think about Neil's offer. Neil asked me not to take too long, since he had spoken to me first and could make few other decisions until I had decided what I would do. I thought about it overnight and decided that I would see him again, this time to put my case for being Shadow Chancellor.

We met again on the following day. I began by saying that I was seeking the job of Shadow Chancellor, not on the strength of my 163 votes, which I realised were perhaps a temporary reflection of my general election prominence, but because of my expertise in economic policy. The only significance of my vote was that it removed what might otherwise have been an obstacle: my junior status within the Shadow Cabinet. I explained how important I thought the job was to our whole political and campaigning stance, and what a difference I thought I could make.

Neil listened carefully and sympathetically, and he in turn promised to think further about it. He asked to see me again later in the day when he said that he had decided to offer the job to John Smith. He explained that he had genuinely been on the point of deciding in my favour when Roy Hattersley had warned him that he, Roy, would insist on retaining the post or even resigning rather than see me get it. I have no means of knowing whether this was true or not, but it would certainly have been consistent with Roy's long-term determination to exclude me from the party's policymaking over economic policy and Europe.

Neil asked me again to serve as Shadow Trade and Industry Secretary. I agreed to do so without further demur. Neil made it clear that he saw the trade and industry job as a major economic portfolio, and that he expected me to exercise a significant influence on economic policy. I have no reason to believe that this was not truly his view at the time.

I make this point because I realised at about this time that it was very difficult to be sure whether Neil was being totally honest. There was always the feeling that he told me what I wanted to hear, but might well be saying different things to others. This is not meant as a criticism of Neil. He was no doubt having to balance many conflicting claims and pressures and he was still having to contend with powerful barons who were always inclined, among themselves at least, to contest his claim to the job.

A few days later, I met Neil again to discuss the membership of my front bench team. I had a number of suggestions to make and Neil also put forward some names. The most important job was that of spokesperson on the City. It was not in any formal sense a deputy's job, but Robin Cook and I had used it to such good effect that it had become recognised as perhaps the most significant appointment outside the Shadow Cabinet.

Neil and I rapidly agreed that the right person for this post was Tony Blair, a young barrister who had entered Parliament at the 1983 election. He had first come to my notice at the time of the leadership election of that year. A meeting of Peter Shore supporters had been called and I remember being gratified to see at that small gathering a young newcomer. We did not see him again at such a meeting; it was only later that I realised he had gone to every candidate's campaign meeting, rather as an Oxford fresher might join each political club.

Tony rapidly emerged over the succeeding parliament as one of the most able of the new intake. I found him personally congenial, and I was always impressed by his interventions at Question Time and his other performances in the House. I was very glad indeed to have him as my lieutenant. The only point on which I mentally marked him down was that on the one or two occasions on which I had tried to interest him in a discussion of the broader issue of economic policy he had made little response.

I treated Tony, as a member of my team, very much as John Smith had treated me – that is, I allowed him plenty of space and in effect simply required of him that he get on with the job. This he did to very good effect. Like his immediate predecessors, he saw the potential of the job, and he made the most of issues like the scandal over the Barlow Clowes affair.

I held a weekly meeting of my front bench team, something John Smith had done only spasmodically. Tony always made an effective contribution at such meetings. His unofficial position as my deputy was confirmed by the fact that he chaired the meeting on those occasions when I could not be present.

My own schedule became, from this point onwards, even more hectic. I was in much demand as a speaker and did a great deal of travelling. The media demands were also insatiable. However, Gill and I did manage to get away for a brief holiday in Tunisia in July.

We had fond memories of our holiday in that country in 1968, when we had danced each night to the strains of 'A Whiter Shade of Pale' by Procol Harum. This time, we arrived at our hotel in Sousse a little late (our flight had been delayed), certainly too late for an evening meal. We were directed to an empty restaurant and promised a snack. As we waited, the broadcasting system suddenly crackled into life and, to our amazement, we found ourselves listening again to 'A Whiter Shade of Pale'.

As the annual conference approached, media interest in me heightened still further. I was asked by Channel Four to make a short film about the issues which faced the Labour Party. I took as my theme the need for Labour to shuck off its image as the party which stopped people from doing things. I recalled the mistake which had been made over council house sales, and warned against the danger of taking a similarly short-sighted view of share ownership – something which Mrs Thatcher was busily popularising through under-priced privatisation issues. I suggested that Labour should try to make the matter our own through employee share ownership plans.

The hard left saw this as further evidence of my keenness to move the party away from its traditional path. They were anxious to exploit any issue which might create a backlash against me and unite all those who had no doubt been secretly fuming at my rise in prominence and popularity.

There was very little I could do to at times to show that I recognised the sensitivities of my colleagues. I remember early on in the conference speaking at a meeting which was being televised for the evening news. The television lights blazed on the platform throughout my speech. I then had to leave to go to another meeting (I was speaking at four or five meetings every evening). As I left, and Robin Cook got to his feet, the television lights were suddenly extinguished and Robin was left to speak in what seemed like symbolic gloom.

I had been asked to stand for the National Executive Committee. I had tried on one previous occasion and had scored something like 12 votes. I took a little persuading that I would do better this time. The results were expected on the Tuesday afternoon. Gill and I sat in the body of the hall waiting for the announcement. Just as the item was introduced, Neil signalled to Gill from the platform that I had been elected.

I attended my first National Executive on the following day. I had been warned by colleagues that serving on the National Executive was a pretty unpleasant experience. The atmosphere, it was said, was hostile and the meetings were often long and acrimonious. I have to say that I was fortunate that my arrival coincided with an improvement in the temper of the meetings. The NEC had become much more co-operative and constructive. Neil in the NEC was even more impressive than Neil in the Shadow Cabinet. In both bodies, he was always tempted to speak more than he should, but he almost invariably spoke to good effect.

My first meeting had, however, been preceded by a difficult moment. I had decided to speak, perhaps unwisely in view of the storm which had raged about my opinions on share ownership, in the debate on the economy. I spoke from the floor for the allotted time of just four minutes. I was given a hostile reception by a small part of the conference and found myself responding to shouts and catcalls. It was not a pleasant experience. It was probably one of the last occasions that the hard left managed to do anything of significance at annual conference.

A week after conference, Gill and I flew out to New Zealand as the guests of the New Zealand government. The invitation had originally been issued to Neil but when he declined, we had been invited in his place. On the day before our departure, we were handed the final version of our itinerary. The first item read 'Met at the airport by the Prime Minister'. I wasn't quite sure what to make of this. I could barely believe that my arrival would warrant a prime ministerial trip to the airport. In reverse circumstances, Mrs Thatcher was hardly likely to slog out to Heathrow to meet a visiting New Zealand MP.

Nevertheless, we were put into something of a sartorial quandary. We had intended, like most people, to travel in sweaters and jeans. I began to think, however, that if the Prime Minister were really going to be there, there might be press – even television. We had better ensure that we looked reasonably presentable.

Rather against our better judgement, we took on to the plane a dress and a suit and about an hour out of Auckland, we slipped into the toilets and changed, still not really believing that the Prime Minister would be there to meet us. When we got off the plane, however, there at the barrier, as large as life (and in the case of David Lange, that is pretty large), was indeed the Prime Minister – in his jeans! I realised that things were indeed done differently in my home country. Not only would Mrs Thatcher not have gone to the airport, but Mrs Thatcher in jeans! It doesn't bear thinking about.

We had a wonderful trip around New Zealand. It revived my love of my own country, and we both fell in love with the South Island, which neither of us had seen much of before. The trip also had its political interest. The Lange government had just been re-elected, but was facing increasing hostility on account of its economic policies. These, in the hands of Finance Minister Roger Douglas, had followed a tough monetarist line and had acquired the tag of 'Rogernomics'.

Much of what Roger Douglas had done was a long overdue deregulation and liberalisation of the economy which had been placed in a sort of corporatist straitjacket by the last National Party prime minister, Robert Muldoon. The monetarist squeeze had initially been popular, particularly with those who found their assets rising in value and who managed to create, for a time, a capital market of some significance in which considerable fortunes could be made.

The productive sector of the economy, however, suffered badly from enormously high interest rates. As farms and businesses folded, and unemployment mounted, people were told that it was necessary to tighten their belts but that they would reap the rewards in due course. This was just plausible enough, after a three-year term, to carry the government through the election. My visit coincided with the growing realisation, however, that the good times might be a long time in coming.

I recall a stimulating evening over dinner with Roger Douglas and a group of 'young Turks' from the Treasury. They had all the conviction of religious zealots. They were convinced that they had discovered the Holy Grail and were seemingly unaware that their prescriptions had been tried and largely abandoned elsewhere.

I saw David Lange later and told him that I thought he was heading for disaster. He listened non-committally. I think he was enough of a politician to know that something had to change, but not enough of an economist to know what that change should be.

On my return to England, I plunged back into a hectic round of interviews, meetings and debates in the Chamber. In November, I was the guest speaker at a Chartist rally in Neil's constituency. Later in the month, I attended the first meeting of the convenors of the policy review bodies.

Neil had decided, following the election, that we had got our presentation right, but had been rejected by the voters because they did not like our policies. He had persuaded conference that the party should engage in a policy review which would allow us to update our policies and make them more attractive to the electorate.

I supported the proposal since I saw it as a means of getting away from the sterility of what I called 'politics by label'. Virtually nothing by way of genuine debate on policy had taken place in the party for years. All that happened was that certain positions were known to be 'left' or 'right' and people were simply required to line up behind their chosen banner. The merits of individual ideas were never discussed.

Neil had, true to his promise, placed me as a joint convenor of the group which was to deal with the productive and competitive economy. In effect, this meant that I was responsible for the development of policy on all issues to do with the macro-economy, industrial strategy and public ownership. John Smith was a joint convenor of a separate group which dealt with taxation and social security issues.

It is fair to say that the report of my group, when it was published in the following year, very much reflected my own views. It was not a complete statement of my views quite, since I was obliged to take account of what others said and contributed, and also of what I believed Neil would want. But all the drafting was done by myself or by Nigel Stanley.

The policy put forward in that 1988 document, which went to annual conference and was published under the title *Meet the Challenge, Make the Change*, put emphasis on the needs of the real or productive economy. In it, there was a commitment to managing interest rates and the exchange rate in the interests of investment and production, a rejection of the monetarist emphasis on financial measures, and substantial reservations about the prospect of joining the Exchange Rate Mechanism.

There was also a solution to the question of what a Labour government would do about those publicly owned industries which had been privatised by the time we returned to office – principally, gas, water, electricity and telecommunications. There was a strong demand from the party that we should commit ourselves to taking these industries back into public ownership. Quite apart from the merits or otherwise of doing so, we had to take this demand – especially from the relevant trade unions – into account, since there would be no point in producing a policy review which was then rejected by the party at annual conference.

We made it clear, however, that a Labour government would not commit real resources – that is, resources which could otherwise be spent on something else – simply to a change of ownership. There were other, better things to do with the money. What we were interested in doing, however, was to secure 'some form of public ownership' – the phrase was deliberately vague, and included a whole range of possibilities falling short of total public ownership – which would not require us to buy back the whole of the equity.

The commitment was a little more specific in the case of water since there was very great public hostility, as revealed by opinion polls, to its privatisation and an expectation that Labour would restore water to its proper position as a public asset. There was also a special arrangement over British Telecom which I negotiated personally with the National Communications Union, the main union involved. The NCU's own policy was to demand full 100 per cent public ownership of BT. I persuaded them to accept a commitment that a Labour government would buy a sufficient shareholding to give us a majority of shares. Since 49 per cent of the shares were still owned by the Government, this was an inexpensive commitment, but one which the union could nevertheless sell to their membership.

The productive and competitive economy group met regularly under my chairmanship. John Edmonds, of the General, Municipal and Boilermakers Union, was a regular attender. John was principally interested in those parts of the report which dealt with the trade unions and was particularly concerned to resist any hint that a pay policy might be necessary. Although John and I did not know each other well, we had no difficulty in agreeing on this point. My view was that pay restraint, in the sense of a sustained but controlled growth in real wages, was certainly desirable, but that anything like a formal pay policy would not work. The best way of securing a sensible approach to pay was to provide real and sustainable growth in the economy so that real wages could grow and the pressure for mere money increases would subside.

Ken Livingstone – elected, like me, to the National Executive in 1987 – was also a member of the group. Ken had begun by assuming that he and I would be at odds. Initially, he was a most unreliable colleague, constantly leaking misleading and highly prejudicial accounts of what the group was up to and making it very difficult for us to discuss ideas – especially ideas which we had every intention of rejecting – without it being reported that they were about to become policy. Over the period of the committee's work, however, he began to realise that I was not the right-wing ogre he had believed me to be and, furthermore, that I actually knew a good deal about economic policy. We became allies in pushing the report through, but we were defeated on a project which we both strongly supported – a fibre optic cable network for Britain.

Another member of the committee was Gordon Brown. Gordon had already made his mark as possibly the brightest of the younger front benchers. He had made his name through being the recipient of a regular number of leaked documents from various parts of Whitehall, but he was also a formidable speaker and debater. He played, however, virtually no part in the work of my policy review committee. He attended only rarely, and spoke, as I recall, on only one occasion. Nevertheless, I somehow gained the impression that he was not fully supportive of the line that the committee was taking on various issues but that he either did not dare or did not know how to put a contrary view.

His unease, if that is truly what it was, was possibly supported by another, more regular attender of committee meetings. John Eatwell was a Cambridge economist who had become Neil's economic adviser. He attended committee meetings, not as a member but as an observer, and as a link between the committee and Neil's office.

John had come to Neil's notice as a result of a television programme he had done on the British economy, in which he had argued strongly for the importance of manufacturing industry and the need to put its interests before those of the financial establishment. This was very much in line with my own view, and I was therefore confident that John would support the general line I took in the committee. What I had not realised, however, was that John was in the course of changing his views, that he was becoming less convinced of the importance or efficacy of macro-economic policy.

The policy review took up a good deal of my time, not only in the work I put in directly on the report of my group, but also in the number of speeches I gave up and down the country trying to urge party members to participate in the review. There was a good deal of suspicion in the party about the review. Members felt that it was likely to become a means by which the leadership pushed through changes – or rather the abandonment of policy commitments – which they would wish to resist. I argued strongly that I saw the review as a means of engaging the party in a policy debate which was long overdue.

At the beginning of 1988, I had suffered another, slightly bizarre blow to my health. We had had Robin and Val Corbett to lunch just after the New Year and had just said goodbye to them when I suddenly found I was unable to stand up. I clutched the wall and lowered myself to the ground, whereupon I was violently sick. I remained like this, unable to get up and retching continuously, for the next couple of hours. Gill called the doctor, who summoned an ambulance.

By the time I was put in the ambulance, I was very weak from the constant retching and virtually unconscious. I was rushed into the Radcliffe Infirmary in Oxford. They did not know what to make of my condition and thought that perhaps I had an ulcer. It was not until the following morning that I was able to explain to them that it was something to do with my balance, that I was unable to stand up and that the retching was like a violent form of seasickness.

It turned out that I was the victim of a mystery virus which had attacked my inner ear and prevented the normal mechanism for establishing balance from operating. It took me a couple of weeks to recover my balance, and I would occasionally experience spells of dizziness for quite some time thereafter. I have always enjoyed robust health, in the sense of being full of energy and free from minor ailments, but – as Gill pointed out – when I did fall ill, I did it rather dramatically.

There was considerable speculation at about this time concerning the deputy leadership of the Labour Party. The possibility of a challenge to Roy Hattersley was widely touted and it was assumed that I would be a likely challenger. I was not very keen to do so, since I had never regarded the deputy leadership as much of a job. I consulted a number of friends, whose advice generally was that I should not bother. I quickly killed the speculation, and expressed my support for Roy. He was duly grateful.

One of those I consulted was Peter Mandelson, with whom I was still on very friendly terms. It was at about this time, however, that I began to detect some cooling in our relationship. This was, I think, due to a number of factors. Peter was a demanding friend, in that he expected a degree of attention and cosseting for which I had neither the time nor inclination. He was also possibly a little irritated at the plaudits I had received for the relative success of the 1987 campaign, and worked quite hard to establish his own very considerable (though rather different) role in the matter.

Peter was also beginning to believe his own myth, and to learn how easily manipulated the media were by someone prepared to use as ruthlessly as he did his particular combination of charm and threats. He increasingly saw himself, not without reason, it must be said, as the fixer of party affairs, and as Neil's mouthpiece on all matters of importance. He became rather contemptuous of most members of the Shadow Cabinet as he also began to see his own fortunes linked to those of the leading figures of his generation – like Gordon Brown and Tony Blair.

Domestically, Gill and I were in the throes of change in early 1988. We had decided that, much as we loved Brook House, it made no sense to have a large establishment in the country which we could hardly ever get to and which demanded much more by way of maintenance and upkeep than we could afford, while we spent most of the week sleeping on a sofabed in a one-bedroomed flat in London.

Accordingly, we sold Brook House. It was the peak of the boom in the property market, and we felt very well off. We bought a new town house in London, at Cherry Garden Pier in Bermondsey, and a smaller house in Gloucestershire, in the converted outbuildings of a country mansion, which we hoped to get to at weekends.

The London house was a dream come true for me. I had always wanted to live on the river, even though this was before I discovered that my forebears had been lock-keepers. I derived great pleasure from watching the Thames as it flowed past our sitting-room window.

My literary agent, Anne McDermid, negotiated a contract for me at this time with Graham Greene of Jonathan Cape. I agreed to write a book for him on my view of socialism, with the help of a young researcher named Charles Seaforth. He worked under my direction over the next few months, principally on the question of how employee share ownership schemes might work. I found myself committed once again to the onerous business of writing so many words each day in order to get the book finished.

The media continued to take a close interest in all that I did. When we moved into our new home, reporters and photographers were in attendance both as our household goods were being packed up for removal from Brook House and as they were being unloaded at Cherry Garden Pier. It is difficult to describe to those who have never experienced it just how intrusive it is to have one's private affairs subjected to scrutiny in this way. We were, after all, doing nothing different from what thousands of people do every day, yet the knowledge that the press were there in order to show us in an unfavourable light made us feel that moving house was somehow shameful.

I was kept very busy in the House by a succession of issues in the industrial field – the sale of Rover to British Aerospace, the demise of shipbuilding, the privatisation of the steel industry and the proposed sale of Girobank, among others. I continued to pursue my interest in macro-economic policy as well. I wrote a paper for Neil entitled 'Why we can't afford a blind spot on the exchange rate'. In it, I described the difficulties which so many Labour governments – under Ramsay MacDonald, Harold Wilson and Jim Callaghan – had suffered through allowing themselves to be hooked on the primacy of some monetary measure, and as a consequence finding themselves defending the financial establishment rather than their own electorate. I was becoming alarmed at how quickly the lessons of the early 1980s had been forgotten. The siren voices of those who urged that Labour must again give priority to showing itself to be 'responsible' were again being heard.

The final stages of the drafting of our policy review took up a great deal of time. Although a good deal of the preliminary work was done by Nigel Stanley, the final draft was my responsibility. We were reasonably content with the outcome, feeling that we had forged a draft policy which would actually work and achieve Labour's objectives in government, and which both the party and the country would find attractive. The final draft of the document to go to conference was approved by a meeting of the policy review group.

After this had happened, on the day that the document was due to go to the printers, I was asked to receive a small delegation. John Eatwell, Gordon Brown and Tony Blair turned up in my office to say that they felt that the document should not go forward in its present form. They objected in particular to what remained of any commitment to return privatised industries to 'some form of public ownership' and to the formula agreed for purchasing the 2 per cent shareholding in British Telecom which would give a Labour government a majority shareholding.

I was extremely irritated at this last-minute *démarche*. I was not clear what Tony was doing there, since he was not a member of the relevant committee. Gordon and John had had every chance to make their views known at meetings yet had chosen to say nothing. I explained to them that the draft had been agreed by everyone involved, particularly by the trade unions, who were ready to support it at conference, and that it was in any case too late now to change it. They left empty-handed, but no doubt, as subsequent events have demonstrated, unconvinced.

In June of 1988, I was asked to go to St James's Palace to meet Prince Charles and offer him some advice on his attempts to involve himself in inner cities policy. I spent about an hour with the Prince and we seemed to get on well. He struck me as charming and genuinely concerned to try to do something constructive without treading on people's toes. I saw him occasionally thereafter, particularly if he needed advice on the Labour Party's viewpoint of some political issue.

In the following month, I became involved in a curious incident which again demonstrated the nastiness of some sections of the press. It was the fortieth anniversary of the founding of the National Health Service and the Labour Party was naturally concerned to make the most of the occasion. Senior people were despatched on the appropriate day to various parts of the country to speak at meetings and generally to attract attention.

I was asked to go to Bath. I spent the day visiting local hospitals and talking to local NHS unions. I did a large number of interviews and concluded with a speech at a large public meeting in the evening, which meant that I had to miss the vote in the House at the end of a debate on the NHS held to mark the anniversary. I got home after midnight, feeling that I had done a reasonable day's work.

The *News of the World* on the following Sunday, however, carried my photograph with those of a couple of others above a story headlined 'Kinnock Carpets Boozers'. The story, from their political correspondent, reported that Neil was furious with some of his colleagues who had missed a crucial vote because they were out drinking on the terrace of the House of Commons.

Even if there had been a semblance of truth in the story, it revealed a great ignorance of the way Parliament works, since drinkers on the terrace have no difficulty in abandoning their drinks when the division bell rings. What had in fact happened, however, was that the correspondent had misinterpreted a speech Neil had made at the PLP that week in which he had berated colleagues for what he called 'terrace-itis' – the habit of depressing morale by telling each other over a drink how badly things were going. The *News of the World* had somehow got the wrong end of this stick, linked it to the fact that some prominent people had been absent for the NHS vote, and produced a badly garbled story which was gravely libellous.

I organised my colleagues, and we jointly sued the *News of the World*. The paper had not a leg to stand on. Typically, however, rather than acknowledge their mistake, offering an apology and perhaps a donation to charity, they tried to make matters worse. I was telephoned at one point by a puzzled party agent in Bath telling me that a journalist from the *News of the World* was going round trying to find out whether I had been drunk during my time in Bath. I took great pleasure in relieving the *News of the World* of a tidy sum in damages for myself and my colleagues.

We had a lovely family holiday in Tuscany that year. We rented half a farmhouse near Arezzo and had a wonderfully relaxing time. Our son Charles brought with him his girlfriend Angela, whom he had met at university, and who was clearly destined to become a permanent member of the family.

On our return, we plunged straight back into the maelstrom of meetings, interviews and constituency affairs, even though it was the long summer recess. It culminated in a hectic week at conference. I was re-elected to the NEC, and fulfilled a demanding schedule of speeches at many fringe meetings. A fortnight later, I was flattered to be asked to join the *Any Questions* panel for a programme in the House of Commons to celebrate the fortieth anniversary of the programme.

At the end of the year, Gill and I had a welcome chance to return to New Zealand. Our niece Karen was to be married, and we had at the same time been approached by a New Zealand television company to make a film about my New Zealand origins and connections. We managed to combine the two projects. Our old friend Linda McDougall, who knew New Zealand television well, flew out with us to produce the film. Our fee was our return fares, so that we could attend the wedding. My sister Ngaire and her husband Doug were able to travel round with us while we made the film. We had an excellent short break, and again enjoyed ourselves – and New Zealand – enormously.

Back in Britain, I worked hard over the New Year on my book. The political situation, from Labour's viewpoint, was dominated by constant media references to dissatisfaction with Neil's leadership. It suited the media very well to keep this story going, ensuring as it did that Labour remained on the back foot. The story would not have survived for long, however, if it had not been fuelled by constant sniping at Neil from within Labour's own ranks.

I frequently lunched with journalists. I noticed how often the moment would come, usually over coffee, when my host would lean forward and say confidentially, 'Now, tell me what you really think – he's not up to it, is he?' I knew from the way in which the question was put that the expected answer was in the affirmative; I also knew that these same journalists regularly lunched most of my senior Shadow Cabinet colleagues. I therefore deduced that they were used to having this sort of conversation.

My interlocutors were no doubt disappointed at my failure to play the expected part. I would give, as was my wont, an honest answer. I did not pretend that Neil was perfect but I would stoutly resist any suggestion that he was somehow a lightweight or not up to the job. Instead, I asserted that he continued to demonstrate amazing resolution and courage, and that he was achieving for the party things which probably no one else could have achieved.

I continue to believe that much of the media attack on Neil had little to do with his supposed intellectual or other deficiencies. It was for the most part good old-fashioned English snobbery on the part of an Oxbridge-educated media establishment which chose to cloak social elitism in a posture of supposed intellectual superiority.

One of my good friends over this period was Tom Sawyer, the highly influential trade union official who was one of Neil's closest confidants on the NEC. Tom was fiercely loyal to Neil, but even he was worried at times over Neil's state of mind and his capacity to stand the immense pressure under which the media attacks put him. I recall a long conversation with Tom at the beginning of 1989 on this subject. Tom would never have done anything to undermine Neil, but it was implicit in our conversation that, if anything happened to Neil (and I believe that there were moments when Tom feared that Neil might throw in his hand), I – as someone representing views quite close to Neil's own – should be ready to contest the leadership.

My own relationship with Neil remained cordial but it was not close. I generally offered him support in both the Shadow Cabinet and the NEC, but we rarely discussed policy, partly because we were drifting apart on the issues that mattered to me. I was becoming alarmed at the extent to which Neil was listening to people and responding to pressures from what I regarded as the old machine politics of the right – the very people who were doing so much to undermine him behind the scenes. I think there was also an element in Neil's thinking, perhaps subconscious, which realised the right's potential for damage and decided to try and buy their support.

I often said to friends at about this time that I felt that Neil and I and a few other brave souls were the only ones who had had the courage to beard the Militant ogre in its den. Now the right, which had been cowering behind us, suddenly looked over our shoulders and realised that the ogre was nothing but a tabby cat. We found ourselves trampled in the rush, as they surged forward to claim the space for themselves.

Neil and I were still sufficiently close, however, for him to ask me in January of 1989 to run the Euro-election campaign later that year. I agreed, out of loyalty to Neil and the party. I did not particularly want to do it, partly because it would be hard work for no very obvious personal reward (since I could not easily enhance my reputation as a campaign manager), but more importantly because my views diverged somewhat from the party's on the central issues of the campaign.

Neil no doubt calculated that not only would my expertise be valuable, but to tie me into the campaign would reduce the risk that one of his senior colleagues would be tempted to criticise the party's campaigning stance. In the event, I was able to resolve any potential division between myself and the party by focusing attention on the much more apparent and damaging divisions among the Conservatives.

The Tories ran the most inept campaign possible. There was open conflict between Margaret Thatcher (who could hardly conceal her boredom and distaste for the whole enterprise) and Ted Heath (who saw a chance to vent his spleen against his successor and give expression to his Euro-zealotry at the same time). From Labour's viewpoint, it was merely a matter of keeping the media focus firmly fixed on this conflict, and ensuring that each day there was some slight development to keep the journalists interested. The Tories co-operated fully in this strategy.

My diary over this period shows a hectic schedule of travelling all over the country to meetings, making speeches and responding to statements in the House, meetings on the policy review, writing articles and continuing with my book, campaigning in the Euro-campaign, doing press conferences and interviews, as well as the usual workload of constituency casework. In April, I was again re-selected by my constituency party.

From time to time, I had the chance to meet visiting politicians. I recall a breakfast meeting with Bob Hawke, then prime minister of Australia, and, on another occasion, I had tea in the House with Helen Clark, then a minister in the New Zealand Labour government and now party leader.

The revised policy review was also a major preoccupation. The 1988 document, *Meet the Challenge, Make the Change*, had been approved by conference, and the idea was that it should be further developed in the succeeding year. In reality little further work was done by way of policy development; mostly, we re-drafted and simplified. In the process, some of the more specific policy commitments were quietly dropped, amidst protestations that nothing of substance was being lost. Party suspicions were, however, mounting, and the divergence of views between leadership and activists continued to widen.

Neil was fighting a number of battles simultaneously over this period. He was now totally dominant in the National Executive. His only opponents were Tony Benn and Dennis Skinner, who were so consistent in their opposition to everything which emanated from the leadership that they lost all credibility. It was always clear to me, in any case, that they had given up any idea of influencing the course of events in the National Executive and were playing exclusively to a gallery outside, a gallery which was itself shrinking in size and influence.

Neil was nevertheless gradually losing the sympathy of ordinary party activists. There was a great deal of residual respect and affection for him from those who had elected him to the leadership in the hope that he would prove to be a great radical leader. But there was a growing disillusionment and apathy as regards the direction in which the policy review and other changes were taking the party. By and large, the party accepted that the overriding priority was to gain power and they were prepared to sacrifice much of their hopes and ideals to this end; however, while they were prepared to do it, they could not pretend to be either excited or moved by it.

At the same time, Neil was fighting a continuing, though largely undeclared battle against the right wing in the Shadow Cabinet.

Throughout the whole time that I served in the Shadow Cabinet, the most important single fact about it, other than Neil's leadership, was the strength and cohesion of the central grouping of right-wing, more senior members.

This group formed around Roy Hattersley and John Smith, with strong support from people like Jack Cunningham and Gerald Kaufman. The group could also rely on the support of lesser figures such as Donald Dewar and Barry Jones. The group did not operate as a cabal in any overt way. It did not need to. The mere fact of its existence gave it an influence over the work of the Shadow Cabinet and the direction of the party which guaranteed that the context in which Neil operated was constantly exerting pressure on him to take a less radical line.

The group was remarkably cohesive and – with the exception of Gerald, who had campaigned for a No vote in the 1975 referendum – largely identified itself by its allegiance to the European cause. Indeed, many of its members had voted against the Labour whip in order to carry the European legislation through in 1972. This common experience of shared tribulations and of being blooded in the same battle gave members of the group, I believe, a sort of confidence in each other which endured and did not need to be constantly reaffirmed. It also explained their almost religious convictions on the European issue and their resistance to anyone who did not share the True Faith. Europe was, after all, the altar on which they had made their initial sacrifices.

Those outside the group lacked any such cohesion. People like Robin Cook, John Prescott, Michael Meacher and myself did not share enough unity of purpose to make ourselves effective as a counter-influence on Neil. This was largely because in my experience Robin and John in particular were very ambitious for themselves and would not willingly have subordinated their own personal ambitions to the wider interest, as the right was willing to do, for instance, in support of John Smith.

But it was also partly because those who were broadly on the left – and this included less influential figures at that time like Jack Straw and Frank Dobson – saw their main purpose as providing Neil with loyal support. Neil was still seen by them as 'one of us'. As Neil himself, whether through conviction or realpolitik, moved more and more rightwards, it was difficult for the left grouping, which defined itself largely in terms of its loyalty to Neil – and in which I definitely included myself – to know how to respond.

It would be wrong to give the impression that anything like hostility existed between the two factions. The Shadow Cabinet's business was usually conducted very amicably, without any overt demonstration of underlying disagreements. This co-operative atmosphere was created, however, on a basis which was very congenial to the right – the tacit concession that, if it came to the crunch, its views would prevail – probably with Neil's support. The left, inhibited by its perceived duty to support the leadership, preferred to blur its fundamental weakness rather than provoke an open conflict which would further weaken both its own position and the leadership.

The Shadow Cabinet, in any case, as a manifestation of the wish to avoid conflict, very rarely discussed policy. Only occasionally did an issue of substance arise. One such instance was at a meeting of the economic committee of the Shadow Cabinet which took place on 27 June 1988. By this time, it was clear that powerful figures in the Shadow Cabinet and in Neil's office were keen to change the party's policy on the Exchange Rate Mechanism.

John Eatwell, in particular, but with strong support from John Smith and Gordon Brown, was convinced that the party lacked credibility on counter-inflationary policy. What he wanted to do, in effect, was to reassure the City and other critics that they need have no fears about inflation under a Labour government since monetary policy would no longer be under the control of government but would be contracted out to an independent mechanism.

This was the issue which was raised at the meeting of the economic committee, a body which met only occasionally and had a somewhat ill-defined membership. I had been alerted to what was in the wind and made a particular point of attending. I spoke powerfully against any change of policy. I again warned that we were in danger of repeating the mistakes made by so many of our predecessors. If we were to commit ourselves to the ERM, we would not be waiting for the City to shackle us. We would in effect be offering up our wrists in advance for the application of the handcuffs.

I carried the day. No one dared really take me on in argument since, I assume, they realised they they would not get the better of it. The only person capable of sustaining the contrary view to mine was John Eatwell and, as an adviser rather than member of the Shadow Cabinet, he was unable to speak. Neil, who stayed above the argument, listened carefully and summed up by acknowledging that no case for changing our policy had been made.

It was, however, a pyrrhic victory for me. I was told that Sam Brittan, the economics columnist for the *Financial Times*, had recently spoken to the PLP committee on economic affairs and had recommended that I be 'put on a slow boat to China' while Labour brought about a change in policy and announced its support for ERM membership. John Eatwell and others must have been listening carefully to his advice, as I was shortly to discover.

These policy differences surfaced only occasionally, but there were rather more frequent expressions of concern about another matter. Some members of the Shadow Cabinet had begun to feel that their positions were being undermined by what they assumed were behind-the-scenes briefings of the press by Peter Mandelson. John Prescott, Robin Cook and Michael Meacher in particular all felt that from time to time their stock would mysteriously plunge as a spate of unfavourable references and stories appeared in the press.

There seemed to me to be little doubt that the source of these stories was Peter Mandelson, who had, by this time, achieved a position of considerable influence with the media by virtue of his ruthless control over access to Labour Party news stories. He seemed able to punish those journalists who refused to do as they were told by, in effect, squeezing them out, while at the same time seeming to reward the more compliant by leaking stories to them. The Sunday press, especially, carried political stories which usually emanated from Peter Mandelson.

One of the main reasons for Peter's influence was that it was widely believed that he acted with Neil's authority in planting stories, even those which were unfavourable to Neil's Shadow Cabinet colleagues. This belief was almost certainly justified in most cases, if Neil's occasional scathing comments to me about our colleagues were anything to go by. I always had the uncomfortable feeling that he might talk about me in similar terms to others.

The relationship between Neil and Peter served them both well. Neil was convinced of Peter's personal loyalty and would often say to critics that anything Peter did was in the best interests of the party (for which, read Neil); Peter's power was immensely inflated by Neil's protection. Neil in turn benefited from the services of a lieutenant with no constituency or party colleagues to please.

My own fortunes took a tumble in the September of 1989. Ann Taylor had been handling the water privatisation measure in committee for us. The share flotation was to take place once the bill became law. She was anxious to deter potential investors, and to exploit the considerable public disquiet at the privatisation of what was seen as a public asset *par excellence*. Although the water industry was not strictly my field of responsibility in parliamentary terms, I had dealt with it in the policy review. Ann suggested that I might write a piece for the *Financial Times* in which I set out Labour's policy on the issue.

I agreed and, in consultation with Ann, wrote a piece saying that a Labour government would regard a privatised water industry as owing its first responsibility to investment in a safe and efficient industry, and secondly, to maintaining fair prices to consumers. Only once these two needs had been met would there be any room for private dividends. I refrained from saying anything about returning the industry to public ownership, since it was clear that this commitment was being quietly dropped.

The article accurately reflected, as far as I knew, the party's policy on the matter and was certainly in line with Ann Taylor's views. It attracted little comment and I thought no more about it. A week or so later, however, I was being interviewed by Jonathan Dimbleby for *On the Record*, when I was asked again about the issue. I repeated, as far as

I was aware, what I had said in the *Financial Times* article. I think, in retrospect, that I may have expressed myself a little more forcefully than in the article and I may have given the impression that, because of the priority to be given to investment and holding consumer prices at a fair level, no dividends at all would be payable.

To my surprise, that interview was headline news on the television news programmes. I was even more surprised when my comments were repudiated by Neil the following day. This was signal enough for the media that I was fair game. I received a pretty bad press, culminating in an article in the *Sunday Times* by Robert Harris which suggested that I was a sort of Jekyll and Hyde figure. It was published complete with graphic drawings showing my face being transfigured under the influence of the full moon!

I could have understood the furore if I had, as a senior Shadow Cabinet member, announced that our policy was to take the water industry back into public ownership, but I was certainly taken aback at the vehemence of the reaction to a statement which would have been popular in many quarters and which was in any case, I thought, in line with party policy.

At about the same time, although I do not have a precise date for it, the party announced a renunciation of its policy on unilateral nuclear disarmament. I had been interviewed on general matters during the course of the day in which the change was announced. In answer to a question, I had expressed the view that if nuclear weapons were to be retained, it was nevertheless inconceivable that a Labour prime minister would actually press the nuclear button, and that the main purpose of keeping the weapons was therefore to use them as a negotiating counter. This view, too, was rapidly disowned by the party's press office.

I was also at odds with my colleagues over another issue of economic policy. The Lawson boom had come to a juddering halt, interest rates were rising to penal levels, unemployment and business failures were mounting fast, and many people were unable to make their mortgage repayments, with the consequence that they were losing their homes. I suggested that a Labour government, rather than rely exclusively on interest rates control to rein back on a credit boom which had got out of hand, would also wish to look at restricting the general level of lending by banks and other institutions in conditions where that lending threatened to become excessive. This view, too, was rejected as being too frightening for the voters.

These differences, and the bad press which I continued to receive, all suggested that I would do rather badly in the Shadow Cabinet elections which were to take place at the beginning of November. I also became aware, however, that a campaign was being orchestrated against me in some quarters. Frank Dobson, who was an assiduous campaigner for Shadow Cabinet votes, phoned me as the date approached to assure me that, as he put it, he had nothing to do with the bad-mouthing of me that was going on and, on that basis, did he have my vote for his own candidature? I assured him of my vote and thanked him for the information.

It did not come, therefore, as a complete surprise when my vote slumped, although I was still comfortably elected to the Shadow Cabinet. Neil asked to see me that afternoon. He came straight to the point and said that he would like to offer me something else. He asked me whether I would again become campaigns co-ordinator. I turned him down without a moment's hesitation. I had no wish to retrace my steps. I could gain nothing by confirming that I could do that job well. I felt that I had been badly treated in the trade and industry job, in the sense that I had not been given the support needed, and I wanted to show that I could handle a proper departmental brief.

I had foreseen that Neil would wish to move me, and had come prepared. I suggested that the only job I would move to would be Environment. Neil leapt at the suggestion and it was agreed on the spot. It was a neat solution to several of Neil's problems. Jack Cunningham had been at Environment for a long time and his usefulness there was declining. After speaking to me, Neil offered Jack the campaigns job, which he was delighted to accept. Jack never knew, I think, that he was second choice.

I suggested to Neil, and he agreed, that I should remain a member of the economics committee of the Shadow Cabinet. This was of little importance, however. I had been removed from an economic portfolio, and could no longer prevent the party from changing its position over the ERM. I was replaced as Shadow trade and industry secretary by Gordon Brown who, with John Smith, proceeded to bring about that change. It seemed to me that those who could not win the argument had nevertheless contrived to have me removed from a position of influence.

ELEVEN

The Parting of the Ways
1990–92

I TACKLED MY NEW responsibilities with enthusiasm. I was genuinely interested in and sympathetic to local government, I had had a long-term concern for housing, the poll tax was clearly the most pressing political issue of the day, and I was keen to make my own contribution to the increasingly important debate over the need to protect and conserve the environment.

I took with me to my new job my two research assistants. Nigel Stanley was an enthusiast on environmental matters and was invaluable to me in developing policy in this area, as well as in the more general political field in which he was so much at home. Henry Neuberger, who had once been economic adviser to both Michael Foot and Neil Kinnock, had joined me while I was doing the trade and industry job. Now that my responsibilities were going to be for Environment, it was not immediately clear what Henry would do for me, but he was a good and original thinker about all sorts of issues and I always found him useful to bounce ideas off.

The problem of paying their two salaries was a constant headache. In one year, I found myself paying a good chunk of one salary out of my own pocket. I was eventually able, however, to stabilise the position, thanks to the support I received from the National Communications Union.

My new front bench team included Ann Taylor, who dealt with environmental matters, Clive Soley, who was responsible for housing policy, and David Blunkett, who was a specialist in local government.

I had known Ann and Clive for some time and found them congenial colleagues. David, however, was someone I knew only slightly. He had had some problems while doing the same job for Jack Cunningham and I was a little apprehensive as to how we might get on.

I rapidly discovered, however, that David was an admirable colleague, provided that he was treated well and taken into one's confidence. His blindness gave him a special sensitivity which was both a strength and a weakness. He had a unique insight at times and a suppleness of mind which was a great advantage. He needed, however, constant reassurance that nothing was happening without his knowledge. We established an excellent relationship of mutual trust – something which stood us in good stead in the difficult times to come.

Within a couple of days of my appointment I was plunged straight into the arcane world of local government finance when the annual statement was made on the subject in the House by Chris Patten, then Environment Secretary. I was well briefed, in the few minutes in which one sees the statement before it is made, and acquitted myself pretty well. I then embarked on a steep learning curve and made myself an expert in pretty quick time.

My political schedule remained as hectic as ever, but was mercifully interrupted by a further holiday in New Zealand over the Christmas period. Our son Charles had graduated in June of 1988 and had turned 21 later that year. We gave him as a joint graduation and 21st birthday present a return fare to New Zealand. He had spent six months in New Zealand, paying his own way and working at all sorts of casual jobs to support himself. We decided that we would fly out to join him for Christmas and to have a holiday ourselves with my sister and her family. We enjoyed ourselves thoroughly and our ties to New Zealand were further strengthened.

The new Shadow Cabinet and National Executive spent some time debating questions of strategy. It was becoming clear that there were two broad approaches to strategy: one, which might be described as 'safety first', and a second, which called for a bolder approach.

The first approach reflected the view that the Tories were unpopular and that the only ground on which they could survive would be that the voters feared Labour even more than they disliked the Tories. The correct strategy was therefore to eliminate anything from the Labour programme which might give the electorate cause for concern, while at the same time keeping the focus firmly fixed on Tory failings.

The second view was that the Tories could not be relied upon to go on being unpopular, that it was very unlikely we would be allowed to avoid awkward questions about our own plans and that it was therefore better to be more positive about what we stood for, so that the voters would have positive as well as negative reasons for voting Labour. We would give ourselves the opportunity to get our message across clearly rather than leave it up to the Tories to distort it.

John Smith was usually reckoned to be the prime exponent of the 'safety first' strategy. Roy Hattersley and I were seen as the leading figures in the second camp. It would be wrong to give the impression that the issue was debated at any length, and it is hard to point to many practical questions which were directly influenced by it. But there was a genuine division of opinion which surfaced from time to time and which underlay some of the tension which inevitably occurs when a group of highly motivated people are engaged in a great enterprise.

Neil usually avoided taking sides – at least overtly. It is probably fair to say that his heart was with the second group but he was persuaded by the first group that it was smart politics to be cautious. Peter Mandelson was certainly in the first group. His influence was always on the side of caution and against those who, in his view, were inclined to 'take risks'.

The rest of the Shadow Cabinet divided on predictable lines. The right wing, with the exception of Roy Hattersley, supported the John Smith line. The left, in a typically less coherent fashion, usually pressed for greater and more positive commitment. As always on issues of this sort, there was an uncommitted range of opinion in the middle which took its cue from the leader and in this case was sensitive to Neil's increasing caution as the election approached.

It was becoming clear to me over this period that Peter Mandelson was working to his own agenda – on what I and others began to call the 'Mandelson Project'. The 'project' was to ensure that Peter's protégés – Gordon Brown as the prime contender, but with Tony Blair as a fall-back – should succeed to the leadership.

Peter was undoubtedly loyal to Neil but I do not think Neil realised that he was merely a player in the Mandelson strategy. It was important to the strategy that Neil should stay in place and, if possible, win the election. This was because Neil tacitly (or perhaps even explicitly) understood that this younger generation of possible successors would be content to wait their turn. They would support him in the interim, protect him against other possible challengers, in the hope that by the time he was replaced it would be too late for their rivals and the succession would be more or less automatic. He, in turn, could promote them safely.

It was assumed that John Smith would be too old by the time Neil gave up. The other threat to the strategy came from people like me. Here, the assumption was that, although I was also older than Neil, I was seen as a sufficiently fresh face to be a credible contender if Neil were to step down for any reason. To a lesser degree, others like Robin Cook and John Prescott were also seen as possible threats. In my opinion, a good deal of the Mandelson strategy therefore concentrated on clearing the way for the eventual succession by undermining as much as possible the credibility of other possible contenders. If this activity were ever challenged, it could always be justified to the leader in terms of loyalty to his cause.

As a member of the Shadow Cabinet I realised that this 'playing of favourites' by the party's communications director caused a great deal of unhappiness, particularly amongst those who felt themselves to be its victims. It probably did more to undermine Shadow Cabinet unity and to distract major players from the job in hand than any other factor.

Some of these underlying factors came into play in the great political issue in which I found myself involved as the new Shadow Environment Secretary. Mrs Thatcher's baby, the poll tax, was becoming extremely unpopular. The rising tide of public concern and outright opposition to the poll tax was of course a heaven-sent opportunity for Labour, but it was not without its problems for us as well.

The party was still engaged in a bitter struggle to rid itself of the Militant parasite. Militant saw the poll tax as a great chance to embarrass the party leadership and to point up the attractions of its own more simplistic approach to politics. They agitated for direct action and a campaign to refuse to pay, oblivious to the problems this would cause for local authorities or for vulnerable people who might find themselves in court. They were also, of course, unconcerned about the propaganda weapon such action would hand to the Tories.

It was clearly much more sensible to keep the pressure on the Tories by allowing popular anger to find its own expression. The Government was undoubtedly greatly damaged by the sight of middle-class demonstrators in the south of England protesting against Mrs Thatcher's favourite measure.

It became clear to me, however, that we could not expect to get through to the next election without answering questions about our own plans for local government finance. I increasingly recognised that, in every one of the many interviews on the iniquities of the poll tax which I did, I would have an easy time dwelling on the poll tax, but that the interviewer would inevitably ask, 'And what would Labour do?' The answer that we were thinking about it lacked something in persuasiveness and merely spurred the interviewer to press me further.

Technically, the answer was that the party had committed itself to an unwieldy combination tax – part property tax and part local income tax – which everyone recognised would terrify the voters and would be unworkable. Neil had specifically asked me, when it was agreed that I should do the Environment job, to disown this inheritance and to find a better alternative.

I reached the view that we should move without delay to deny interviewers and the Tories their favourite riposte about our lack of an alternative. My preparatory work in this direction ran into a great deal of opposition, however, particularly from the party's press officers, who were convinced that we would simply distract attention from the Tories' difficulties.

GOODBYE TO ALL THAT

I was equally convinced that, if we failed to say anything, the question of what we would do by way of local government taxation would become a big issue in the next election campaign. The Tories and the media would hound us mercilessly and would convince the electorate that whatever we had to hide would be much worse than anything the Government may have done. Much better to get our ideas out in the open in good time, so that we could explain them properly, correct Tory misrepresentations, defuse the issue in the minds of the voters, and keep attention focused on the poll tax.

I was to speak at the party's local government conference in Cardiff in early February 1990. I proposed to set out the principles on which we would devise our poll tax alternative. However, my plans to hold a press conference on this issue were very nearly sabotaged by Peter Mandelson and his office.

I remember being asked in the conference hotel by Philip Stephen, the political correspondent for the *Financial Times*, why I thought Peter Mandelson was 'out to get me'. I expressed surprise, quite genuinely, that this was Philip's perception. He in turn seemed surprised that I did not know that this was the case.

A week later, I spoke briefly to Neil about my concern at the press treatment of our preparations of a poll tax alternative. I complained particularly about a piece in the *Daily Mirror* written by Alastair Campbell, who was the well known recipient of direct briefings from Peter Mandelson, usually, it was assumed, on Neil's instructions.

Neil promised action and shortly afterwards I was invited to lunch by Alastair. I had no further reason to complain of my treatment by Alastair after that meeting, but the sustained sniping in other parts of the press continued.

The next few months were as busy as ever. The usual round of engagements continued without let-up, but there was the huge additional burden of working through our plans for local government finance. I had decided that we should adopt a phased approach, promising in effect to replace the poll tax as quickly as possible by returning immediately to the tried and tested rates system, but moving quickly to reform the rates by instituting a new and fair revaluation of property and by relating the rebates system more closely to the ability to pay.

In the course of working our way through to these conclusions, however, we naturally considered a number of different options. Many of these, such as a 'floor tax' – a property tax based exclusively on the size of a property – were considered only to be immediately rejected. Each such idea was faithfully reported by the press as being the proposal which Labour would adopt. It took a great deal of time and effort to persuade the media that we were going through a genuine process of inquiry and consultation, and that the mere fact that an idea was suggested did not mean that it was going to be adopted.

My own role in this was bedevilled by constant reports that John Smith and I were at odds over the issue and that John was pressing upon me a coherent plan of reform which was contrary to my own ideas but to which I was being forced to yield. I still have no idea of where these reports came from. The truth was that John had no ideas at all on the subject and never made any proposals. I was particularly irritated by a leading article in *The Times*, headed 'Sensible Mr Smith', which congratulated John on his wisdom in persuading me to abandon the notion of a property revaluation based on capital values. The decision to abandon the commitment to a capital values basis for revaluation, which I had inherited from Jack Cunningham, was mine and mine alone.

The only issue on which John and I disagreed was my belief that the rates system, while infinitely preferable to the poll tax, was nevertheless a pretty crude reflection of people's ability to pay, and that to remedy this through an extension of the rebates system threatened to impoverish large numbers of people by subjecting them to what was in effect a means test. I therefore wanted to show that, as a further stage in reforming the rates, we wished to consider an automatic adjustment of liability to rates, calculated according to taxable income revealed by income tax returns. The Inland Revenue assured me that, with their new computerisation, this could be done without difficulty.

David Blunkett and I were keen on this idea and thought we should indicate that this was where we wished to go. We felt that it would meet the most obvious attack that was made on the rates – the fact that people like widows on low incomes could find themselves saddled with large rates bills on the strength of the value of the properties they lived in. John Smith and others, however, were opposed to the idea, fearing that it would frighten voters in some way, and would throw up problems of confidentiality and complexity.

In the event, we compromised, by retaining the idea in a general sense and as a rather distant ambition, but nevertheless making it clear that we were not proposing a simple return to the rates as we knew them. We agreed to call our proposed local government tax 'Fair Rates' to signal both its similarity to the old rates system and the fact that it was an improved and fairer version. As our subsequent experience showed, bringing forward our proposals at that time and in that form was successful in defusing the endless questions and counter-attacks about our alternative to the poll tax, and we were able to concentrate attention on the Tories' difficulties.

The whole episode involved great stress and intensive effort, however, which was not helped by the endless intrigue and speculation which went on while we were trying to bring our plans to fruition. Peter Mandelson was briefing the press regularly (there was intense media interest in our plans) and they were clearly being given an account which suggested that my views were likely to be rejected by my colleagues.

When this turned out not to be the case, Peter reacted by trying to prevent me from talking to the press about our conclusions. He presumably feared that I would be able to demonstrate that the briefings they had been given over the previous few months were simply wrong. When we reached agreement in the Shadow Cabinet on the proposals, I offered to brief the press on what we had come up with. Peter insisted, with Neil's agreement, on handling the briefing himself. I still don't know what he told them.

When the proposals were finally agreed by the National Executive, I assumed that, in line with usual practice, we should hold a full-scale press conference to launch 'Fair Rates'. (This was at a time when we held a press conference to announce that the leader had got up in the morning.) Peter first resisted this idea, and then reluctantly agreed. The press conference, however, flopped because most of the journalists had unaccountably failed to hear about it.

The *Six o'Clock News* that day carried a tendentious and misleading account of what we had agreed. I rang the news editor and managed to get a slightly more accurate version on to the *Nine o'Clock News*. He in turn phoned me the following day to say that his journalists, in filing their story for the *Six o'Clock News*, had reflected the briefing they had received from the party's press office. I was furious. I went to see Neil to complain that the launch of an important policy initiative had been undermined. I also offered proof that party officials were working against the party's interests. Neil appeared to be concerned and promised to take the matter up with Peter Mandelson. I heard no more about it.

Relations between me and Peter remained cordial on the surface but I was increasingly aware that he was working against me behind the scenes. On another occasion, a friend of mine at Walworth House overheard Colin Byrne, the party's deputy communications director, who was generally assumed always to do Peter's bidding, 'bad-mouthing' me (his word) to a journalist over the telephone. He was sufficiently concerned to report the matter to me and to authorise me to use his name in raising the matter with Neil. Neil, however, was more concerned to know the identity of my informant than in registering the substance of my complaint.

The general atmosphere, so far as matters of this sort were concerned, is illustrated by another incident. Neil asked to see me. When I arrived in his office, he asked me if I knew the novelist and screenwriter Hanif Kureishi. I was slightly surprised but replied that I knew who he was but did not think I had ever met him. Neil seemed to accept this and then explained that it had been reported that a Shadow Cabinet member had been heard to opine that Neil was 'no good on television'. Inquiries had been made, the report had been traced to Hanif Kureishi, and he had in turn apparently said that he had heard the comment from me. This was a ridiculous assertion, I thought, which not only displayed Neil's increasing paranoia but also that the walls were whispering all sorts of nonsense to him.

This atmosphere of mutual suspicion was very much encouraged, I believe, by the activities of Peter Mandelson, but it was also a reflection of the fact that people held their positions in the Shadow Cabinet only by virtue of annual elections by the PLP. For some of my colleagues, remaining in the Shadow Cabinet became the most important political aim. So long as they retained their Shadow Cabinet seats, its real long-term purpose, to gain and exercise power for political purposes, seemed to matter little.

The system engendered a year-long and therefore perpetual campaign for the votes of parliamentary colleagues. It also meant a constant preoccupation, not only with one's own fortunes but with those of one's colleagues. It was hardly conducive to team spirit or to constructive policy-making.

Despite all these pressures, the Shadow Cabinet functioned reasonably well on a day-to-day level. Although a general election was only a distant prospect, the imperative of presenting a united front suppressed any open expression of conflict or disagreement. Anyone who rocked the boat in any way would have been roundly condemned by his or her colleagues.

It would also be wrong to give the impression that I was constantly embattled. A great deal of my time was spent on activities – press conferences, meetings, interviews and so on – which were widely seen as helpful, sometimes essential, to the party's cause. I remained, I believe, one of the party's most effective campaigners and spokespeople.

I was constantly involved in a range of issues apart from the poll tax. The environment was a matter of great political interest, and global warming in particular attracted a great deal of attention. With Nigel Stanley and the help of the voluntary bodies, I developed a comprehensive policy for the party on these issues.

I was also very much involved in the whole range of local government issues. Local government was under severe attack from a Thatcher government which regarded it as an outpost of insurrection and was determined to reduce its resources, powers and independence. I spent a good deal of time talking to local government officials in various forums and defending their interests, on issues like charge-capping, in Parliament.

The question of some form of city-wide administration for London, following the abolition of the GLC, also attracted my support. In April of 1990, we launched our local government election campaign in London by taking a boat on the river with a number of London celebrities in order to publicise our plans for a new London-wide authority. The campaign on this issue remained one of my preoccupations over the next few years.

In mid-year, the party selected a new communications director. Peter Mandelson had decided to seek a parliamentary seat. Neil was furious, as he understood that he had been promised by all senior officials that they would stay in post until the next election. I remember Charles Clarke telling me that, for the first time, Neil's relations with Peter deteriorated sharply over this issue.

The question of Peter's successor was hotly debated. Those on the NEC who felt that they had been badly treated by Peter were very keen to ensure that the new appointee would be more even-handed. They were therefore reluctant to endorse Neil's favourite, the deputy communications director Colin Byrne, who was seen as very much Peter's man.

In the event, an outside candidate was the comfortable winner. John Underwood had had wide media experience, was personally very likeable, and interviewed extremely well. Unfortunately for John, his appointment was a poisoned chalice. He never enjoyed Neil's confidence, and he was constantly undermined by Peter Mandelson and Colin Byrne, who stayed on for a time as deputy. Eventually he was forced to resign.

In July of 1990, the Shadow Cabinet was visited by Nelson Mandela. It was a great privilege to meet in person such a legendary figure, one of the few people I can bring to mind for whom unreserved respect and admiration are entirely appropriate.

Meanwhile, my frenetic activity on issues within my brief did not distract me from my long-term preoccupation with economic affairs. The development of our policy on the economy and Europe occasionally surfaced at the NEC and the Shadow Cabinet. I was always in a minority in urging caution on the party in its growing belief that our economic salvation lay in handing over the powers of policy-making to Brussels.

By this time, Neil had become convinced that we must join the ERM. He was helped to this conclusion by the difficulties in the Tory party over the same issue. It was almost as though he believed that if Mrs Thatcher was against our membership, it must be a good thing.

He was encouraged in this direction by the new economic team of John Smith and Gordon Brown. They had immediately set about changing the party's policy on the issue. I was powerless to stop them. I remember Gordon Brown addressing the PLP on the great advantages of joining the ERM, using arguments which I knew to be erroneous. He suggested, for example, that by fixing the parity within the ERM, we would somehow be applying a form of socialist planning of the economy, rather than leaving such an important issue to the mercies of market forces. The party responded warmly to the notion that the speculators would be disarmed. He, and they, seemed unaware of the fact that the only thing which gave speculators their chance was if governments were foolish enough to defend a parity which was seen by traders to be out of line with a currency's real value.

The whole debate about the ERM, in every party, was bedevilled by an astonishing ignorance of economic history. People like John Major and Gordon Brown truly believed, I think, that the ERM was a new and magic device which would somehow insulate their decisions about the currency against reality. They could not see that the ERM was in the end no different in its essentials – and its probable outcome – from any other attempt to use the reserves of one or more countries in order to defy the market.

Because I was no longer in the economic team, I was unable to express a view publicly on these issues. The rules of collective responsibility meant that I could express a dissenting view in public on something as important as this only from outside the Shadow Cabinet.

I was therefore obliged to sit silently in the PLP while Gordon secured the agreement of his largely ignorant colleagues to a step which I knew would be disastrous from every point of view.

I suppose that I had the option of resigning from the Shadow Cabinet and speaking up at that point. I had decided, however, that a Labour victory was the most important goal. A public break with my colleagues would not have persuaded them, or anyone else, that I was right and they were wrong. It would merely have given our opponents the chance to exploit our disunity.

I also felt that the real crunch would come, not in opposition, but in government. I foresaw that, within a few weeks of taking office, Neil would be faced with a sterling crisis, as Harold Wilson had before him, in which he would have to decide which to defend, the pound or his voters' interests. I wanted to keep my powder dry until that point.

I was not confident that I could win the argument, or at least win enough support, to be able to prevail at that point, but it would be at least worth a major effort. I was in any case genuinely undecided as to Neil's true view. I knew that he was persuaded of the case for joining the ERM as a pre-election stratagem, but he assured me in private that he had no intention of being impaled on the hook of defending an indefensible parity. There seemed to me therefore to be everything to play for, even though I suspect that Neil may have been saying different things to others.

My inability to speak publicly on these issues eventually of course meant that there was little point in continually harping on the same themes in the privacy of the Shadow Cabinet. There is a limit to how often one can irritate one's colleagues by fighting over and over again the same losing battles. My views were well known, and the issues were no longer within my own portfolio of responsibilities. On important occasions, however, such as when the Shadow Cabinet drafted policy statements, I would speak up and at least influence the drafting so as to avoid unnecessary excesses.

I was at odds with Neil over one or two other issues as well. The most important of these was defence. It was by now clear that the Soviet threat was rapidly diminishing and even the Tories were talking about the possibility of scaling down our defence spending. It seemed to me ridiculous that we should allow ourselves to be outflanked by the Tories on this issue, yet, because of fears that the voters felt that we were soft on defence, Neil was determined that we should not be seen to commit ourselves to a lower level of defence spending. I and others who normally supported him in the NEC voted against him on this issue. We lost narrowly, but conference that year endorsed our view. Neil responded by making it clear that he would pay no attention to conference, something which in previous years he would never have dared to do.

My vote in the Shadow Cabinet that year held up reasonably well, but I was nevertheless the victim of other factors. Ann Taylor was elected to the Shadow Cabinet for the first time. The obvious vacancy that needed to be filled was defence – Martin O'Neill had been doing the job but from outside the Shadow Cabinet – but Neil was reluctant to give that particular job to Ann. There seemed nowhere else for her to go, so Neil proposed that she should continue to do what she had been doing – taking responsibility for green issues – but this time inside the Shadow Cabinet and as head of her own team rather than as part of mine.

Neither Ann nor I was happy with this arrangement but we agreed to try to make it work. It was seen as some sort of demotion for me, and it certainly reflected my diminished value to Neil.

These Labour Party concerns dwindled into insignificance, however, by comparison to the cataclysms which beset the Tory Party. Mrs Thatcher had lost the argument over the ERM, Geoffrey Howe had made his famous speech from the back benches, and Michael Heseltine had launched his challenge for the leadership. Gill and I were driving through the gates of our Norman Shaw office building at 9.30 on the morning of 22 November 1990 when we heard the staggering news on our car radio that Mrs Thatcher had resigned. I wound down the window of my car and shouted the news to the policeman on duty.

I was pretty much incredulous as the Tory Party proceeded to elect John Major as their new leader. My first recollection of John Major was of an evening several years earlier when I had been waiting to wind up a debate and the opposition whip had approached me to see how much time I wanted. I remember thinking that the rather grey figure whom I noticed then for the first time seemed pleasant enough, but was probably rather dim. When he had surfaced in the Cabinet, first as Chief Secretary, then briefly and unconvincingly as Foreign Secretary and finally as Chancellor, he had seemed to do little to suggest that he was the stuff of which party leaders are made.

From my own viewpoint, the immediate consequence of the change at the Tory top was the return of Michael Heseltine to the Cabinet as the defeated contestant and as my new opponent at Environment. Heseltine had made it clear that he would abandon the poll tax and had forced the other candidates, including Major, to agree.

No one in the Tory Party, though, least of all Heseltine, had a clue how they were going to extricate themselves from the poll tax nor what they would replace it with. The matter was to be debated on 3 December. The debate was a great occasion, not only because of the intrinsic importance of the issue, but because it marked the return of Michael Heseltine to the parliamentary arena proper.

It is hard for those who have never experienced it to understand what it is like to speak from the despatch box in a debate which has been built up as a great parliamentary occasion and which engages the passions of the opposing sides. The chamber is full to overflowing. The atmosphere is heightened by tension and excitement. Every tiny incident is magnified and amplified.

The peculiar nature of the occasion is most apparent, naturally enough, to the main protagonists. On most occasions when one is required to speak, there is at least the assurance that the audience one is addressing is mildly interested in what one has to say. This is not the case in the House of Commons.

The speaker's supporters are all behind him or her. The only people actually in view are the opposing side. They not only do not wish to hear the speaker but will positively try to prevent the speaker from being heard or from making a speech at all. Every tactic is resorted to – loud conversations, constant interventions and interruptions, organised barracking, physical gestures, spurious points of order. The slightest slip or hesitation is greeted with ironic cheers or unkind laughter.

The speaker's only weapons are the merits of the speech, humour and force of personality. A good and experienced speaker will usually manage to command the House. But, once lost, the House is very much like a bear pit and the despatch box can be a very lonely place.

There was enormous interest in Michael Heseltine's return to the despatch box, both in his own personal performance and in the substance of what he had to say. I was apprehensive at facing such a renowned debater, but I was reassured when I noticed, rather to my surprise, that his hand was visibly shaking as he spoke. He performed adequately, but not brilliantly. It is very easy to lose one's edge without constant exposure to the parliamentary atmosphere, and the continual round of Tory Party dinners, addressing the adoring faithful, was hardly good preparation for such an occasion. It took Michael Heseltine several months to get back to full form.

My own speech went well, and I was pleased with its reception. I had begun to learn the importance of humour as a weapon on such occasions and I included what I thought were some pretty good cracks at the Tories.

Although the Tory Party and the poll tax were dominating the media, the Labour Party was not, as I knew myself, free from internal intrigue, although very little of it had surfaced in the press. The Tory success in changing their leader seemed to provoke a sudden surge of interest in some quarters in the possibility of a similar manoeuvre in the Labour Party.

I began to notice that the discontent with Neil which had been simmering beneath the surface in the Shadow Cabinet now became more visible. Some of his colleagues could barely conceal their contempt for him. Neil always had a tendency to go on a bit, and I remember on one occasion in the Shadow Cabinet John Smith muttering to me, 'When is he going to shut up?' I recall thinking that if John was prepared to say such a thing to me, whom he had no reason to expect to take his side, how much more open he must have been to his particular friends.

I began to detect some worrying signs that John's friends were urging him to make a challenge for Neil's leadership. John himself became more overt and confident in making public his criticisms of Neil. At the end of November, I found myself sitting next to John on the front bench. He took the chance to talk to me at length about Neil's excessive enthusiasm for the ERM and how he, John, believed in a much more cautious approach.

It was an odd tack for John to take with me, since we both knew that we had traditionally taken very different views of this particular issue. I got the distinct impression that I was being sounded out on the issue and that a bid was being made for my support. I believe that if I had responded eagerly, and indicated my preference for John's rather than Neil's approach, the conversation would have gone further.

I concede immediately that I had little hard evidence to go on, but I was sufficiently disturbed to go to see Neil to tell him what I thought was going on. Neil seemed to take seriously what I said. The episode led nowhere, and the atmosphere of conspiracy subsided before Christmas. It was symptomatic, however, of the difficulties and pressures with which Neil constantly had to contend.

Christmas saw Gill and me, this time with our daughter Helen, setting off on what was by now our annual trip to New Zealand. We had our usual delightful holiday, and on this occasion bought ourselves a small farm. My sister had been telling us that she and her husband could do with a 'run-off' on which they could raise the surplus calves from their dairy herd. We had a little money saved and land prices in New Zealand at the time were very low. We were shown a 90-acre bare block on the slops of Mount Pirongia and promptly fell in love with it, not so much because of its virtues as a farm, but because of its stunning beauty. It backed into the native bush, there were crystal-clear streams running down its slopes and one could see a hundred miles south to the distant snow-clad peaks of the great North Island volcanic mountains. There were many times, usually moments of great pressure or crisis, in the next few years when Gill and I would mentally make our escape and transport ourselves to the peace and tranquillity of our mountainside paradise.

The New Year carried on much as the old one had left off, with the poll tax very much dominating the political agenda. Our announcement of our fair rates proposals had done a great deal to disarm our opponents and the commentators, but we were still asked, and with increasing persistence, what our proposals would cost the average poll tax-payer. Every interview on the subject would end with this question, which was of course very difficult to answer. Interviewers like nothing better than being able to take a cheap trick.

I resolved that we would confound everybody by coming up with the answer. We did a great deal of work, with the aid of expert researchers, and we made sure that the methodology we used would command the support of the professional organisations who specialised in public and local government finance. We were confident that our conclusions would stand up to critical analysis. Our figures showed the fair rates bill for people in different classes of property in every local authority district in the country, and revealed that our bills would be on average £140 per person lower than the poll tax.

On the morning of 10 April 1991, I was interviewed by John Humphreys on the *Today* programme. The programme was always important in setting the news agenda for the day and John was an excellent interviewer. However, he always liked to have the last word by wrong-footing his interviewee with a difficult question at the end. He asked me, as I expected he would, what our plans would cost. I replied that I was holding a press conference later that morning at which I would release detailed figures, but that I could tell him now that our figures showed an average reduction of £140 per person and in some cases a good deal more. I waved the lists of figures in front of him. He seemed impressed.

Chris Patten, by now Tory Party chairman, was telephoned by the programme and asked for his comments. When he was told what our figures showed, he said that he was 'gobsmacked'. I have always thought that Chris probably meant to say that he did not believe our figures but that, with his taste for – but less than complete understanding of – the demotic, he had not quite said what he meant on this occasion. The word was seized upon by the commentators. It gave a very satisfactory impression of a Tory Party which had been completely wrong-footed by our initiative.

The press conference went well, and our figures stood up to scrutiny. The press the following day was favourable. It so happened that the Shadow Cabinet was having a full-day strategy meeting on that day, and my colleagues were clearly impressed at the front page headline in the *Guardian* to the effect that 'Gould Pulls Rug From Under Tories'. I felt that my advocacy of a more positive campaigning stance had been vindicated.

I often cited this episode when, on later occasions, I was challenged on my criticisms of what seemed to me an excessively cautious approach. It was never my view that we should be indiscriminate in what we said or disclosed. But we should be ready to choose our ground, prepare it carefully, and then launch what we had to say with great confidence. I still believe that this is the right way to campaign.

By this time, we were virtually on general election alert. It was generally assumed that the Tories would like an election in the spring or early summer of 1991, about four years after their last election victory. A failure on their part to go for an election during this period would be seen as an admission that they dared not do so. Our strategy, therefore, was to keep the pressure on them, so as to make a 1991 election difficult for them, and thereby create the impression of a government which was running out of time and options.

It meant a hectic work schedule for all the leading campaigners in the party. I was involved in press conferences, for example, three or four times a week. Each one had to be carefully prepared and would be followed up with substantial interviews.

I was being drawn more into the party's general campaigning as well. I had been sounded out much earlier on whether I might serve again as one of the party's principal strategists and I had given my cautious agreement, but I was not keen to thrust myself forward. My work load was already about three times too great.

Gill and I had a brief break in Portugal in May before returning to a political agenda crammed full of poll tax, housing matters, the Citizen's Charter, inner cities, local government for London and a myriad of other issues. I think it is hard for outsiders to understand how hard and long senior opposition politicians have to work.

Because of the imminence of a general election, we realised that we were unlikely to have the time for our by now annual New Zealand holiday at the end of the year. We decided at short notice, therefore, to take advantage of the summer break, when there was very little likelihood of a snap election, to have a holiday in New Zealand in early September. We flew out via Singapore, had a delightful stay in New Zealand, and returned via a week in Bali, feeling much refreshed.

I was again fully booked up during conference week, and spoke at a large number of fringe meetings. I also had to wind up one of the main conference debates. Gill and I had been invited to the Royal Box at Twickenham for the opening match of the Rugby World Cup on the same day. I made my speech at 12.30, jumped into the car at 1 p.m. and drove to Twickenham as fast as I could so as to arrive in time for the match. We were just about the only occupants of the Royal Box who were pleased with the outcome – a New Zealand victory over England.

I was again elected to the National Executive during conference week, and prepared for my fifth year of membership. I had also been approached by George Howarth with an offer of help for the forthcoming Shadow Cabinet elections. I had never previously bothered with anything much by way of campaigning, but George persuaded me that my result would be much improved if people felt that I was taking the trouble to court them. He was in touch with what he described as 'networks' of people in the PLP – people who talked to each other and often moved and voted together, identifying themselves often on regional but sometimes on other grounds as well.

The effort proved to be well worthwhile. My Shadow Cabinet results improved substantially and I felt that my fortunes were on the mend. George Howarth, Peter Hain and others began to talk to me in guarded terms about the possibility of running for the leadership if, by any chance, we were to lose the election and Neil should stand down.

The new parliamentary session was dominated, as far as I was concerned, by the new council tax legislation. I found myself facing on this occasion Michael Portillo, at this point number two to Michael Heseltine, who quickly revealed himself as formidably intelligent and well-briefed.

Portillo had been one of the staunchest defenders of the poll tax but he managed to embrace its successor with equal fervour and without apparent embarrassment. He had been responsible for the detailed work on the council tax proposals and he knew the legislation intimately. I had to work very hard to make sure that he and the bill were subjected to proper scrutiny. I again enjoyed the cut and thrust of committee work, where I managed to embarrass Michael Portillo on only one occasion; he had a sufficient conceit of himself to resent it very much. We developed a healthy respect for one another and remained in touch long after the committee stage had been completed.

As we turned into the New Year, the general election loomed ever larger. The Government was still in deep trouble over mortgage repossessions, business failures and the deepening recession, all of which, I believed, had been made much more difficult by John Major's continuing commitment to the ERM. This time, we began to believe that the Tories might really be beaten.

Our language in public was of course entirely upbeat and confident of victory. In private, however, there was a deep-seated pessimism which was hard to shake. Despite our growing sense that the Tories might not recover, there was a reluctance to believe that we might actually win, at least outright. Most of us expected that the outcome would be messy, a minority government perhaps, with the possibility of another election before too long.

My concerns were reinforced by a special all-day Shadow Cabinet meeting which was held on 7 January 1992. I had long since given up raising issues of economic policy, especially the ERM. I was reconciled to Labour fighting the election on a commitment to the ERM, but foresaw that I would have to fight my own battle on the issue if and when we formed a government.

At the Shadow Cabinet meeting, however, Michael Meacher, who had not previously been very active on the issue, asked Neil directly (and perhaps unwisely) whether it was his intention to devalue if we won the election. Neil rounded on him savagely and declared that he would tolerate no mention of devaluation. The subject was not only taboo, he said, but the suggestion that devaluation might be necessary or desirable was entirely mistaken. A devaluation would mean, he asserted, not lower interest rates, as some seemed to believe, but higher interest rates as a consequence of the loss of confidence the foreign exchange markets would feel.

I was somewhat shaken by Neil's vehemence, which seemed to me to exceed what might have been necessary if his intention had been merely to put an end to any further discussion. I concluded at that point that Neil had now been entirely converted to what I regarded as the specious reasoning of the ERM supporters.

At the end of January, I joined the election campaign committee for a day of simulated election events. The day went well and my own contribution seemed to be regarded as helpful. I was a little surprised, however, to see how large the committee was. There were 17 or 18 people present – very different from the tight little ship which had run the 1987 campaign so well.

In my view, this issue of the size of an executive committee is crucial to the success of an enterprise such as an election campaign. If the committee gets too big, it is incapable of acting as a unit. The attendance fluctuates, with different people turning up from one meeting to the next. Decisions taken at one meeting are counter-manded or misunderstood by a different gathering at the next. Because the group is too unwieldy, smaller groups form at the margins and meet informally in order to make progress. This adds to the sense of discontinuity. Many of these problems manifested themselves in the 1992 campaign.

In March, we had dinner with the Kinnocks. Neil was in good form and seemed more relaxed than usual. He was more prepared to share the conversation with others. I was impressed by his confident state of mind. A few days later, John Major announced that he had asked the Queen for a dissolution of Parliament and there was to be a general election on 9 June 1992.

I had been asked to direct the campaign in London, where it was thought we would face particular problems. The preparations for the London campaign were fine, but there was some ill feeling amongst those who shouldered the responsibility for carrying them out. I made it clear that I would tolerate no personal bickering and that the only thing that mattered was that the team should work together. This approach seemed to work, and the campaign in the capital went well. Our results in London were no worse, and in some cases better, than those in other parts of the country.

I was also by now a full member of the main campaign committee and deputised for Jack Cunningham as chair of the committee on the quite frequent occasions when his constituency duties took him out of London. There were two meetings daily of this main committee, the first at seven in the morning, preceding our main press conference of the day.

I found my participation in this committee a frustrating experience, however. The structure of the campaign, following the model established in 1987, had been fixed many months earlier, long before I came on the scene. It was never clear to me precisely why we had committed ourselves so rigidly to that particular structure, whose merits were by no means self-evident. I found myself pursuing a strategy whose purpose and rationale were obscure. The party's campaigning over this period had been in the hands of David Hill, who had been appointed as communications director when John Underwood resigned. David was a good and experienced campaigner who was particularly good in his handling of the press. He lacked the flair of a Peter Mandelson, however, and there was a certain sameyness about our campaigning, in both concept and practice, as a result.

I found myself out of sympathy with the strategy, too, on what I believe is the most difficult issue for any campaign – the question of whether to use one's time in promoting one's own strong points or in defending oneself against the attacks of one's opponents. The answer to this question lies in an understanding of how the ordinary voter views political issues, something it is easy for political professionals to get wrong.

Political activists usually have political views which are coherent and consistent, and they are inclined to think that all people are like that. In fact, most people do not have consistent political views. They have instead sets of mutually contradictory prejudices. They resolve the contradictions when it comes to polling day according to which issues, which prejudices, have the greatest salience in their minds at the time.

This is very well understood by the tabloid press, which is now expert at tweaking at the right moment those issues, such as tax, scrounging, race and immigration, which are likely to favour the party they support. That is why the support of the tabloids has been so important to the Tory Party. Much campaigning is therefore about who controls the agenda. The party which can dominate the campaigning agenda with favourable stories and issues is likely to gain a crucial advantage.

I favour, for these reasons, always campaigning as far as possible on positive issues, and leaving our opponents to make the running on their own stories so as to give them no help. This approach had, however, been ruled out in the 1992 campaign on the crucial issue of tax.

John Smith had committed the party to a rationalisation of the anomaly which meant that national insurance contributions ceased to be paid by people who earned just over the average industrial wage. This change, and one or two other tax increases on higher incomes, was to fund increases in pensions and child benefit. The mistaken obsession with financial responsibility – the perceived need to show precisely how every commitment was to be funded – meant not only that our commitments were very few and relatively unattractive, but also that we were obliged to go into excessive and self-defeating detail about the tax increases they made necessary,.

John was clearly concerned about this and resolved that we should take the fight to the Tories. It was agreed that we should launch our election campaign with a Shadow Budget, at which John would set out with crystal clarity precisely what our tax proposals were. Great confidence was reposed in John's ability to reassure the public that they had nothing to fear from our tax plans.

I was always dubious of this strategy. It seemed to contradict all that I knew about campaigning. We were playing into our opponents' hands, by using our own time to direct attention to our weakest area. I was even more aghast when, during the campaign, if ever the tax issue looked like flagging, we would go back to it by holding yet another press conference on the subject.

I was also critical of the tax proposals on the ground that they were too timid. If we were to impose tax increases, then they should at least have spared those middle income people whom we hoped to attract. There was no point in again threatening to place a cap on the aspirations of those voters, particularly in the south of England, who had found Mrs Thatcher's appeal so irresistible precisely because she had offered them new horizons. A progressive tax policy should have imposed greater increases on a smaller number of people at the top end of the income scale. These were, after all, the only people who had enjoyed tax gains under the Tories and there would have been little public sympathy for them if they had been required to pay some of it back.

I also felt that we concentrated so much on tax because we had nothing to say on other economic issues. Our shared commitment to the ERM meant that we could not attack the Tories – at least, not with any credibility – on the wider issues of economic management. Any such attack could easily be deflected by pointing out that, like the Tories, we would hand macro-economic policy over to an outside agency. Indeed, our constant call for the same policy but with lower interest rates was especially lacking in credibility, since a Labour government would have had, if anything, to pay an interest rate premium, due to lack of market confidence, in order to maintain the same parity within the ERM.

For all these reasons, therefore, I was not entirely convinced that our strategy was correct, and I was not therefore totally surprised when it failed to deliver. We found ourselves bogged down on an issue which, notwithstanding Tory ineptitude, our opponents were bound to capitalise on in the end.

We did not fare much better when it came to developing our own themes. The National Health Service was clearly a big issue for us, but our attempt to exploit it with the story of Jennifer's ear came badly unstuck. This was mainly the result of inexperience. We should never have revealed that the story of the little girl who had had to wait so long for an ear operation was based on a real case, and should have stuck to the perfectly sensible line that it was a fictionalised but representative story which tallied with the real experience of many thousands of people. Instead, we allowed ourselves to be impaled on the hook of whether or not Jennifer's parents had given their consent and whether the story was accurate in every detail.

The campaign was very nearly derailed by the backwash from this incident. I remember chairing one 7 a.m. meeting of the campaign committee when Neil arrived at the door, livid with rage, demanding to see whoever had spoken to the press on the subject the previous evening. A terrified party official rose and followed him out of the room. A day later, Robin Cook declared in a fury that he would cancel a follow-up press conference and, in effect, concede the Tory charge that we had invented the whole thing. I managed to calm him down.

A number of factors have been identified by some people, with the benefit of hindsight, as responsible for our defeat. The finger was pointed, for example, at the role played by the Shadow communications agency, and in particular Philip Gould. It is alleged that these paid servants of the party took over the campaign, lacked political judgement, and substituted their own narrow ad-men's view for what should have been broad political themes.

I do not share this view. It is certainly true that Philip Gould played a large part in the campaign, but he did no more than he was asked to do. In fact, the information he provided was pretty accurate and reliable. He warned us throughout the campaign, for example, in his daily account of the polling evidence, that we were vulnerable on tax and that we would be in trouble on the issue if the Tories got their act together. It has always struck me as unfair to require Philip to provide information to the committee, and then blame him because the committee is alleged to have paid too much, or too little, attention to what he told them. It was the politicians' responsibility to direct the campaign, and to decide how to respond to the information they received.

It is also said that the decision taken late in the campaign to open up the issue of electoral reform cost us victory. I reject this view as well. I agree that the decision was inept, or at least ineptly handled, and that, far from attracting wavering voters, it suggested that both Neil and the party were lacking confidence in their prospects of forming a government of their own.

It was not, however, a decisive factor. The attempt to blame the electoral reform issue, and those who were alleged to have taken the decision to raise it, was part of that unattractive tendency in the Labour Party to scapegoat.

Then there was the Sheffield rally. Popular wisdom has it that the triumphalist tone of this event turned off the voters and converted victory into defeat. This, too, is a rationalisation with the benefit of hindsight. If we had won the election, most people would by now be declaring that they knew we were on course for victory when they sensed the party's confidence at Sheffield.

It was certainly a heady occasion. The opinion polls had shown during the course of the day that we had suddenly surged ahead. We were given leads of four, five and seven per cent in three of the main polls. It looked as though we had made the decisive breakthrough. Those who arrived in their thousands at Sheffield were in a high state of excitement. By the time of the rally itself, however, I and a few others knew that the latest poll had put us just one point ahead. It was therefore unlikely that the decisive point in the campaign had been reached, as so many of those present fervently believed.

The event itself was well-organised and succeeded in its main aim of enthusing party workers. The atmosphere was electric, and it has to be said that some of our leading people succumbed to it. Roy

Hattersley, for example, who had vowed in advance to avoid any suggestion that we had already won, could not resist addressing the rally in the language of victory.

The members of the Shadow Cabinet were required to walk down the central aisle of the huge arena to take up their places on the stage. It was an extraordinary experience, with all the lights, music, cheering, to walk what seemed hundreds of yards through a forest of clutching hands and rosettes, a cacophony of noise in our ears, with people in tears of excitement, shouting and waving and slapping us on our backs.

Little wonder that, by the time Neil reached the stage, he too was in a high state of excitement. He bounded on to the stage and strode to the lectern. 'Y'awright?' he bellowed into the microphone. 'Ye-e-es,' the crowd shouted back. 'Y'awright,' he bellowed again, and again. 'For God's sake, shut him up,' I muttered to whoever was standing beside me.

It is easy to say, as so many have done, that the Sheffield rally was a mistake. It is certainly unlikely that we will see a repeat performance for some time. But to blame that single event for our defeat is again far too simplistic. The real reasons for that defeat lay in deep-seated policy issues and in the way we tried to position ourselves in relation to our main opponents. Paradoxically, the Sheffield rally was an expression of our lack of confidence in ourselves. We were trying to achieve through pzazz what we dared not try to achieve in substance. If we had been braver on policy and on breaking from the monetarist consensus, we would not have needed the Sheffield rally.

By the end of the campaign, I was again physically exhausted. At least I had managed to spend more time in my constituency than in 1987, and I had been buoyed up by the affectionate reception I had received from the people of Dagenham wherever I had gone. I was confident of a good result in my own seat, but anxious about the overall outcome.

Neil and others have claimed since the election that they knew a few days before polling day that we had lost. I think this is unlikely. My guess is that Neil could not allow himself to believe in victory, as a sort of protection against the possibility of disappointment, and then transformed that natural caution *ex post facto* into a reasoned conviction.

On the evening of polling day, I was on duty at Walworth Road to handle the media at that end. I had a quick meal and was back at party headquarters by about 10 p.m., waiting for the first results. Looking back, I suppose that what I expected was a mixed result, but one which would at least see the Tories leave office.

The first result, from Basildon, produced a familiar sinking feeling. I knew at that moment that we were in for a long, hard night. I remember the night as being punctuated by a series of blows, each one presaging a worse overall result than had been promised by the one before. One by one, our last hopes were extinguished. It was immediately clear that we had no chance of an overall win, then the prospect of being the largest party also disappeared, then the chance of denying the Tories an overall majority slipped away, and finally, by about 4 a.m., it was clear that John Major would have a working majority.

I was interviewed at each stage of this progressive destruction of our hopes. I did what I had become very good at – keeping a brave face and seeking what crumbs of comfort I could find. But there was no disguising the bitter disappointment of defeat.

At about 1 a.m., I broke away from Walworth Road and went out to Dagenham for my own count. Although I trebled my majority, the mood was sombre. It was clear that the enormous effort of so many people, sustained over more than five years, had come to naught. I returned to Walworth Road to a party headquarters which was coming to terms with the scale of the defeat.

By about 5 a.m., the long night was coming to a close. The majority of party workers had gone home. There was nothing more for them to do. The planned celebrations had been stillborn.

There was, however, one last act of the drama to be played out. We had had a telephone message that Neil and his entourage had left his constituency in Wales and were driving back to London. We organised a welcoming committee which gathered on the steps of the Walworth Road building to greet him.

The mood was subdued as Neil, Glenys, Charles Clarke and about nine or ten other members of Neil's immediate staff arrived. We went up in virtual silence to the offices on the fourth floor which had been set aside for Neil. No one had any appetite for conversation.

Neil looked tired, grim and determined. He announced that he would make a speech to journalists on the steps of Walworth Road at about 6 a.m. We all stood around (for some reason no one sat down) while he drafted a speech in longhand. My recollection (which must be faulty) is that there was virtually no light, except for the cold, ghostly glare of the street lamps outside. Occasionally, as the work progressed, there would be a brief, muttered conversation. Once or twice, there was an audible sob.

There was a brief discussion of one or two points that Neil might wish to make. Charles Clarke and John Eatwell both offered thoughts. Finally, Neil was ready. Charles Clarke asked me, as the only other member of the Shadow Cabinet present, to go with Neil. Glenys, Neil and I travelled down in the lift together.

Glenys said, as the lift doors closed, 'I don't think I can go through with this.' Neil said, 'You've got this far. You can do it.' I said to Neil, 'The party owes you everything.' As the lift doors opened, Neil said, with pardonable inaccuracy, 'This is the last speech I will make as party leader.'

A sizeable crowd had gathered as we emerged into the glaring lights and television cameras. As Neil appeared, a muffled cheer broke out but he quickly quelled it. He read out his speech in a strong voice. I cannot remember much of what he said. Glenys and I were both in tears.

TWELVE

Leadership and Resignation
1992–94

NEIL TELEPHONED ME on the Sunday after the election. I had spent the Friday and Saturday sleeping and resting. I had scarcely had time to ponder on the implications of our defeat or of Neil's cryptic remark that he had, in addressing the crowd at Walworth Road, made his last speech as leader.

I suppose that I had always assumed that, if we lost, Neil would not carry on. Two successive defeats as Leader of the Opposition were certainly enough for anyone – for his supporters as well as himself.

It still came as a surprise, however, when he told me that he intended to resign as party leader and would do so on the following day. I began to talk him out of it, at least in terms of the timing, but he was so adamant that I rapidly gave up. He had lived with the situation, and no doubt with the prospect of defeat, for so long that it could safely be assumed that he knew his own mind better than anyone else.

He must have asked me about my own intentions. I replied that I would probably contest the leadership. Neil advised me strongly against doing so. 'Smithy has got it all sewn up,' he said. 'You'll get only a fraction of the vote. Better to let him have it. He won't last the course. It's important that you're there to pick up the pieces.'

As always with Neil, it was difficult to know whether he was telling the whole truth as he saw it. In particular, I don't know whether, by saying that John would not last the course, he meant that John would run into political or health problems. I have no doubt that his advice was well intentioned and it certainly proved to be remarkably prescient.

I was also pretty convinced that, whatever Neil's true motives, he would not have seen himself as serving John Smith's interests. Relations between Neil and John were superficially cordial, but Neil would have needed superhuman qualities to remain unaffected by the support offered to John by the press in contrast to the vicious treatment he had himself received.

Glenys, I know, bitterly resented the way in which John had been used by the Tory press, over a long period, as a stick with which to beat Neil. I suspect, too, that she resented even more that John, as she believed, had done little to discourage this. Although Neil never revealed anything of this himself, I always felt that Neil and Glenys were likely to think alike on the subject and that Glenys was the more reliable guide to their true opinion.

I pondered Neil's advice, but it did little to help me resolve my central dilemma. Neil was almost certainly correct in predicting that John would easily win any leadership contest. Indeed, he had for so long been written up not only as the next but as the preferred leader that an unstoppable expectation had developed. This expectation had been reinforced throughout the election campaign, during which John had been treated as our trump card. Great emphasis had been placed on his qualities of prudence and trustworthiness. The failure of the campaign, and particularly of our tax initiatives, did nothing to dent this confidence in John's virtues. Images, once set, are often remarkably impervious to the facts.

The problem as I saw it was this: Neil would make his announcement on Monday; John would certainly declare his candidature almost straightaway. It was hard to see that anyone else, at least anyone serious, would risk a challenge. Without the immediate declaration of a challenge, the press would rightly assume that the succession had been decided. By Wednesday, the party would to all intents and purposes have a new leader.

This would have been achieved within five days of a stunning election defeat. There would have been no opportunity for a *post mortem*, no time for reflection, no debate within the party, no chance of canvassing options. The party would simply wake up one morning to find that it had a new leader. No 'magic circle' could have produced a more instantaneous result. However inevitable it may have seemed at the time, it would in the longer term have been greatly resented.

I was determined that this should not happen, for the sakes of both the party and myself. In my own case, I had quite consciously spent the last two or three years suppressing my own opinions in what I saw as the wider interest. Not only had my reputation suffered as a result, but so too had the party's. Suppressing political debate is never a good idea, particularly for a supposed party of the left. We had become fixated, in my view, with the idea of winning power and had lost sight of what we wanted to do with that power. That loss of focus had communicated itself to the electorate, who were less convinced than they should have been on what we were about, and were less likely to support us as a result.

Anointing John as leader without a contest would have meant that I and the party were plunged straight back into that situation. All the pressure would have been to support the new leader. Dissent of any sort would have been frowned on. We would have faced another five years of iron discipline and emphasis on unity. And our new leader, for reasons of temperament and political conviction, would have reinforced this pressure with his own personal preferences for caution and conservatism.

I felt that I owed it to myself and the party to ensure that there was a contest. I knew that I had little or no chance of winning it. But I also felt that I could attract enough support to make my candidature a serious one and to offer the party the chance for proper debate and a proper choice. If this could not be done at that precise moment, when could it ever be done?

I was reasonably confident that I could get enough support to make my challenge possible. This was despite the rule which required any candidate for the leadership or deputy leadership to be nominated by 20 per cent of the Parliamentary Labour Party. The rule had been put in place a year or two earlier in an attempt to ensure that Neil did not face an annual challenge from Tony Benn. The threshold requirement had, however, been set at a figure which was too high for the good of democracy within the party and which acted as a real bar to candidates who might never have a chance of winning but who were nevertheless legitimately entitled to throw their hats into the ring.

I had been assured by various people that, come a leadership contest, I would have their support. I had good reason to expect the support of others. My calculation was that I could get the required number of nominations. I consulted a number of close colleagues, including Nigel Stanley, David Blunkett, Michael Meacher, George Howarth and Peter Hain, all of whom pledged their support. They did not try to discourage me, but it is fair to say that neither did they offer me any great expectation that I could win.

I decided to announce my candidature and held a press conference for the purpose on the afternoon of Tuesday 14 June, the day after Neil had announced his resignation. John had already declared. Two days later, our son Charles announced his engagement to his long-time girlfriend Angela Maxwell. We were delighted and had a celebratory family dinner at The Marsh Goose, our favourite restaurant in Moreton-in-Marsh.

The early stages of my leadership campaign were encouraging. The opening press conference went very well. The first meeting of supporters was well attended. We were made immediate offers of financial help. David Mills, brother of my Fabian colleague John, and husband of Tessa Jowell, the newly elected MP for Dulwich, generously wrote out a cheque. Richard Faulkner, the former parliamentary candidate who now ran a parliamentary consultancy, offered to pay the rent of office premises for the use of the campaign. In due course, Harsh Kumar, businessman and Labour Party supporter, made a generous contribution to campaign expenses. This support meant that, while we were not flush with money and could not afford, for example, expensive printing, we were assured of enough financial backing to keep the campaign going. We were determined to play by the rules – not, for example, to use House of Commons premises as campaign offices – and to keep proper accounts.

Political support was also forthcoming. I was gratified by the support I seemed to be picking up, especially from women colleagues and from those who had been newly elected. In the early stages, there was an air of great optimism and even a sense that, once the nominations hurdle had been cleared, a real momentum might be established that would surprise the pessimists.

The obstacles were nevertheless very real. The assumption that John was unstoppable meant that it was difficult to persuade the undecided to do anything other than back the certain winner. There is always in any contest of this sort a large number of people who will jump on whatever bandwagon is established. And because the new parliament had not yet assembled, it was not easy to contact colleagues, especially new ones. I and others spent a huge amount of time on the phone.

John, by contrast, had immediately been backed by a large number of senior colleagues and, more importantly, by leading trade unionists. The support pledged by John Edmonds, for example, long before any ballot had been taken or members consulted, appeared to guarantee John the votes of the General, Municipal and Boilermakers' Union. Other trade union leaders did likewise.

I was disappointed, however, at the attitude taken by Rodney Bickerstaffe, allegedly of the left, who took it upon himself to make his own personal recommendations to his executive, without allowing the candidates to address the executive or otherwise communicate with them. The executive followed his recommendations. As proved so often to be the case, a number of leading figures from that union, the National Union of Public Employees, indicated to me privately that they would have liked to support me but, since I could not command a majority, they could not.

By this time, I had declared that I was also standing for the deputy leadership. I have been criticised for this decision, by friend and foe alike. My opponents lost no time in saying that it was an error which showed a wider lack of judgement. My friends pointed, with justification, to the confusion it produced in the minds of those who wished to support me. Many of those felt that, in voting for me for one or the other, they had done their duty by me, with the result that my support was split between the two contests. It was difficult to persuade my supporters that they should vote 'Gould–Gould'.

In my defence, I should point out that there were good precedents for my standing in both contests. Roy Hattersley had done precisely that, for example, in the leadership contest in 1983. More importantly, the argument of many of those who, with hindsight, said I should have gone for only one of the two offices was that I should have concentrated my efforts on the deputy leadership, that this would have avoided confusion and would have allowed the John Smith campaign to offer me tacit support – or at least refrain from overt opposition – in the deputy leadership battle.

But this was to ignore the reason which had impelled me into the contest in the first place: to have gone for the deputy leadership only would have been to concede the leadership to John without a contest.

Why not, then, just concentrate on the leadership?, which is what my wife Gill wanted. The argument here was that I needed to secure enough nominations to enable me to proceed. We feared that, doubting as they no doubt did my chances of winning, people might be reluctant to give me that support unless they could see that I would – even though defeated for the leadership – be in a position to protect them against any backlash they might suffer as a consequence of their failure to support the new leader. If they could see that I was standing for the deputy leadership as well, with a reasonable chance of winning, then they would be more likely to feel comfortable about nominating me for the leadership.

Fighting the two campaigns was quickly complicated by the entry into the deputy leadership contest of two more contestants: Margaret Beckett and John Prescott. Both were likely to prove formidable opponents: Margaret because it was thought that she enjoyed the support of John Smith and John Prescott because of his support from the trade unions.

The Smith campaign felt, of course, none of these concerns. Robin Cook, who had volunteered to run John's campaign, was able to relax while I struggled to obtain the required number of nominations. He contented himself with the odd spoiling story, suggesting, for example, that he was persuading some people to offer me a nomination simply in order to ensure that there was a contest. Not only was there no basis to this, as far as I know, but it was in marked contrast to the hostile reaction of the Smith camp to the initial announcement of my candidature.

The only time I saw Robin embarrassed throughout the contest was when Gill and I happened to come across him in the Red Lion pub one lunch time, closeted in earnest conversation with Peter Mandelson, who was by now an MP. In the light of Robin's earlier comments to me about Peter, I thought he looked a little uncomfortable.

In the event, I secured the required number of nominations in both contests with relative ease. The support of a fifth of the Parliamentary Labour Party was a considerable achievement, and should normally have been the springboard for further advance. There was no concealing the fact, however, that John had the support of a much greater number of MPs, and that the main trade unions were also committed to him. By the time I had got the nominations, the contest was virtually over.

My problems were illustrated by my attempt to get the support of the Transport and General Workers' Union. It was known that general secretary Bill Morris was inclined to back John Smith, believing that this was what the party, trade union hierarchy and his own members wanted. The Broad Left group on the executive, however, was less keen and came to see me. We had a useful discussion, but they felt unable, when it came to the crunch, to make a fight of it.

One of my handicaps, in trying to get the support of trade unions, was that I did not have a clear image in right/left terms. I believe that this has always been a problem for me. I am not easily categorised. Attempts have been made to pigeon-hole me, and when I fail to conform to the ascribed stereotype, this is thought to demonstrate inconsistency on my part. People feel comfortable with those who can be easily summed up. They feel less comfortable with those who present a more complex image.

Despite these problems, I threw myself with energy into the campaign. I was determined to do as well as possible in electoral terms, but, more importantly, to stimulate the sort of debate about economic policy and the party's general political stance which I believed had been absent for too long. I travelled all over the country on a punishing schedule of meetings, interviews and other engagements.

It was gratifying to discover that it was often the younger and brighter activists who were keen to support me. It was also pleasing that, whenever I was able to speak to people, they seemed to warm to my message. It became clear, however, that getting my message across directly in this way was only a minor factor in a campaign dominated by the images created by the media. The perception that John was a certain winner grew stronger as the campaign developed. This meant that I was able to attract less interest than I had hoped, and even the debate which I had wanted to stimulate did not really get off the ground.

The importance I attached to the debate increased in the light of the deepening recession and the growing problems arising from our membership of the ERM. I watched these events with growing despair – despair not only at what the Tory government was doing to the British economy and to the lives of millions of people, but also at the failure of the Labour Party to identify the cause of the problems and to speak up on the issue.

Alongside the ERM, there was also the prospect of our commitment to the Maastricht Treaty, which would in my view entrench the ERM difficulties. It became clear that the Shadow Cabinet saw no problem in accepting Maastricht, and that unless I could somehow exercise a leading influence over the issue, we would drift into acquiescence.

The leadership campaign did of course offer me many opportunities to explain my views on these issues, but very little of what I said was ever reported. The only reports which were made tended to concentrate on the course of the campaign in electoral terms and predictions about the outcome.

One of my best performances took place, in any case, behind closed doors. The PLP had agreed to hold a hustings meeting, at which the candidates would each address the meeting and then answer questions. I spoke well and answered questions effectively. I did not hear John, but I was told that he was nervous and uncertain. This was not, of course, reported. So entrenched were people's views that I don't think my superior performance, attested to by many of those present, swayed a single vote.

There were many other occasions – Fabian debates, trade union conferences, public meetings in Manchester, Liverpool, Sheffield, Birmingham, Norwich, Leeds, Plymouth, Newcastle, Bristol, Glasgow, Torquay – when I had the chance to put my case. I generally acquitted myself well but I felt a growing sense of frustration as the hopes of my supporters faded. I was especially disappointed that I could not deliver for so many of those younger activists, in particular younger women, who took a chance by supporting me.

On 16 July, I gave a party for my supporters, just two days before the results of the contests for leader and deputy leader were to be announced at a special conference. It was an enjoyable occasion which gave me the chance to thank so many of those who had supported me so loyally. Everyone knew, however, that the cause had been lost.

The day of the special conference was always likely to be a difficult experience for me. A group of my supporters had arranged to accompany me to the Horticultural Halls, where the conference was to be held. As we approached the hall, I noticed that there were a number of people at the entrance selling copies of the *Morning Star*. I was asked by several journalists if the story in the *Morning Star* were true. I replied that I had no idea what they were talking about.

Somone then showed me a copy and I saw a front page story headlined 'Gould Withdraws and Urges Supporters to Back Beckett'. The report went on to say that I had decided to withdraw from the deputy leadership campaign. I was astonished. The *Morning Star*'s political correspondent was someone I knew; normally I would have expected him to consult me at the very least before publishing such a potentially damaging story.

I smelt a very large rat. My first concern, however, was to ensure that none of the delegates would be misled. By this time, I knew that I was unlikely to win the deputy leadership contest, but there was no point in allowing my vote to be unfairly diminished by a deliberate ploy of this sort. I therefore persuaded John Evans, who was chairing the meeting, to make an announcement at the beginning to the effect that the story was completely without foundation.

In the event, the story had little or no impact on the outcome, but the episode does cast an interesting light on the morality of the contest and of whoever was responsible. My first thought was that the story had been planted to aid the Beckett campaign. I was puzzled, however, since Margaret was the almost certain winner and did not need the help of such a disreputable tactic, which would in any case have been completely out of character for her.

I was naturally preoccupied with other matters but after the conference, I was approached by someone close to John Prescott who asked me where I thought the story had come from. I said that I did not know. 'Ask yourself who was the most likely beneficiary,' I was told. 'It was the person who needed the votes that would otherwise go to you. John's campaign hoped to give the impression that you were acting to head off a last-minute surge of support for him, so that he could maximise all the anti-Beckett votes.'

The results at the conference were duly announced. They were even worse than I had feared. I secured just under 10 per cent of the electoral college vote. I also came third to John Prescott in the deputy leadership contest.

The 10 per cent figure was often thrown at me subsequently by commentators who wished to show how little support I had in the party. It is not just special pleading, however, to point out that it is in fact a quite misleading figure. Because of the electoral college system, I got no credit from those many contests – in constituency parties or trade unions – where I polled well but failed to get a majority. I was constantly being told that in this constituency or that, I had narrowly failed to win but had secured perhaps 47 or 48 per cent of the votes. All the votes in those contests would then be credited to John.

It is also worth pointing out that many people voted for me in the contest for one office and then, thinking that they had done their duty by me, voted for someone else in the contest for the other office. I also suffered from the rolling nature of the contest. The ability of John's campaign to release in sequence the results of a series of contests, particularly in the trade unions, gave the impression of an unstoppable momentum. This would not have been possible if the results had been announced all at once.

All in all, therefore, I believe that the true extent of my support in the party was much nearer 35 per cent or even 40 per cent than the 10 per cent figure so often quoted – still undoubtedly a minority, but a substantial minority. For the purposes of 18 July, however, the day of the special conference, there was no disguising the beating I had taken. I had told Gill, my faithful partner and supporter on so many occasions, not to come. There was no point in putting her through an ordeal. I was glad when it was over.

The Shadow Cabinet elections had taken place in parallel with the leadership contest and the results were announced five days later. I did quite well, but not well enough to compel John to give me an important post, or at least a post in the economic field. To be fair to John, it would have been impossible for him to have given me an economic brief, in view of all I had said on economic policy during the leadership contest, without signalling a change in his own policy which he was clearly unwilling to make.

John nevertheless treated me quite equitably. He telephoned me with the offer of a choice between Health, Education and the newly created post of Shadow Heritage Secretary. I was, for some reason, not particularly attracted to the first two, but intrigued by the scope which appeared to be on offer with the Heritage job. I was also interested in the Citizen's Charter job, on the ground that it would offer me the chance to roam quite widely, but John had apparently promised that to someone else.

In the event, I decided to do the Heritage job, shadowing David Mellor. David had by this time become a figure of some notoriety, as a consequence of his well-publicised affair and other difficulties. He was a high-profile and ambitious politician whom I thought it would be fun to shadow.

My first thought, however, before grappling with my new portfolio, was to get some rest. I had been working non-stop at a killing pace for a year or more. Whereas most of the people who had played a major role in the election campaign had had some respite after polling day, I had been plunged more or less straight into the leadership contest. The disappointing outcome of that contest meant that I did not even have the exhilaration of success to buoy me up. I was therefore keen for a break.

Fortunately, my sister and brother-in-law arrived for a holiday at the end of July, and a large party of family and friends went off in August for a fortnight's stay at a farmhouse in the Dordogne. It was a marvellous holiday. We all vowed that we would gather again for a similar holiday in New Zealand for Christmas of 1994.

The dominant political issue on our return was the growing crisis in the economy. There was increasing pressure on the pound and consequently growing doubt as to whether it could sustain its parity within the ERM. The Prime Minister and Chancellor both maintained that there was no alternative to membership and that they would do whatever was necessary, through interest rates and spending the reserves, to defend sterling. The atmosphere of crisis heightened daily. There was a good deal of interest in my own views, since my stance as a long-term critic of ERM membership was, as a consequence of the leadership contest, by now well known.

I was, however, in something of a dilemma. I was merely a middle-ranking member of the Shadow Cabinet and so bound by the ordinary rules of collective responsibility. For as long as I stayed in the Shadow Cabinet, those rules allowed me to speak on my own portfolio, but precluded me from speaking on the economy. Yet the economy was the great issue of the day, and my views – well-known as they were – were of great interest to the media. I could hardly pretend, having campaigned so publicly on the economy just a few weeks previously, that I no longer had any views or that they had somehow miraculously changed.

I was also caught up in a wider debate on the general style of the party. I had again made very public my belief that the party should be bolder and more positive. Our failure to speak up on the ERM issue was not only important in itself but seemed to illustrate perfectly the wider issue.

My forays into these fields were treated with considerable equanimity by John. He could, I suppose, afford to be generous to a defeated opponent, but he was nevertheless remarkably tolerant, and I was well aware that I was pushing that tolerance to its limits. Unconcerned about my own political future, which seemed of little importance by comparison with the magnitude of the issues we were confronting, I was by now preoccupied with the ERM drama unfolding before our eyes.

On 12 September, Gill and I went to the Last Night of the Proms, where I found myself sitting next to Norman Lamont. Norman was always entertaining company. For our amusement, he made a great show of patriotic fervour for 'Land of Hope and Glory' at the end, and made it clear through numerous asides that he had no sympathy for the European entanglement in which he found his economic policy. He did not, however, drop his public commitment to the ERM until the débâcle of our enforced withdrawal just a few days later.

I confess that when the news finally came through that we had left the ERM, I shed a momentary tear. I felt that an issue on which I felt so passionately and had sacrificed so much, on which I had allowed myself to be divided from my party and my colleagues, had finally culminated in a total vindication of all I had stood for. It was a heady moment, but even in that moment, I suddenly knew that nothing would change and that the game – for me – was up.

I had watched aghast as the party, and particularly our Shadow Chancellor Gordon Brown, had maintained an even more intransigent line than the Tories throughout the ERM crisis. Gordon had even gone so far as to say that if the Germans had revalued the mark as a means of stabilising the ERM or at least relieving some of our difficulties for a time, he would want to see the pound revalued in line with the mark. This was economic lunacy. It has always been a puzzle to me that people who make mistakes of such magnitude and reveal such a total inability to understand the issues of which they are supposed to be masters nevertheless sail serenely, on, unscathed by any suggestion that they might not be up to the job.

What was even more difficult for me, however, than watching my party and colleagues make these mistakes was to realise that, even when the mistakes became apparent beyond doubt, the fundamentals of the situation would not change and the mistakes would be perpetuated. For a couple of days I believed that perhaps the force of events would compel a change, but I rapidly sensed that such optimism was misplaced.

As I wrote in the *New Statesman* at the time, the events which forced us out of the ERM had for a brief moment bathed our affairs in the harsh light of reality, stripping away all the pretensions and illusions which normally pass for policy. Our political leaders were compelled in that moment to yield publicly and unequivocally to that reality, with no chance of concealing or misrepresenting what had happened. But, I predicted, it would only be a matter of days before the clouds of obfuscation, self-serving and illusion rolled back in over the political landscape, and we would again conduct our affairs in a fog of ignorance and prejudice.

That is indeed what happened. The political establishment, which had been proved so wrong, continued as before. The Tory government, which had inflicted such damage with the proclamation, repeated until the very last moment, that there was no alternative, carried serenely on with a quite different policy which they barely understood and had previously condemned as 'fool's gold'. The Labour opposition did not allow events even to check its stride. As far as I am aware, none of the major figures in the drama on the Labour side ever hinted for a moment that they might have been wrong or that their attitudes or policy might change as a result.

Indeed, I ran into immediate problems on precisely this issue. The question was discussed by the NEC at the end of September, with a view to producing a statement for conference. The statement made no reference to our earlier stance or to the fact that we had been even more gung-ho than the Tories in wanting to prolong the agony of

ERM membership. I angered my colleages by commenting that a little honesty would not have come amiss.

The whole episode was a classic example of the British establishment at work. Virtually all of the opinion-formers – the political leaders, the leader writers, the captains of industry, the Civil Service mandarins – had been united in their views of the key to economic success. That unanimity had convinced the vast majority, who knew nothing of the actual issue, that they must be right, and that those who took a different view were charlatans. When they were shown to be wrong, the fact that they had all been implicated in the mistakes meant that they averted their gaze and comforted each other with various excuses to conceal their embarassment.

I was deeply depressed. I realised that if I could not win the argument, and bring about a change in policy, at a time when events themselves had conspired to support me so strongly, then I could never hope to prevail. For me, a future career in British politics would mean constantly observing a process with which I had no sympathy but which I was powerless to influence.

I should make it clear that the issue for me was not Europe but the economy. The claim that my views on the economy should be discounted because they were informed by a deep-seated anti-Europeanism was constantly made by my opponents. This was, however, a calumny. I was as convinced as anyone that our future lay in Europe. The question was not Whether or not Europe? but What sort of Europe?

There seemed to me to be a clear agenda we could pursue with our European partners which concentrated on the things that made sense. We could try to co-ordinate a Europe-wide reflation of the economy, promote a European environmental policy, democratise the political institutions, establish a Europe-wide energy policy, co-ordinate defence and foreign policies, and so on. What was a mistake, however, on both political and economic grounds, was the attempt to create a single European state, a sort of nation state writ large.

This concept stood little chance of success and was fundamentally contrary to the wishes and interests of the people of Europe. It threatened to subject the whole of a diverse European economy to a monetary policy which may or may not have suited the Germans but was unlikely to suit anyone else. Even if it did succeed, it would dangerously divide Europe, through the erection of new economic barriers to replace the Berlin Wall. Instead of the democratic, decentralised, outward-looking Europe we should have been building, we were intent on creating a bureaucratic, centralised, inward-looking European super-state which matched the vision of an élite but did nothing to command the allegiance of the people.

For me, however, the ERM episode was an important illustration, not of European folly but of an age-old illusion about economic policy. It was a repetition of the mistakes made by so many earlier British governments – based on the belief that monetary measures matter more than the real economy in which ordinary people live and work and that one can take a short-cut, through fiscal policy and the mere assertion that we have a strong currency, to the economic success which we see others enjoying.

The ERM experience also showed me that, even when such illusions were totally shattered by events, they were so deeply entrenched in the British psyche that it was unlikely that they could be displaced. I began to think for the first time that the task of rejuvenating British society, of freeing the British people from the weight of their own history, would not be accomplished. The British seemed to me to be like one of those great beached whales, whose size and strength were of no use to it because of its determination to swim in the wrong direction.

These impressions were very much reinforced by the debate which was taking place concerning the Maastricht Treaty. I confess that, like most people, I had not taken a great deal of notice of the treaty when it had first been negotiated. There had been so much on the domestic political agenda at the time that yet another European initiative had seemed to be of little import.

The result of the Danish referendum, in which the Danish people withheld their consent to Maastricht, however, alerted me and many others to the true significance of the treaty. I had become increasingly concerned about its provisions, especially as the ERM saga – which seemed to offer an illustration of the problems that Maastricht was likely to bring – unfolded before our eyes.

I could hardly believe that, at the same time as the ERM débâcle was delivering its brutal and unmistakable message, the British government and the Labour Party were using the same arguments and the same language to try to convince the British people that there was no alternative to Maastricht. The long battle I had fought over the ERM was merely a prelude to a similarly long and unsuccessful battle over Maastricht, and after Maastricht there would be yet more battles.

In the course of the 11 days between our withdrawal from the ERM on 16 September and the beginning of the Labour conference in Blackpool on 27 September, I moved from a sense of elation to one of gloom. I should make it clear that this was not a matter of mood – I have always been blessed with a very stable temperament – but simply of conviction. Rationally, I could see it was highly unlikely that I could divert the British political process from making yet another fundamental mistake. Nor did my own political prospects look very bright. There are no prizes for being right.

I was particularly unhappy at the idea of being locked into a Shadow Cabinet role which prevented me from speaking up on these issues. Despite my disappointment at the outcome of the leadership contests, I had enjoyed the freedom to debate the issues which I thought were important. The thought of serving another four years in what I increasingly regarded as the straitjacket of Shadow Cabinet membership was not an attractive one.

For all these reasons, I decided that I would resign from the Shadow Cabinet. I consulted virtually no one, apart from Gill and Nigel Stanley, and even then I simply informed them of my decision.

I had accepted an invitation to speak at the fringe meeting of the Labour Common Market Safeguards Campaign. The meeting was traditionally held on the opening Sunday of conference and I had spoken at it many times over the years. There had been a time in the 1970s when this fringe meeting was one of the most important at conference, but, as its name indicated, the campaign had got rather caught in a timewarp, and support for the meeting had ebbed away. I nevertheless decided that I would announce my resignation during the course of my speech.

Nigel Stanley was critical of this decision, since he felt that it would convey the wrong message about the reasons for my decision. He was right, in that it certainly made it easier for my opponents to portray my decision as founded in some sort of hostility to Europe rather than as an expression of my long-held views on the economy. But I was anxious to get the issue out in the open as quickly as possible, and the LCMSC meeting presented a good opportunity to do so.

However, I wanted to achieve as much impact as possible, which meant that I would have to keep my decision absolutely secret until I was ready to announce it. Although I spent the few days before conference thinking about the speech I would make, I was unable either to tell friends and colleagues about it or to warn John Smith. I knew from bitter experience that leaks always occurred in such cases, particularly where those unsympathetic to me would have the chance to put their own spin on a story before it was properly launched.

I attended a meeting of the NEC on the Sunday morning and felt rather bad about concealing from John my intention of announcing my Shadow Cabinet resignation that afternoon. After lunch, I delivered a letter to John which I intended that he should receive before I actually made my speech. As I handed the letter in at the hotel reception desk, I was filmed doing so by television news cameras – another illustration of the goldfish bowl in which British politics is conducted.

Despite my best endeavours, rumours about my decision had flown around the conference and a large audience, together with many journalists, had packed into the hall. I had told my colleagues on the platform that I had something significant to say, and I think that some of them guessed what it might be. The announcement, however, when it came at the end of a speech in which I reviewed the history of the ERM débâcle and the prospect of an equally damaging entanglement with the Maastricht Treaty provisions, took most people by surprise. I concluded by saying that I had no illusions as to how quickly I would be marginalised by my colleagues but that I felt an obligation, as long as my voice was heard, to speak up on the issues I believed were so important.

As I left the hall, I received a standing ovation from a largely sympathetic audience and a gratifying amount of media attention, reflected in the television news and papers the following day. Throughout those few days, however, I felt curiously detached and – although it is quite contrary to my usual attitude – almost fatalistic. I had a sense of events moving me to an inevitable outcome.

There was a further drama yet to be played out, however. Members of the National Executive sit on the conference platform, in full view of the delegates and of the television audience. They sit there throughout the conference, including the session in which the results of the elections to the NEC are read out. The results are known just a few minutes before they are made public.

Joyce Gould, the Party's organisation director and, incidentally, someone who was often assumed to be related – if not actually married – to me, discreetly approaches any NEC member who has lost his or her seat and whispers the bad news in the defeated candidate's ear. I had, in preceding years, often watched this absorbing little ritual, as the black spot was delivered to its victim, in full view of an audience of millions oblivious to the significance of the brief and muttered conversation.

I had often sat on the platform in earlier years and expected, as Joyce moved among my colleagues, that she would come to me. In 1992, she did. I showed no emotion as the results were read out. Indeed, I felt very little. My support from the constituencies had fallen quite sharply, not, I think, as a consequence of my resignation from the Shadow Cabinet (since delegates are usually mandated some weeks before conference) but because of my earlier leadership challenge to John Smith. With John now established as leader, many in the party were inclined, retrospectively, to see the contest between us as an act of disloyalty on my part.

The week, which in some senses had been so traumatic, nevertheless ended on a high note. It is a further part of the brutal and public ritual which is so often an intrinsic part of top-level politics that defeated NEC members nevertheless remain on the conference platform for the rest of the week and are required to address conference on behalf of the NEC as needed.

I was asked to wind up a debate on environmental matters towards the end. I made a very good speech, on housing, the best I had ever made at conference. I spoke entirely without notes, which I had increasingly found was the style of speaking which suited me best. Conference was impressed and, as I resumed my seat, teetered on the brink of giving me a standing ovation. Some sense that it would seem disloyal to the new leader, however, prevented delegates from doing so. Nevertheless I was pleased with my reception and even more pleased with my own response to what had been a hard week.

In truth, it had been a hard six months. I had seen the prospect of high office in a Labour government disappear with the general election defeat, I had immediately engaged in a gruelling and crushingly unsuccessful challenge for the leadership, I had resigned from the Shadow Cabinet and I had lost my seat on the National Executive.

I emerged from this period in remarkably good spirits, however. I was, as always, sustained by the love and support of Gill and the family. I was also buoyed up by the sense that I was at least in charge of my own destiny and that, despite the reverses I had suffered, I was still regarded as a significant political figure whose views were worth listening to. I had always felt that, unlike so many of my colleagues who relied on constructing power bases, my position in politics depended solely on the value of what I had to say. My ability to speak up had never depended on holding any particular office. As long as I was listened to, I felt that I had a role to play. In any case, as I often said to myself and others, there are never any final battles in politics.

My family has always been very important to me. An account of my public life over this period can give little impression of the things which really mattered to me at the time. I found, as I grew older, that the company of family and friends, and the simple pleasures of eating and drinking and walking in the country, were the things I really valued. Although I never doubted my commitment to politics, I was not one of those politicians obsessed with politics who have nothing else in their lives.

It was a family occasion which next engaged Gill's and my attention. Our son Charles married Angela on 26 October 1992. It was a wonderfully happy occasion, and a timely antidote to the adverse tide of circumstances I had recently encountered.

There was, however, little relief from the press of political events. The Maastricht issue was becoming more and more dominant. The matter was debated on several occasions at meetings of the Parliamentary Labour Party. I spoke effectively at some of these meetings; however, I knew that I was in a familiar minority, confronting a majority who did not want to think too hard about the implications of what they were doing. Most politicians decide their positions according to short-term considerations, usually to do with immediate personal or party advantage, and are unwilling to take the longer view. As always, too, the majority were content to follow their leaders rather than think for themselves.

It was in any case the Tories who were in the greater trouble over Maastricht. The Labour Party preferred to observe its opponents' problems rather than take a strong position itself. The view of most Labour MPs was that if the right wing of the Tory Party was against Maastricht, that was good enough reason to be for it.

I spoke in the second reading debate on 4 November and was disappointed in, but not surprised at the Government's wafer-thin three-vote majority at the end of the night. I went to Denmark at the end of that month to speak to the annual meeting of the Danish June Movement – the anti-Maastricht coalition which had won the referendum. I was also active in the British media.

The end of the year saw a welcome break in the shape of our annual trip to New Zealand. This time, we went out before Christmas. For the first time, we felt that our children, especially with Charles married, could arrange a Christmas without us. In the New Year, Gill and I went on a motoring trip with my sister and her husband in the South Island. We were overcome by the beauty of the scenery and the sense of space and peace.

As we drove past a small settlement on the shores of Lake Hawea one fine morning, we decided to linger and look around. The lake shimmered in the sunshine and the mountains at the far end still shone white with snow. We discovered that there were several small building plots for sale, at prices which were equivalent to our modest savings. In a state of excitement, and in the space of about an hour, we bought the one which we thought had the best views. We had no idea what we might do with it, but the mere thought of owning a small piece of such a paradise was enough.

Our return to Britain meant plunging back into the Maastricht debate. I spoke on 1 February, during the committee stage of the bill (which was concluded on the floor of the House), on the issue of citizenship. I took the opportunity to review the whole concept of Europe, the progress that had been made towards the creation of a European super-state and the dangers which I felt this gave rise to. The speech went very well and seemed to impress those who heard it. I received many notes and comments from colleagues, some of whom said it was the best speech they had heard in the House of Commons.

I was nevertheless extremely frustrating to speak on such an occasion. The debates were largely held late at night. The press and most MPs had gone home long ago. The debates were not reported and so the wider public had no idea of the issues which were discussed. Even many MPs remained in blissful ignorance of what they were about, being content to rely on the pitifully inadequate and partisan accounts reported in the press. The main concern of the press was in parliamentary tactics and the outcome of particular votes, not in understanding the fundamental issues. It is fair to say that the British people and parliament sleepwalked into Maastricht.

This state of affairs was not helped by a sort of conspiracy between the two front benches. They were both determined that the Maastricht Bill should get through, but, for their own reasons, they pretended they were at each other's throats. And so, it was convenient for both of them to focus attention on an obscure part of the Maastricht Treaty which dealt with social policy.

The Social Chapter dealt with important issues, but whether or not those issues were incorporated in our treaty obligations was of comparatively little consequence. It suited John Major to inflate the significance of this question, however, so that he could show his right wing how tough he was being in resisting the socialist ambitions of Jacques Delors. It suited John Smith to do likewise, so that he could divert the attention of his party – with his much-trumpeted determination to back the Social Chapter against Tory opposition – from the embarrassing fact that he was keeping the Tory government in office.

In February, I had two lunch meetings which were eventually reported in the papers. Michael Portillo had, rather surprisingly, suggested that we might lunch together and had booked a table in the Churchill Room in the House of Commons. We lunched in full public view and had an interesting but straightforward conversation in which we exchanged views on the political scene from our respective viewpoints. This quite unremarkable event nevertheless made main front page headlines in several newspapers.

On the following day, I was invited to lunch by David Jordan, the editor of *On the Record*, the BBC's main weekly current affairs programme. He broached with me the impending decision of Jonathan Dimbleby to give up his anchor-man role, and enquired whether I might be interested in replacing him. I promised to think about it but phoned him back a day or two later to say that I was not. I could not really contemplate a career other than in politics. Despite the setbacks I had suffered, I still felt that there was an important role for me in British politics, and I knew from my earlier experience that, despite its attractions, a television job did not offer the same chance of pursuing political goals.

At about this time, I was also approached by some colleagues about a new political initiative which they wished me to take. John Mills and Bob Harrison, both long-standing friends and colleagues with whom I had worked on European and economic matters, suggested that the time was ripe for an attempt to put full employment back on the political agenda. We put out feelers to a number of political friends, sympathetic academics and trade unionists and received an encouraging response.

The result was the launch on 12 March of the Full Employment Forum, of which I was founding chair. The Forum was meant to provide a focal point for all those in the Labour movement who were concerned at the monetarist emphasis of our economic policies and who wished to see a more interventionist position adopted. It was an immediate success, in terms of both the support it attracted and the impact it had on policy statements from the Labour leadership. The subscription was set at £25 for an individual member. This relatively high figure meant that only serious people joined and that subscription income became our most important source of funds. Membership climbed steadily into the hundreds, and was then followed by a surge of interest from trade unions and constituency parties who began to affiliate in large numbers.

The Forum concentrated on publications and seminars, and drew heavily on the support of academic economists. It was not long before we began to set the agenda. Within a few months, the Labour leadership, in the shape of John Smith and Gordon Brown, were using the language of full employment in all their speeches and statements. Many of our members felt that we were making real progress.

I was not so sure. I worked hard for the Forum and was, I think, its major asset for a time. But I was under no illusion about the nature of our success. Full employment was an easy goal to sign up for. People could support us without making any real commitment to a change in policy and without any real understanding of what was required to achieve full employment. When Gordon Brown wrote, as he did, in a pamphlet on full employment that the prime purpose of policy was to set conditions of monetary stability in which the economy could then respond to micro-economic stimuli, it merely showed how far we had to go before we could even begin to speak the same language. The notion that government might actually intervene to manage the economy, not according to monetary criteria but in order to achieve real goals like full employment, was still alien to our policymakers. As a party we had swapped sides in the historic argument between those who saw monetary stability and the protection of assets as the major goal of policy and those who set full employment and the real economy as our proper objectives.

I was also conscious that, in parallel with the progress we felt we were making with the Full Employment Forum, the Parliamentary Labour Party, the House of Commons and the country's governing institutions were all supporting the entrenchment of Euro-monetarism on a virtually permanent basis through the Maastricht Treaty. We were still light years away from changing opinion on this central issue.

It was not so much that we could not win the argument as that people preferred not to have the argument at all. When the House of Commons gave a third reading to the Maastricht Bill in May, most of those who trooped through the lobbies had deliberately absented themselves from the Chamber for most of the debates and had little idea of what had been discussed.

I was appalled that people who had put themselves forward to serve their constituents in the House of Commons could so casually give away to an outside unelected agency such substantial powers of self-government on a permanent basis without bothering either to inform themselves of the arguments or to consult those on whose behalf they exercised the power of decision. I concluded that only a House of Commons which was already merely a shadow of its former self could act in such a way and that, by so carelessly betraying its own history and the responsibility it owed to the British people, it was merely confirming the diminished value it placed upon itself. My confidence in the prospects of national renewal received a further blow.

My gloom at these developments was relieved by a rare moment of triumph when, on 1 April, our West Highland White terrier, Angus, became Westminster Dog of the Year! It was the first time the competition, sponsored by the National Canine Defence League and a dog food company and open to any dog with a Westminster connection, had been held. It attracted an entry of over 80 and Dame Janet Fookes judged a short list of about a dozen. Tory and Liberal dogs were sent off with their tails between their legs. It was a well-deserved Labour triumph and an overdue shot in the arm for a Labour Party which, after four successive election defeats, had long been starved of victories of such significance.

I remained very active on a wide front: *Any Questions* in Paris, a television debate on the monarchy, a Commonwealth Parliamentary Association regional conference in Gibraltar, an appearance on *Clive Anderson Talks Back*, the Commonwealth Parliamentary Association annual conference in Cyprus, as well as my usual round of engagements to do with the Full Employment Forum, the Fabian Society and so on. I was enjoying my politics, but my pleasure at being able to say and write what I thought was tempered by the realisation that, while I was respected for what I had to say, I was essentially operating at the margins and had only a peripheral influence on events.

I was in touch with a range of people in the party and the Labour movement generally who were unhappy at the course of events and who shared my wish to see a bolder and more radical approach adopted. There were frequent meetings of such small groups, and occasionally events of greater size and significance such as a conference on the future of the welfare state and another entitled 'What's Left?' at which I spoke, but the outcome was always the same: uncertainty as to whether anything could be done to stem the tide of caution and reaction.

It was a source of some amusement to me that over this period my public image went through one of its periodic changes. I had long since ceased to be the 'golden boy' or, according to interpretation, the yuppie who would sell every last principle for the sake of a vote. I now emerged as a dangerous leftie, the principal standard-bearer of old-fashioned socialism. Most commentators seemed blithely unaware of the fact that I had remained consistent over a long period and that the main elements in my political belief had developed organically over twenty years or more. The changes in my public image reflected their rather than my own inconsistency.

At the end of November, I received a phone call from the Association of Commonwealth Universities. They were acting for a firm of headhunters who were trawling on behalf of the University of

Waikato in New Zealand. The university, it seemed, were seeking a new vice-chancellor. Did I know anyone who might be interested? I suggested a couple of names of people with New Zealand connections. 'I don't suppose you would be interested yourself?' I was asked. I said no.

'I think I may just have been approached about a job in New Zealand,' I said to Gill when I came off the phone. She seemed disappointed when I said that I had rejected the overture. We had increasingly begun to think of spending more time in New Zealand, perhaps in retirement, but I had not seriously thought about living and working back there full-time.

A fortnight later, Gill took another call. This time the caller made it clear that the university had me very much in their sights and would like to send a headhunter to talk to me. Gill advised them to send me all the material about the job. When it arrived, and I read it, I began to think seriously for the first time about making a move. I agreed to see the headhunter.

Ian Taylor duly arrived from Auckland and we had a long and informative conversation on 7 December. The upshot was that I agreed to speak in confidence to the university when we went out to New Zealand in January. I made it clear that I could not apply for the job in the ordinary way – the merest hint that I was contemplating a return to New Zealand would have meant death to my political career in Britain – but we agreed that if the university wished to offer me the job after talking to me then I would consider it and give them an answer.

Gill and I approached our trip to New Zealand with the realisation that this time we were visiting the country not as holidaymakers but as potential immigrants. The step would be even more momentous for Gill than for me, since I at least knew the country well and felt at home there, whereas she would be giving up her own home country for a totally new life. We resolved to look at New Zealand through different eyes, and to judge whether we could give up all that our life in Britain meant to us for the sake of what we saw.

We found New Zealand, and the New Zealand way of life, as

attractive as ever. The country had developed and matured enormously since I was a boy. It had become an altogether more stimulating place. All the familiar virtues were there – scenic beauty, a sense of space, a relaxed lifestyle – but there were now added social and economic developments of genuine challenge and interest. New Zealand was in the process of re-orienting its economic and geographical outlook on the world. Domestically, it was re-discovering itself as a bi-cultural society with all the added complexities and challenges that that meant.

The conversations with the university council went well. It was astonishing that there was not the hint of a leak of discussions which directly involved over 20 people. By the time we had concluded our holiday, the university and I had reached agreement. We would co-ordinate our announcements in early February, when I would return for a formal presentation to the university and the wider community.

I was tremendously excited by this quite unexpected turn of events. Yet, in retrospect, there seems to have been a certain inevitability about it. In Britain, my decision, when it was announced, was seen as a comment on my disillusionment with Britain and with British politics, and I suppose that was certainly a factor. But much more important in my own mind was the sudden realisation that I could do something constructive in my own country, rather than hang around on the margins of a political system which no longer offered me a real role.

The British establishment is very good at marginalising those with whom it disagrees. I could have maintained an honourable position in British politics – a respected voice representing a valuable view of where we should be going. But I was aware that I was increasingly being typecast as the licensed radical who could be trotted out whenever a contrary and literally eccentric view was needed. I had always been serious about my politics, in the sense that I wanted to use political power to make real changes. I would not have been content with a role as critic and carper, constantly lamenting the things I could not change and out of sympathy even with my colleagues.

The dreams I had harboured since childhood of a rejuvenated Britain, perhaps leading the world again as an efficient, humane and democratic post-industrial society, seemed unlikely to be realised. My own hopes of making a real contribution to that change had been dashed. The British themselves seemed finally to have given up and to have accepted their leaders' estimation of their worth. They no longer had the energy or self-belief to free themselves from their history.

Even the Labour Party, which of course continued to offer an immensely preferable alternative to the Tories, had nevertheless closed its mind to the possibility of radical change. More compassionate and competent government, yes, but a new vision, a conscious attempt to change society, to project Britain into a new era – that was definitely off the agenda. Rather than challenge the establishment view, Labour now seemed intent on earning its approval and was willing to pay the inevitable price – denying itself the goals of greater equality and freedom for ordinary people. The fundamentals of a class-based, privilege-dominated society would remain unchanged.

The announcement of my move in February was followed by a growing conviction that I had made the right decision. That conviction was unshaken by the shocking news of John Smith's untimely death and the brief thought, surfacing in the minds of some of my friends, that perhaps there might have been the chance for one more effort. My thoughts had already turned towards my new life in New Zealand.

Returning to New Zealand and to the Waikato region felt like coming home. My parents had retired and ended their days in Hamilton, my sister and her family lived and farmed in Te Awamutu, my brother had gone to school there and had been a solicitor in Matamata, my grandparents had lived in Cambridge, we had ourselves bought our farm at Pirongia. But it was more than returning to my roots.

It was a recognition that I could make a contribution to the country to which I owed so much. And it also reflected a view I had increasingly held, as I had travelled more and more frequently through Asia and the Pacific, that the world now looked more in focus when viewed from the Pacific rim than from Europe. I discovered that I was, in essence, a New World person. The blood of my pioneer forebears still flowed in my veins. They had decided to leave the old world, disenchanted with its unwillingness to change, and to seek new challenges in a new land. I was proud to follow in their footsteps.

INDEX

Except for entry under his name Bryan Gould is referred to as BG